In the Name of God Almighty, the Most Compassionate, the Most Merciful

The Opening, Photo Credit: Anton Khlopotov

"By (the Token of) Time (through the ages),
Verily Man is in loss.
Except such as have Faith,
and do righteous deeds,
and (join together)
in the mutual teaching of Truth,
and of Patience and Constancy."
—Surah Al-Asr, The Declining Day

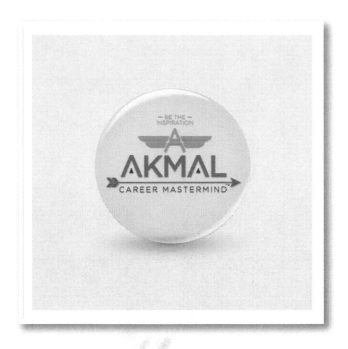

This symbol represents the Mastermind Agreement and Code defining the journey of the Career Mastermind™. It is inspired by the falcon—a bird gifted with intelligence, speed, and accuracy. It has been associated with visionary power, wisdom, and guardianship—a guide to each individual's life purpose. The letter A evokes the falcon in its appearance of upward flight, like an arrow. It signifies aspiration and the ascent of career and personhood, guided by the Master's strong wings of experience.

ALSO BY HASSAN AKMAL

Career Bucket List™

Foreword by Jullien Gordon

May 2020

www.CareerBucketList.org
#CareerBucketList

Hassan's 5 Principles of Mastery

1. Mindfulness
2. Repetition
3. Self-Confidence
4. Patience
5. Will Power

PRAISE FOR *HOW TO BE A CAREER MASTERMIND*™

"I can't type. This failure of mine has led me to recording my thoughts and having them transcribed. I decided not to take notes, which led to an enormous improvement in my memory connecting what I hear to other experiences and knowledge and a visual mental web of understanding. Both of these things have become a piece of the design in my life. This book is quite a surprise to me, not only because its author is an academic, but also in its endorsement of passionately designing your life.

The big design problem is the design of your life. Not the design of a car, or a house or even a curriculum—it is the design of your life. What you do in your life takes up most of your day and that design should not be left to others. This is a book about participating in your own learning. It is a remarkable, passionate guidebook—dense, but easily absorbed because you hear this rather wondrous man talking to you as you read. It feels like he is sitting next to you and delivering this wisdom for your understanding and your memory without notes; without a typewriter, without the formality of the educational system, giving you a plan that leads to the design of a personal learning system.

I particularly like his metaphors about tennis—I congratulate him on his efforts!"

—RICHARD SAUL WURMAN, CREATOR OF TED; AUTHOR OF OVER 90 BOOKS ON WILDLY DIVERGENT TOPICS; RECIPIENT OF THE LIFETIME ACHIEVEMENT AWARD FROM THE SMITHSONIAN, COOPER-HEWITT MUSEUM; CONTRIBUTOR TO GENIUS: 100 VISIONS OF THE FUTURE, A PROJECT SPONSORED BY THE EINSTEIN LEGACY PROJECT, WHICH FEATURES ESSAYS SUBMITTED BY THE 100 GREATEST INNOVATORS, ARTISTS, AND SCIENTISTS

For more information on Wurman's most recent book, *UnderstandingUnderstanding,* please visit: www.uursw.com.

ADDITIONAL ACCLAIM FOR ONE OF THE MOST INFLUENTIAL CAREER BOOKS OF THE 21ST CENTURY

"While many of us are caught up in the habit of thinking about the next job we want, if we want a truly fulfilling life, we should be thinking about what kind of life we want instead. Hassan Akmal encourages you to take control of your destiny and discover a new way to look at life and a clear approach to unearth new opportunities that maybe weren't possible. You will learn how to use your own Kantian life lenses to create value versus focusing on just a positive mindset where you look for the value in what the world is offering you."

—FRANCESCA LAZZERI, PHD, AI & MACHINE LEARNING SCIENTIST, MICROSOFT

"In a rapidly changing work environment where all generations are forced to adapt, Hassan provides timeless strategies into how to think about career and future prospects."

—BEN ROYCE, HEAD OF PERFORMANCE DATA SCIENCE, GLOBAL AGENCY, GOOGLE

"Akmal chronicles relevant personal experiences and provides an insightful primer on navigating the difficult path to career success in a challenging time."

—SALMAN AZAM, ESQ, ATTORNEY; ENTREPRENEUR; MANAGING PARTNER; COMMUNITY ACTIVIST

"Akmal demonstrates the true meaning of personal passion. He explains away the purpose of a life's work, and how it impacts those around us. This book is exemplary standards for the leaders of today, who find themselves in an ever-changing environment. This book will be the 'go-to' career book of the next decade."

—DR. MARTIN J. BOYLE, DM, MBA, CFE, LPD, CEB, CHS-III, DABCHS; AUTHOR; SECURITY SUBJECT MATTER EXPERT; UNIVERSITY DEAN; PROFESSOR; CEO; EXECUTIVE CORPORATE PARTNER

"A pure, creative—visionary genius! Akmal transforms your global impact lens—enabling you to find your zenith or "Z", and empowering you to 'trust the truth' within you: That cannot be sought, which grows not in heart."

—AMMAR LATIF, PHILOSOPHER AND PROFESSOR

"The book How to be a Career Mastermind™ by Mr. Akmal, has the capacity to be a classic for many reasons. It includes the compelling world view of an elite athlete with compassion and a toughness of mind that engages the reader throughout. The lessons learned are shared generously, they champion the vision of a Career Mastermind™ through a synthesized strategy that generates traction. Original, pertinent, and perhaps timeless; this book provides readily accessible pathways for professionals in various stages of development. The lens of positive mindset, coupled with building your alliance and Career Mastermind™ groups, are value added interpersonally and professionally. There is a lot to read and retain; however, the book flows with humor and ease, with snapshots of 'career and life hacks' that keep you stimulated, learning and moving forward with new tools and perspectives."

—PEDRO MANRIQUE, PHD, CEO, DRP SYSTEMS; AUTHOR AND INVENTOR; ORGANIZATIONAL DEVELOPMENT CONSULTANT; STRATEGIC ANALYST

"One of the most important books out there on career and life vision."

—**NATHAN CANNING**, FOUNDER AND PRINCIPAL
STRATEGIST, PARADIIIGM, LLC

"How to be a Career Mastermind™ guides the reader in how to find their 'Ikigai,' i.e., reason for being, and how to align and unlock their career and life visions. Akmal's insights particularly resonated with me as a science PhD who found fulfillment in a 'non-traditional' career path. This book is a great read for anyone seeking meaning and purpose in their career!"

—**DEVANG K. THAKOR**, PHD, FOUNDER AND PRINCIPAL
CONSULTANT, ANIOPLEX, LLC

"Considering how much of our time we spend on our careers, it's shocking the lack of innovative thinking in career guidance. Akmal effectively and inspiringly responds to this need with a thoughtful, creative, and enjoyable guide to achieving career success."

—**DAVID DABSCHECK**, CEO AND FOUNDER, GIANT
INNOVATION

"Akmal delivers a great work—a compass for the wandering mind, looking for direction. While encouraging readers to find their inner 'Ikigai', the author challenges the reader to follow the heart's ambition through the art of self-discovery. A powerful read!"

—**TYRONE ROSS**, MANAGING PARTNER, NOBLEBRIDGE
WEALTH™ & ASSET MANAGEMENT SERVICES *(NAMED THE TOP
TEN TO WATCH IN 2019 BY WEALTHMANAGEMENT.COM)*

"If you want to take control of your career and find happiness and meaningful success, look no further. Hassan shares his genius about building relationships that will change the arc of your career in the best ways possible!"

—**MARK J. CARTER**, CREATOR OF IDEA CLIMBING™

"Akmal is a revolutionary in the fields of Career Services and Professional Development. He demonstrates the art of building a global alliance of positive mindsets, combined with—'forward momentum'—that brilliantly masterminds career clarity."

—**MURWA FARAH**, HUMAN RIGHTS ACTIVIST; CAREER AND LIFE VISION CONSULTANT

"Akmal lays the foundation for taking your career vision and making it a reality. Each of his seven lenses will inspire your path forward."

—**GREGORY COSTANZO**, CAREER CONSULTANT AND EDUCATOR; DIRECTOR OF CAREER SERVICES

"A life changing journey complete with a roadmap. A must read for anyone at any point on their career path."

—**CHRIS MARSHALL**, PRESIDENT GRADUWAY NORTH AMERICA; FORMER ASSOCIATE VICE PRESIDENT FOR ALUMNI AFFAIRS, CORNELL UNIVERSITY

"Akmal inspires us to design a life with no borders. He helps you reimagine your career trajectory as a passionate portfolio of living."

—**NICOLE ARNDT**, CAREER CONSULTANT; INDUSTRY RELATIONS LEADER; WRITER

"The best career and life guide from a true thought leader and Mastermind in the industry!"

—JESSICA RODGERS, HIGHER EDUCATION PROFESSIONAL

"Hassan provides the key to creating a career you'll love."

—CATHY GIBBONS, CAREER EDUCATOR

"Hassan brings his vast experience and lifelong passion for career mentorship together beautifully to deliver an essential read for today's rapidly changing job market."

—THOMAS DEELY, EXECUTIVE DIRECTOR OF CORPORATE PARTNERSHIPS; ANGEL INVESTOR; FINTECH SPEAKER; FORMER VICE PRESIDENT, GOLDMAN SACHS

"Hassan provides a powerful tool to approach career and life in a new innovative way."

—TASHA CHOI, CEO AND FOUNDER, HIGHIRE

"It is impactful to have Hassan, someone who has not only lived through harrowing challenges and has overcome tremendous odds, dedicate himself in sharing his knowledge and positive experiences so others will be motivated to ignite their own passion and life purpose."

—ERIC DI MONTE, TALENT ACQUISITION EXECUTIVE, UNIVISION COMMUNICATIONS INC.; NETWORKING STRATEGIST; D&I ADVOCATE

"This book is full of great advice and strategies for anyone looking for a healthy and meaningful career-life balance. It should be required reading for anyone graduating from college and embarking on their career."

—DR. MICHAEL OUDSHOORN, FOUNDING DEAN OF ENGINEERING, HIGH POINT UNIVERSITY

"In this book, Hassan shares the secrets to masterminding a career in today's Gig Economy through the lens of his own personal and professional experiences.

In sharing his story, Hassan shows the reality of ambitious pursuits: that life can present challenges at any moment and learning how to move past these obstacles can be critical for developing our career.

Through the intimate details of his own challenges and his path to shaping his career, Hassan's story feels relatable and provides a real world context for understanding how to become a Career Mastermind™."

—**JENNIFER SHIN**, WORLD-RENOWNED DATA SCIENTIST, ENTREPRENEUR, AND INFLUENCER; PRODUCT DIRECTOR, CONTEXTUAL, NBCUNIVERSAL MEDIA, LLC

"Understanding the connection between purpose and intrinsic motivation, and the forward momentum these create in the actualization of our Ikigai (the Japanese concept of "Reason for Being"), is the start of a lifelong journey the author Hassan Akmal paves for us in this timely How-To book. How to be a Career Mastermind™ encourages us to clear our dual lenses and realize the intricately woven, helix-like bond between our professional and personal visions for ourselves, and offers important lessons about the power of mindset in creating our most authentic career and life narratives."

—**DORCAS LIND**, PRESIDENT AND FOUNDER, DIVERSITY HEALTH COMMUNICATIONS AND ASSISTANT VICE PRESIDENT, HEAD – DIVERSITY AND INCLUSION, MONTEFIORE MEDICAL CENTER

SOCIAL MEDIA

LinkedIn.com/in/hassanakmal
Facebook: @CareerMastermind
Instagram: @CareerMastermind
Twitter: @LifeMastermind

Learn more about the book:
www.CareerMastermind.org

Learn more about the Author:
www.HassanAkmal.com

Learn more about Career and Life Vision:
www.CareerandLife.Vision

Podcast: "Behind the Scenes"

The Career Design Lab's "Behind the Scenes" Podcast is a year-round series that consists of a number of in-depth interviews with industry professionals discussing provocative career-related topics—to set the stage for students and alumni.

www.SoundCloud.com/Columbia-sps/sets/Behind-the-Scenes

THE CAREER DESIGN LAB

The #ASKCDL Show
FACEBOOK and INSTAGRAM: @CareerDesignLabNYC
www.CareerDesignLab.net
#CareerDesignLabSF

CAREER
MASTERMINDS

GIVE BACK

Nonprofit 501 3 (c): www.InvitationRelief.org

Hassan Akmal is available for speaking engagements including fireside chats, panels, and keynotes.

To inquire, please visit: www.CareerMastermind.org or get in touch by e-mail: ha2049@Columbia.edu.

Believe.

HOW TO BE A
CAREER
MASTERMIND™

HASSAN AKMAL

Purpose Series

Published in the United States.

Names: Akmal, Hassan, author.

Title: How to be a Career Mastermind™: Discover 7 "YOU Matter" Lenses for a Life of Purpose, Impact, and Meaningful Work / Hassan Akmal.

Includes references, glossary, and index.

Description: First Edition. | New York, 2019.

ISBN: 978-1-7335593-1-7 (paperback)

Subjects: Vocational guidance. | Self-realization. | SELF-HELP / Motivational & Inspirational.

Book Cover Design by JCNB

DEDICATION

◆◆◆

*D*edicated to my late father, who left us in 1987. We miss you dearly. May you be united with us in paradise, ameen.

And to my mother—the most selfless woman on the face of the earth. May God Almighty elevate your place and rank in the Hereafter, ameen.

Muhammad Akmal   Imtiaz Akmal

To my students and clients all over the world:
Thank you for inspiring me to write this book.

Your stories and success are interwreathed in front of me
and beside me, and will crystallize—*beyond* me.
Our story is not over, it has just begun to unfold...

"A person is a fool to become a writer. His only compensation is absolute freedom. He has no master except his own soul, and that, I am sure, is why he does it."

—*Roald Dahl*

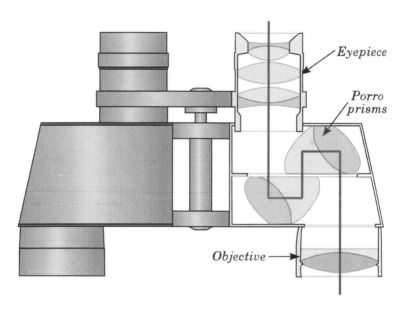

Look into your future, and focus.

CONTENTS

MINKAMAN, SOUTH SUDAN: Amel, 45, throws her hands up indicating she has not received food at a distribution center for displaced families, Oct. 16, 2014. (Alissa Everett, Humanity United)

"Don't blink when humanity stares you in the eyes."

—*Hassan Akmal*

[Inauguration of Invitation Relief's Kids of the World Project, 2010]

Every **Master** has experienced **disaster**.
Career and Life Masterminds *create their own freedom.*
How you move will influence how you feel.
Repetition is the *Mother of Mastery.*

A masterful swordsman *never* drops his sword.
Practice your technique over and over until they become
a part of *you.*

PART 1: THERE IS NO MAJOR IN CAREERS

What's driving you?

AUTHOR'S NOTE

THE MASTERMIND AGREEMENT

*T*he essence of life is multidimensional.

Every morning we open up two gifts that we often take for granted: our eyes. With these two complex lenses, we see life and the beauty of the surrounding world.

Light is a particular type of electromagnetic radiation that can be seen and sensed by the human eye, but this energy exists at a wide range of wavelengths. The electromagnetic radiation emitted by the sun is a very narrow section of electromagnetic energy—70% of its wavelengths are between .3 and 1.5 microns. Within this band, there are three types of light; visible, near-infrared, and ultraviolet.

The only part of the entire electromagnetic spectrum that our eyes are sensitive to is the visible region. Yet, there is so much more out there to see and feel.

If what we are actually seeing with our eyes is only a fraction of reality, there must be another way to visualize and internalize this magnificent existence.

A Crossing of Moments

Life is a crossing of moments. Moments may be fleeting, but we can cherish, savor, and preserve some of them in our memory. Each moment has its place in our lives: those that impact us positively, and those that we try to avoid.

No matter what moment in time we find ourselves in, each instance matters and affects us differently.

Many people fear death, but there are some that fear living. Some live empty lives, and some live rich lives—and some, give up. They stop living because of a life-changing moment, oftentimes a catalyst of sadness or despair. Circumstances affect people, but so do perspectives.

Life is about Focus

Most people don't see clearly without an outlook and perspective that is sharply defined. They have difficulty focusing. Whether they are easily distracted, or their mind is constantly wandering, they struggle to maintain focus if what they are looking for isn't distinctly perceptible.

As babies, we open our eyes to new colors and perspectives every minute. Clarity exists intuitively; it's innate. And love fills our being with the desire to see and experience more.

Over time, we lose this gift. Our minds get confused, and self-doubt enters. But *certain truth* still exists around us and *within us*.

Have you ever woken up in the morning with a powerful thought racing through you, a thought that seemed like the missing piece of the puzzle? It answered a question you harbored in your mind which you couldn't understand. It happens in a moment of calm, stillness, and emotional mastery.

What if we could each harness the ability to command moments in time and transform them into inspiration? A commitment to a constant pursuit of self-improvement that reaps immense rewards and dreams unimagined—transforming dreams unrealized into being.

Welcome to the art of Career Masterminding!

The Lens Ball: Contact Juggling

Eternal Vision

The activities and illustrations in this book will teach you to see with your heart, not just with your mind.

Most people believe that they take actions based on their *conscious mind*, but the truth is their *subconscious mind* is the principal motivator behind the decisions they make. It can read messages much faster than your conscious mind. In fact, it can process 500,000 times more than what the conscious mind can.

I will help you to use both *eyes*—your inner vision and your outer sight, when focusing on your future. Together, we will turn the page in our lives and look ahead.

The Sacred Gateway to Mastermind

This book is a *career and life manual* that will home in on your ability to shape sustainable and positive change—and find purpose. *Purpose is the sacred gateway to Mastermind.*

Charity is a purification of the soul. It's Purpose in motion. It begins at home and is integral (in all of its forms) to Purpose.

Purpose is defined as an object or an end *to be attained*. However, for a Career Mastermind™, purpose is less about what you want, and more about what you give.

As we design our lives, let's redefine Purpose. Purpose, for a career designer, is not an *end towards a means*; purpose is a *means towards an end*. Purpose is Perspective.

"Our lives begin to end the day we become silent about things that matter."
—*Martin Luther King Jr.*

Meaningful Work and Purpose

We all want our lives to have meaning. But for something to be meaningful, one has to own it and individualize it. It has to be *personally* inspired.

The impetus for this book is to celebrate that journey and to craft a purpose that fits your life's lens. It doesn't matter what that purpose is—as long as it's true *Purpose,* and it fills you with joy.

First things first—commit to yourself and forget about everyone else. Own a cause.

The Career Mastermind™ journey is a personal journey. Pace yourself. Start with this book's core elements. Some aspects will shock you, some of them will unsettle you, some will spark your interest—most will provide you with balance.

We all have a mission in life. What's yours?

Mastermind Secrets and Groups

All masterminds have secrets. It's these secrets that help them succeed and redefine who they are.

This book takes the mastermind concept to a whole new level, challenging the traditional sense of the word, setting boundaries, and at the same time, opening up new frontiers.

Let's start with this misconception: you join a mastermind group only to mentor others, so if you are already successful, you shouldn't be in one. This is simply not true. We are all students of students *of students,* and even if you are an expert or scholar, or a student of one, the quest for knowledge never ends.

You're probably wondering what a mastermind group really looks like, and more specifically, what a mastermind group feels like. It sounds fancy, huh? Maybe you have no clue, so you're interested in knowing how to build, facilitate, and/or participate in one of your own. Or, you may have taken part in a few groups with varying degrees of success, and you're intrigued to learn more.

Perhaps you want to know what you've done wrong, how you can make things better, or how to take them to the next level. You're in good hands, because I'm going to help you with all of those needs, plus introduce you to a brand new, unconventional understanding of what is called—"The Career Mastermind™."

"Real knowledge is to know the extent of one's ignorance."

—*Confucius*

Career Masterminds are leaders, not followers. They haven't paved paths for others—they have blazed them. Are you ready to blaze your own trail?

Home Sweet Home

Where do you start?

Everyone needs a center. Let's call it "home." After all, home is where the heart is. A powerful mindset is homemade.

Your home base and purpose are one and the same. Your *home* will become your *Purpose. This is a virtual or safe space, a place to reset.*

You'll need a focal point. When we pray or meditate, many of us have a target—our center of gravity.

From now on, think of yourself as a life archer. It's where and how you will find balance.

The same applies to *mastering* masterminding. It's your starting point. There is no finish line. However, the road ahead is far from linear. So let's personalize it.

Here's how: take your first initial and write a sentence or phrase using that initial and the word *change.* "H" is my letter. Your letter will be your base, stabilizing your career and life compass—you will learn how it does this in Chapter 7. Mine is below:

HASSAN: I (H)arness change

Now, looking ahead on your roadmap, turn to your final goal. Let's call and label that imaginary dot or point, "Z." Most of us won't know where that is or what it leads to, and that's alright.

Once you become a Career Mastermind™, that "Z" will be clear. It will become one of your life's treasures.

Focus on that imaginary "Z" for now. Try to visualize it. Map out the distance from your starting point to that destination, wherever it may be. Ask yourself, "How will I get there?"

Each destination will lead you on a new route to a new destination. Every destination is a point on the map, a dot that leads you closer to where you are meant to be, and what you are meant to do.

The Mastermind Agreement

You and I are entering into an agreement to tackle all of these questions and challenges. Everyone needs a team. Congratulations, you've just formed your first Mastermind Group. It only takes two people!

BE THE INSPIRATION

Sign: _____ Date: ___/___/___

Inner Viewing

The more you invest in this book by "inner viewing" yourself—reflecting, exploring, uncovering, and discovering the things or people that move you—the closer you move to that Purpose.

As you read:

a. Re-read each title, word, and sentence with pure reflection and progressive understanding.

b. Complete the worksheet at the end of each of the 7 "YOU Matter" Lenses, chapters 1-7. Revisit them monthly.

c. Underline the concepts and *Career and Life Hacks* that resonate with you.

d. Take notes throughout the book.

e. Visualize how you will apply each principle in your life.

f. Challenge yourself to build (not find) that purpose, and if you already have it, refine it.

While there are many books on the topic of personal career development, this book takes on a much broader perspective, helping you envision personal goals that have global impact.

Observation, philosophy, discovery and experience meet in a workbook that helps define ultimate meaning and purpose with *self* as a component of humanity.

We all need a Purpose greater than ourselves. Let's begin the journey of finding yours.

—H.A., January 1, 2019

"My alma mater was books, a good library… I could spend the rest of my life reading, just satisfying my curiosity."

—*Malcolm X*

FOREWORD

◆◆◆

THE PATH TO MEANINGFUL WORK

*I*n my twenty years educating college students and alumni and helping them launch their careers, I have witnessed a change in what helps people become masterminds of their life and career paths. Following a linear path and relying on traditional steps and services is no longer effective. In today's economy, competition among talent is too stiff, employment sectors are more diverse and intertwined, and education is not catching up with the evolving needs of employers. While employers are spending more resources than ever before to find, train, and retain talent, the job market still feels like an abyss for most job seekers and career explorers. But it does not have to be. Finding meaningful work is possible for most people. It just requires a different set of strategies from the traditional job search linear plans that we are all accustomed to.

Building a path towards life and career success can be achieved with a mindset shift, a bit of courage, lots of experimentation, and just a few key relationships to open the right doors of opportunity. These may sound like simple strategies, but I am often surprised at how many people ignore them and instead opt for career quizzes that predict future job title, plans that are often uninformed, and online job boards that rarely generate responses. While they have proven to be ineffective, these strategies continue to be widely used by job seekers and career coaches because they provide more certainty and clarity about the path forward, and because they give the illusion of being actionable.

The most successful career advancement strategies can be learned from those who have achieved success themselves. When I ask people about how they became successful at achieving meaningful work, they often share their stories of "luck," which typically seem to emerge from risk taking and mentoring relationships. It turns out that experimentation and relationships are the biggest predictors of career success, and those who apply them often throughout their lives, not just when they need a job, tend to achieve the highest levels of career success. Hassan Akmal exemplifies these traits. I first met Hassan while networking at one of the annual conferences hosted by the National Association of Colleges and Employers (NACE). He thanked me after my presentation and told me that I inspired him to strive towards becoming and training the "new breed of career professionals." Years later, I see he has done just that as an educator, author, speaker, and founder of Columbia University's Career Design Lab.

For most people, experimentation and mentoring can be challenging because they are ambiguous. How do we ask someone to be our mentor? And how do we choose the right opportunity that would be worthy of experimentation? The answer is simple: follow curiosity and join a community. Think about a subject area, a field, an industry, or a type of work which has intrigued you for a while. Chances are you have been busy and involved with life distractions and haven't had a chance to explore this further. This is your moment! Join a community around your area of curiosity and start experimenting with different tasks and building relationships. A community can be a meetup group, non-profit organization, a class or even school, or a part-time job or internship, even if you don't need the money. The point is to be in the same space as people with similar interests who tend to know more than you and are connected to a larger network. If you do this right, a few things will begin to happen fairly quickly:

1. You will begin to feel personal fulfillment because you are engaged in an activity that matches your curiosity and with people who support it.

2. You will be able to experiment with various tasks and develop skills that will open the doors for more opportunities down the road.

3. You will build relationships with people who have similar interests; among them will be the mentors who will guide you and connect you with their networks.

I have witnessed countless college students, alumni, and professionals transform their lives and careers with these strategies, and I have seen their impact firsthand on my own career. As Dean of Career and Experiential Education at Stanford University, I changed the career center's mission to focus on meaningful work and supported the creation of the Life Design Lab. These experiments and the many relationships and mentors I had over the years eventually led to my transition into the inaugural role of Vice Provost of Integrative Learning and Life Design at Johns Hopkins University. Experiments and relationships have transformed my life and career, and I believe they can transform yours too.

Running experiments with your career and building a network of mentors are not shortcuts to success. They require patience and a genuine investment of time and resources. The process may feel a bit long for some, but the return on investment is much higher than the short-term gains we usually experience from the traditional job search. The time to be the Career Mastermind™ of your life is now. Stop chasing jobs. Join a community. Surround yourself with mentors who can guide you and open doors of opportunity now and in the future. And when you get there, remember to pay it forward and give back to the communities and mentors who helped you achieve success.

Dr. Farouk Dey, Vice Provost for Integrative Learning and Life Design, The John Hopkins University

LinkedIn's Top Ten Voices in Education, 2018

TEDx Speaker (TEDx Johns Hopkins DC; Title: Life Purpose Reconsidered)

"Don't give in to your fears. If you do, you won't be able to talk to your heart."

—*Paulo Coelho,*
The Alchemist

PREFACE

———◆◈◆———

TAKING STEPS TO ADVANCE YOUR PERSONAL VISION

"You can't connect the dots looking forward; you can only connect them looking backwards. So you have to trust that the dots will somehow connect in your future. You have to trust in something — your gut, destiny, life, karma, whatever. This approach has never let me down, and it has made all the difference in my life."

—*Steve Jobs*

We often use the word "career" as a synonym for occupation, trade, profession, or vocation. This definition refers to what a person does to earn a living. It is formally defined as "an occupation undertaken for a significant period of a person's life and with opportunities for progress." Yet, in the modern age we are seeing people change careers more and more frequently. Longevity at any one place, in any one career, has significantly decreased. Thus, change is long overdue.

Career Disruption and Impact

The future of work is uncertain. In our current economic landscape, we are seeing people questioning their careers more often—in search of meaningful work. They are also seeking purpose-driven organizations that foster engagement, commitment, and the motivation to make an impact. Is the secret ingredient of extraordinary companies purpose?

There are thousands of careers, both traditional and non-traditional, not to mention the wealth of niches. Many of them require extensive education and training. Many others require little or no experience. **This book will completely subvert the historical concept of a career.**

Against the Trend

This book is about defining and developing "the new career"—mastering diverse occupations that can't be reduced to one title or trajectory—and surrender only to genuine merit.

My present role is the Inaugural Executive Director of Industry Relations and Career Strategies. However, it's a career with an expiration date. This is not a story about my work at Columbia University. This is a story about being a Storyteller with no end date in sight.

What is a Career Mastermind™?

A Career Mastermind™ is *a master of mindset—someone who has torn down the barrier between work and life—and developed a positive mindset.* This can manifest in seconds or years, depending on what level you reach. Think of all the events (good or bad) in your life as having lessons to teach, each one unique and a stepping stone towards the next challenge.

Adversity shapes character, and the struggles you endure define your future path. At the same time, the love for what you do adds to your aura. It's something that every Career Mastermind™ has and commands.

Welcome to "YOU Matter"

Many people don't love themselves. This needs to change. Forgive yourself for the past and promise yourself a new future. It's time to see things and yourself differently. *The reason the lenses in this book are called "YOU Matter" Lenses is because each lens belongs to you, nobody else.*

Throughout the process of designing and crafting your career and life vision, I will be right here to help guide and challenge you. I have shared these 7 lenses with thousands of students who to this day still write to me with appreciation about how it has changed their lives. You will need these lenses to build a game-changing growth mindset that will kick-start and prioritize your new career and life.

Close your eyes. *Turn to clear your vision.* Now open them.

NEW YORK, NY: From the "YOU Matter" Design Your Career Crown (Signature Series) at Columbia University. This event series teaches students how to activate a transformational mindset.

"Remember that wherever your heart is, there you will find your treasure."

—*Paulo Coelho*

Every Moment Plants a Seed in Your Soul

We each have to define our moments and *live in them*. We must understand them from the outside looking in, as well as from the inside looking out. Some moments last forever, and some you may not realize even happened. But they are still there. What about the "now?" Before you begin this journey to career masterminding, you must focus on the present and know where you are.

As seekers of our own truth, we must remember to stop and close our eyes every once in a while. We can't keep racing and competing with one another. That is not what life is all about: in fact, life will pass you by. We must reflect upon everything with much deeper lenses to broaden our perspectives. We must work to challenge our distorted views, including the challenges impeding our work and life balance.

The teachings of the 7 "YOU Matter" Lenses, each of which is dealt with in chapters 1–7, will help you cultivate the right mindset to approach those challenges with resilience and insight.

The overarching theme of this book is cultivating mindset and perspective. We must start with a *bird's eye view or drone perspective* as we begin to focus on what really matters to us. Later, this form of seeing will help us zoom in on what's happening and force us to be accountable to ourselves—as our footsteps fall wherever they may be. It will act as a checkpoint, as well as a benchmark. You will be able to see where you land in the larger scheme of things, and then make adjustments based on your life's radar.

You are the one living your life, not anyone else. Through deep reflection, something my father taught me, we can find clarity and begin to understand what is truly important to us as human beings: Purpose.

NEW YORK, NY: Pigeon on top of the Empire State Building

To *clear my vision*, I had to endure adversity, learn perseverance, and reflect and join the right mastermind groups—both formal and informal. Through this process, I was able to tackle new career directions, and overcome self-limiting beliefs and preset notions that were holding me back. I could reframe and reverse-engineer my thinking by mastering my passions and using them to help people solve difficult problems—then help them realize their goals. This attitude kick-started my journey of eliminating the separation between work and life, culminating in my present role as a Career Mastermind™—coaching others to be Career Masterminds too.

I will always remember David G. Allen's words as I go through life: "Patience is the calm acceptance that things happen in a different order than the one you have in your mind."

The worksheets in this book are focused on helping you identify the situations that bring out the best in you. They will assist in your evolution as a Career Mastermind™. When you work on them, picture your life in a way you would want to live if money or time wasn't an issue. The key here is not finding a job, but helping you refine your worldview, to help you pave your way to personal and career development. Are you ready to activate your transformational mindset?

It is important to consider the "personal" first, because all endeavors begin with a person. This is, after all, a form of Human-Centered Design, another term for Design Thinking. You must also start learning through this design to take risks, examine your career, explore your curiosity, and get out of your comfort zone. We will explore this in more detail in Chapter 2.

The Power of Clarity

Having a career and life vision is essential for you to find job satisfaction and success. It is a roadmap for where you want to go, keeping you focused on your long-term objectives so that you're not pushed in other directions.

It can be challenging to define your career and life vision on your own. To guide you through that process, a Career and Life Vision Consultant may be your best resource. It will take time for you to develop this reframing habit, but it's an investment that will pay dividends over your entire life.

In this book, you will learn how to build and navigate your own Career Mastermind™ Group while sharpening your ethos and tracking your progress on your own personal mission of career masterminding using the collective intelligence of others.

The Light at the End of the Tunnel

You might be thinking, *I still don't know where to start.* Let me help you take the first step. You need formidable confidence. Repeat after me, "My heart is a tunnel, but where's the light? You have no passion, but mine shines bright." Excellent, now we can continue this journey!

Clearing your vision is a never-ending process. It's like cleaning your car's windshield. When it's clean, you can drive with much more ease. For some of us, like me, driving is an "escape." It's therapeutic, as long as it's not on the 405 freeway during rush hour in Los Angeles! And when it's stop-and-go, it's stressful and you need patience. When it's pouring outside, you need the windshield wipers. On other days, you just need to wipe it down.

But despite where you travel or how bad the weather conditions, you always need to be alert and use your peripheral vision and mirrors. You have to be able to see and know your blind spots. The same applies to your career and life vision. Sometimes there is haze or fog, but you see it through.

Begin by searching for the highest point in your current or closest city, preferably one that has a coin-operated binoculars, or if not, a great view. Go there.

To be a Career Mastermind™, you must be able to clearly see with both eyes. One represents your career vision (left eye), and the other represents your life vision (right eye).

Your vision must be balanced, and we will explore this concept deeply in the book. I have also included *Career and Life Hacks—tips that will help you understand and grasp each of the "YOU Matter" Lenses.*

Personal vision begins with a reset. The following pages have instructions on how to reset the focus of your career and life vision one at a time, and then refocus them together after calibration.

CAREER AND LIFE HACK #1
Turn to clear vision. Positive change is clarity in motion.

Your Life and Your Big Screen

Think *big picture.*

Be a global visionary. Your positive mindset must be in place before the show begins, before you set foot on stage. Perspective will follow a positive mindset.

In the end, I hope that this book will be a place where people come and learn to better understand the world, as well as *a sanctuary for self-reflection*—where people come to better understand themselves.

Career and Life Mastery awaits, take your ethereal wings.

CALIBRATING YOUR CAREER AND LIFE VISION IS LIKE CALIBRATING BINOCULARS

The diopter adjustment is a control knob on your binoculars. It is designed to let you compensate for differences between your own two eyes. Once you set the diopter, then the two barrels should stay in proper relation. From then on you can focus, just by turning the central focusing knob.

Close your eyes, clear your mind, now open them.

CAREER VISION
Create a career bucket list in your imagination, what would it look like if time or money wasn't an issue? Where would you be working? What would you be doing and why?

LIFE VISION
Imagine your life in the far future, as clearly as you would visualize the rest of your day today or the week ahead. How much time would you have after work for yourself or family?

Turn off your racing thoughts. Take a deep breath. "Reset"

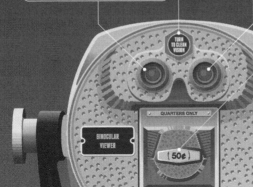

TURN TO CLEAN VISION

QUARTERS ONLY

BINOCULAR VIEWER

50¢

TO OPERATE TURN HANDLE ONE FULL TURN

5876

Infographic available for download at www.CareerMastermind.org/Resources

☑ CHECKLIST

- ☐ ⊕ Focus on a middle-ground object, using the central focusing ring.

- ☐ 🏅 Focus on your life vision or the point in your future where you want to be, before connecting to the next.

- ☐ ◎ Change the lens cap so that you can see through your right eye.

- ☐ 🌱 Look again, focusing now, on just your career vision.

- ☐ ⊕ With both eyes open, and staying in the same position, focus on the same object by using the diopter adjustment on the central column.

- ☐ 🏃 Focus on your vision or the point in your future where you want to be, before connecting to the next.

- ☐ 👁 Remove the lens cap and enjoy the matching view through both eyes at once.

- ☐ 👥 Now, see and visualize your new career and life vision into the future.

To calibrate the diopter, you must bring the binoculars up to your eyes, open both eyes and place your right hand on the diopter. When this concept is applied to you as a Career and Life Designer, the diopter is your "pause" or reset button (it is normally set to zero); it's time to adjust. If you turn it prematurely, it makes the binoculars ineffective, as the two eyes can never focus at the same distance, at the same time. You use the binocular's central focusing knob to focus both barrels at the same time.

Then, to adjust for differences between your eyes, you use the diopter adjustment one time to fine-tune the focus for the right barrel only. Like with binoculars, you just focus on your career and get caught up in your job, or just on your personal life; you don't close one eye and squint. When the eye is squeezed closed, the pressure on your eyeball temporarily changes it shape and makes it focus differently. That, can throw your adjustment completely off. Keep both eyes open, as you should be aware of your career and life vision (together), both short-term (nearby) and long-term (far away).

From then on, the two sides will stay focused together, whether you're looking at objects near or far. This applies to your career and life vision, as they need to be assessed collectively and together, to ensure they are always balanced.

Designed by **Hassan Akmal** and Illustration by **Ahmed Zaeem**

Infographic available for download at www.CareerMastermind.org/

Double Down On What You Love

People who love their jobs tend to live happy and prosperous lives. This aligns so well with a concept called "Ikigai" and will be dealt with in Chapter #1 for Lens #1. This is not opinion; it is based on data!

According to Gallup, only 13% of people love their jobs, which means that 87% of people do not. My job is to bring you into that 13%, or to raise that percentage. Remember that this 13% percent also crafted their own job; they didn't find it. My goal is to help equip you with the tools to build yours.

Consider the example of Steve Jobs. He was determined to do what he loved to get what he wanted, and look what became of him. He followed a dream and combined it with a formidable work ethic, and became the chairman, CEO, and co-founder of Apple Inc., as well as the chairman and majority shareholder of Pixar. He once said:

"You've got to find what you love. And that is as true for your work as it is for your lovers. Your work is going to fill a large part of your life, and the only way to be truly satisfied is to do what you believe is great work. And the only way to do great work is to love what you do. If you haven't found it yet, keep looking. Don't settle. As with all matters of the heart, you'll know when you find it. And, like any great relationship, it just gets better and better as the years roll on. So keep looking until you find it. Don't settle. Your time is limited, so don't waste it living someone else's life. Don't be trapped by dogma — which is living with the results of other people's thinking. Don't let the noise of others' opinions drown out your own inner voice. And most important, have the courage to follow your heart and intuition. They somehow already know what you truly want to become. Everything else is secondary."

Many people tell us to "follow our passion," but I will admit that this is bad advice! Most people do not just land a job and then build and design their life. The small percentage of people who are happy in their jobs have paved a path for themselves. They managed to change their jobs because they changed their lives.

I recommend changing yours by following the 5 Life Design Strategies below that helped me change mine:

Life Design Strategies That I Recommend

1. Test drive your future.

2. Trust your gut.

3. Play to your strengths.

4. Craft your job.

5. Shop for the right boss.

The process of mastering your mindset begins with clearing your vision, and it never ends.

"Every single one of you has a purpose—it's developed from your passion.

And when one is on point with that purpose, it can help change the world for the better."

—*Hassan Akmal*

INTRODUCTION

CAREER ALIGNMENT

"And think not that you can guide the course of love. For love, if it finds you worthy, shall guide your course."

—*Kahlil Gibran*

*E*veryone has a bucket list, right? You know, the things you want to do before you die—like jumping out of an airplane, or competing in a triathlon. Are there places that you always wanted to go? Perhaps you wanted to visit the Taj Mahal or see the Amazon rainforest one day?

What about a *Career Bucket List*?

Most people say "yes" to the first question only; they have never heard of a career bucket list, let alone have any idea of how to prioritize one.

This book introduces this new concept of "Career Bucket List" to the world and will help you create one. Regardless of your bucket list, it must be *your* list, not anyone else's.

Do we have a deal?

Designing Your Career Crown

I realized early on that I should stop worrying about what others think. You should realize this too. Your career crown was meant for you to wear. It must be tailored to your size, your build, and your comfort. You might grow out of it, but if that happens, you can design a new one.

My Wish for You

To make an *impact*. I relate careers to the chapters of a book's legacy. You always want to make a difference.

You might outgrow your position, or get bored at some point, but it's your right to move on when you want and need to. Maybe you enjoyed doing something for years, but now you don't feel you are adding the same value. Or, it's time to move on to something new.

Maybe you even mastered your art, but that doesn't mean you have to do it for the rest of your life. The process of designing is continuous. You may have many careers, each equally important and meaningful.

This may all sound like a lot to take in, so I would like to answer some common and anticipated questions now and throughout this book. I will start with five frequently asked:

1. Where do I begin?

2. How do I connect passion to purpose?

3. How can I develop a career strategy when I am not sure what my passion is?

4. I have many passions, but which one do I focus on?

5. How do I transition and/or advance my career?

These questions are difficult and complex to answer, but when I contemplate how I ended up where I am today, I know it came from my adherence to a few principles and reframings that I will cover in this book.

How Do You Begin?

You always begin where you are.

That's where I began. I immersed myself in the deep, long, and continuous process of self-reflection and purposeful thinking. Whether you do this while you perform yoga, take long walks, drive, meditate, or pray, it doesn't matter, as long as it's not rushed, and it's genuine. You will find yourself in a moment of truth (or truths) and find it to be rewarding.

For me, I never found long self-assessment tests to be very conclusive. I don't recommend them. Keep in mind, I am not your typical career coach. I believe in counsel, not just advice. I also believe that students need to stop looking at career centers as their "answer all" solution or as a placement center. This couldn't be further than the truth.

The process to master your career begins and ends in self-discovery; it begins and ends with you.

CAREER AND LIFE HACK #2
You first.

Articulate Your Reflections

Reflection is a kind of reality test for understanding our experience. Reflection is the way we discover and compose the meaning of our experience. Having a career and life vision gives you the ability to see your work and career—what you do and where you do it—in a way that is personally meaningful, stimulating, inspiring, fulfilling, *and* in alignment with who you are.

Many successful managers and executives will tell you that they did not plan their careers or have specific career goals. Rather, they had an idea (an image) and an understanding of what they liked and did not like, as well as some general guidelines for how to lead their work and personal lives. People that think like this are more likely to be flexible. People that are flexible are more likely to adapt and grow. So, guidelines are good, but meticulous plans, although they have their merits, can be detrimental.

I've learned that there is a difference between having a career and life vision versus being able to define a specific job in a specific industry at a specific company. Although you could consider that a career goal, it is not a career and life vision. This brings me to my next point.

Career development is a lifelong project of exploring our personal experience, naming its meaning, and living in a way that translates this meaning into action. The more I learned about myself, the more I knew I needed to learn from the world. You will find this to be true too.

CAREER AND LIFE HACK #3
**Make your career and life lens
a panoramic lens**

Connecting Passion to Purpose

Jullien Gordon, Freedom Finder and Business Coach, and someone who has mentored me both directly and indirectly, speaks of the "missing link" between passion and purpose. He says, "You must find your passion, master it, then use it to solve another person's problem." If you can do that, you have a business proposition. Create a positive result in someone else's life—that's value.

You can't just wake up and find one evergreen single and identifiable passion, because you have many. Your passion or passions need a focal point; they need roots—something that you are good at, or that you want to (and can) get good at. Let's be honest; if you don't like doing it, you are likely not passionate about it or very good at it. When it's laid out, it becomes simpler. You must understand it and agree with it conceptually. Then, you let that seed grow as you work on it. Every day that you water this idea, it will grow. Before long, your seed will be a fully-realized tree. Its fruit will be your successes; its taste, your happiness; and its growth, your pride.

What about Purpose?

How can you identify it?

In *The 8 Cylinders of Success*, Jullien shares the 8 "P"s to help you align purpose. I have found them extremely useful in my life, so take a moment to reflect and answer the following questions in Part 1 and 2 below:

Part 1: Where am I?

1. Principles » Your dashboard

   What beliefs equate to success to me?

2. Passions » Your keys

   What do I love doing and why?

3. Problems » Your fuel

   What social, scientific, technical, and/or personal problem do I want to solve?

4. People » Your motor

   Whom do I want to serve and how?

Part 2: Your Destination—Where am I going?

5. Positioning » Your lane

   What do I want to be #1 at in the world?

6. Pioneers » Your pace cars

   Who are my models, mentors, and/or guides?

7. Picture » Your road map

   What's my vision for myself and my world?

8. Possibility » Your destine-nation

   What is possible in the world with me that would not be possible without me?

How to Transition and/or Advance Your Career

A quick-fix, for both cases (and often missed), is to focus on transferable skills! You must reposition yourself, using them as cornerstones when building your career profile.

But before that, here's what I did to prepare myself for these scenarios: I read every book that was out there on purpose, career, and life. I read books like *The Art of Happiness at Work*, *What You're Really Meant to Do*, and *The Rhythm of Life*.

I was a visualizer: I liked to visualize goals and actualize them later. Whether it was foreseeing where I would ace my opponent on the tennis court or anticipating a volley, I imagined it happening first. I considered every little detail—where the ball would land—and what my next step would be. I applied this same concept to my life.

I have learned lessons from hundreds of mentors and from my own experiences that have helped me capitalize on best practices over the course of 10+ years as a director of career services. I have included many of them in this book as a guide for you.

Be a Hub of Connectivity

To fully understand career masterminding, and to assist you in a transition, you must have a strong grasp of dynamic collaboration. You must know who your informed connectors are at all times.

I surrounded myself with people that would nourish my inquiring mind. A mastermind group focused on masterminding careers, including mine, became for me—*a magnet of acquisition.* I needed a catalyst to accelerate my dreams, a peer-to-peer mentoring group that could help its members troubleshoot their inner and outer challenges.

Have you ever heard the expression: a true friend is brutally honest? Well, that's what a mastermind group is—except that these peers help lift you out of life's ditches.

Over the course of your life, you will navigate many transitions, both personal and professional. As you do, it may be helpful to align mastermind groups with your goals.

The term "mastermind group" was coined in 1925 by Napoleon Hill in his book, *The Law of Success*, and described in more detail in his 1937 book, *Think and Grow Rich*.

The peer-to-peer sharing and loyalty in these groups will help you articulate and reconnect with your career and life vision. This creates an action-oriented bias. This "bias" should be something that moves you, or sparks your inquisitiveness, and commands your thirst for knowledge. It should drive you forward and prevent you from looking back. It should motivate you. You may be shy at first, you may hesitate, or you may not even want to take this seriously. I know that it can be daunting, but that is what the group is for: to keep you sailing against the strong winds and currents.

The Intersection of Your Talent and Calling

Career Masterminding centralizes where you're at mentally in order for you to better understand how your talents can make the world a better place. It's the intersection of your talent and calling. Humanity comprises each and every one of us, and each one of us belongs to and is humanity. We are all unique and special in our own right. Every single person on the face of the planet needs and has Purpose.

From a young age we are instructed in both school and at home as to what we must do and how we must act. We are taught to follow socially accepted and traditional paths, and if we do that, we will be rewarded with "success." This not only limits our beliefs, but also our possibilities. The transformational and transitional path is the path less traveled. It's up to us, not anyone else, to justify what *success* means. Is success loving who you are, what you do, and how you do it?

Silent Wins

The gift of success in my life has had its roots sprouting since I was young. For example, cultivating my enthusiasm for my career in tennis was transformative. It's interests like these, when filtered, that impel us toward the necessary actions to improve our lives.

As a former professional tennis player, I have seen the enormous pressure athletes face. This includes the fears, the expectations, the mental toughness, and concentration it takes to survive a competitive tennis match and win. Every match changes you. Every "near win" helps you refocus and improve.

Inscribed above the entrance to Wimbledon's Centre Court is an inspirational line from Rudyard Kipling's poem, "If": "If you can meet with Triumph and Disaster, and treat those two imposters just the same." That line greets those ready to battle for one of tennis's most treasured trophies in one of my favorite tournaments.

Tennis taught me about life and love. It wasn't about goals or success, but a constant pursuit of excellence, and more importantly, mastery. *Akmal* means "to be the most complete" but not perfect or 100%. Mastery is the 99% that keeps motivating you to get better. It will play a role in your journey just as it has in mine.

"Tennis uses the language of life. Advantage, service, fault, break, love … every match is a life in miniature"

—*Andre Agassi*

In life, sometimes you're winning, and sometimes you're losing, but you're always loving the game.

The Balance of a Life Worth Living

Our careers, like life, can be volatile. You can be down and almost out, then make a comeback. There are ups and downs, but you control how you react to them. You have to make things happen. It's like having break points: you take a risk and go for it! Sometimes you have your day, and sometimes nothing goes your way, but both experiences generate thoughts and feelings that influence you.

Tennis players are thinkers. We analyze, we reflect, we explore, and we learn. It's our nature as human beings to turn things over in our minds. When we escape our comfort zone and act under pressure, we test our capacity and reach. But so much of it is timing. There is a saying in tennis: "Are you working hard enough to get lucky?" This book will guide you in becoming a thinker too.

We can play on the offensive or defensive in a tennis match, and the same applies in life itself. We are generally more comfortable on one side versus the other, but you need both in life, and you need to know when to change things up.

The Quest for Love

The quest for love changes us. It helps us mature and learn our capacity to love. *The more you truly love, the better you can see.*

Havencrest Castle is one of America's best-kept secrets. Purchased in 1976 (the year I was born), it was originally known as Greenleaf Mansion. More importantly, this castle is the source not only of an amazing love story, but of finding one's calling and fulfilling a lifelong dream.

The artist and owner of Greenleaf Mansion, Alan St. George, met his wife Adrianne when he was just 13. He said that it was love at first sight, and married her ten years later, at the age of 23. Together, they bought a 22-room home along the Mississippi River, which they turned into 63 rooms, each room dedicated to their love.

The minute I heard my first love story,
I started looking for you, not knowing
how blind that was.
Lovers don't finally meet somewhere,
they're in each other all along.
—Rumi

Today, the castle has over 60 rooms, some secret and never seen by the public. Their credo: "Reality is for those who lack Imagination."

SAVANNA, IL: Alan St. George doing what he loves, sculpting!

St. George explains one of the quirks of his house:

"Our anniversary clock on the table is stopped at three o'clock. You'll see a lot of clocks throughout the house stopped at three o'clock—that's the time we got married."

SAVANNA, IL: Mr. and Mrs. St. George

Both Adrianne and George were artists. George was the creator, and Adrianne, the visionary. Every carving, every detail was envisioned and designed. George explains:

"We weren't practical. But this is kind of the result of two impractical people."

They constructed their house on their own, but they made every piece for each other. George put his heart into his work.

"For those 30 years, there was almost never a time you didn't hear a hammer or a saw somewhere in the house because we just kept adding."

But just as quickly as it began, their love story was cut short by Adrianne's death. The two made a promise, a phrase they lived by. "Our motto (is), *semper nos.* It's Latin for 'always us'—it's the idea that marriage goes beyond life," says St. George. The phrase is everywhere in their castle, painted on the walls and even carved into dishes.

"Marriage goes beyond life. We are married, we're still married, not till death but eternally. She's always on my mind and in my heart, and she always will be."

It's a promise they made then, and one that he's keeping forever in his castle in the forest. This love story has no end, and that is inspiring.

"Adrianne taught me how to love and be loved and to give all of yourself and then you get everything back."

SAVANNA, IL: Their love sealed by their motto, "Semper Nos".

After 30 years of meticulous work on their beloved property, Adrianne died of heart failure, leaving Alan alone with the monument of their love. Since then, Alan has opened the house to viewers on select weekends. This is a story of two passions colliding, and the realization of two people's calling.

"Being deeply loved by someone gives you strength, while loving someone deeply gives you courage."

—*Lao Tzu*

This place was special to me because I proposed to a (now-ex) fiancé there, who accepted. I told Alan about the proposal, and he was so touched, he wrote me a card on my way out to thank me. This was a moving gesture, even though my marriage did not go ahead as planned. But I proposed here because it was a place of love and magic, and Alan's class was a validation of its truth. Nothing would change that. And that's magic.

"The greatest happiness of life is the conviction that we are loved; loved for ourselves, or rather, loved in spite of ourselves."

— *Victor Hugo*

My mother said she never wanted to remarry because she is waiting for my dad and believes she will see him again in paradise, where they will be reunited. Alan believes the same, and I was honored to share this story with him.

Like my mother, Alan never remarried. I have always been a die-hard romantic, but it's rare that I meet someone who outdoes my romanticism. Just imagine it: every single artistic structure in their castle is handmade as a testimony of their love. If this isn't the next best Bollywood movie, what is?

And here it is, the Havencrest Castle:

SAVANNA, IL: Havencrest Castle

CAREER AND LIFE HACK #4
Make your love your process, not your outcome.

Your True Self

I found my love as a pro tennis player. It was not romantic love, but tennis is certainly a game of love! It filled me with pride and afforded me the most balance. During training, I felt this love: it was like a feeling of euphoria when I got the most pop on my shots. It became my rhythm of life. Much like a tennis player finds his pace, we do the same in this mysterious world. We call it "being in the zone."

Imagine being in the 5th set at Wimbledon. You just came back from two sets to love, you are in the finals, and millions of people are watching. Imagine that you have lost all sense of time and place. Your legs keep running, the shots keep landing. You feel like you can outrun anyone in the stadium. You anticipate your opponent's next move, almost like a tease, and you just can't miss. You are in the zone. Alan was in the zone when he built the Havencrest Castle. No matter how long it took, there was no stopping him. Very few of us have that kind of deep motivation. We often spend too much time focusing on the wrong things.

"When you are good at something, make it your everything."

—Roger Federer

Most people search for happiness. However, the search for happiness can make people unhappy. But we are obsessed with the search. Think about it. Alan didn't describe success as the key to happiness. There are plenty of famous actors who landed the biggest roles of their careers, yet they were unhappy. Many have reached the top of the career ladders, have millions in the bank, but are suffering from deep depression. Suicide is still one of the leading causes of death in the developed world. So if success isn't the key to happiness, what is?

On my way out of the castle, I was invited to see a room that isn't normally shown to the public. I had just come out of the doll room, a room that felt almost haunted, so when I was asked, "Do you really want to see it?" I said to myself, "Well, what could be more nerve-racking than the doll room?!"

There I saw a different theme, the pieces after Alan's loss of Adrianne.

SAVANNA, IL: Alan St. George holding one of his sculptures from the series
"With These Hands"

Alan used pain as his motivation, and what surfaced was self-awareness and success. Alan took grief, and made it his friend and motivation. He used the series *With These Hands* to cope with his loss and to help put things into perspective. This inspired me, as I'm sure it will inspire you. We all carry sadness. It's always there, though some of us just deal with it better than others.

"When it is dark enough, you can see the stars."

—*Ralph Waldo Emerson*

The way to happiness is through struggle and self-reflection. The key to happiness is meaning, not success. Happiness is deeper than that.

I have kept in touch with Alan and my respect for him has only grown. He taught me what true happiness is. He describes it as a "life well-lived." He still practices his labor of love. Why? You may ask. Well, because he loves it.

I asked him to write his love story, many asked—and he did! I received this in the mail on March 8, 2019:

Havencrest's Love Story, "Always Us"

There are not many people like Alan in this world—there never have been, and there never will be.

If the key to happiness is meaning, then what is the key to meaning? *Purpose.*

Take a couple minutes to read and answer the questions on the following pages:

Master of Perspective

I wrote this book because I wanted to discuss the merits of humility, self-awareness, and purpose, including how you view yourself. It's my attempt to help others *dream while awake*, both personally and professionally. Both personal memoir and practical counsel that can be implemented in order for you to become a Career Mastermind™, a Master of Perspective.

We all need to belong and have meaningful relationships. Purpose allows us to use strengths to serve others, and this drives you forward. You must then transcend the hustle and bustle of daily life, elevate yourself, and discover a worldview, a holistic perspective. A holistic perspective is fundamental to both career masterminding and storytelling.

Beyond Redemption, Growth, and Love

Happiness fluctuates. It comes and goes, much like money. But the things that remain despite this flux are meaning and purpose. These are the ropes you hold on to when times are tough.

Throughout our lives, especially in America, we are deceived. We are told that in order to be happy, we have to be successful. This is not necessarily true.

There is data that indicates that chasing happiness actually leads to unhappiness. Modern society is enamored with success and happiness, and often neglects other central tenets of life. The problem is that these two words are entirely subjective. Is there more to life than chasing happiness? Is there more to life than success?

Of course there is.

THE KEY TO MEANING IS PURPOSE

Happiness comes and goes—like money, but meaning and purpose remain. Lift yourself above the New York City hustle and bustle by finding "flow". Flow is the psychology of optimal experience, it's when you are "in the zone" as a tennis player or athlete. When you are in a state of mind when you lose your sense of all time and place, and everything falls like dominos in the right direction. It's when it clicks, when the aces happen and the serve "pops", and when you find the sweet spot in your form and energy.

Infographic available for download at
www.CareerMastermind.org/Resources

MOMENT BY MOMENT
How can you experience life the way you
want to experience it?

_____

_____

DESIGN YOUR PURPOSE
How does one find or create his/her calling?

_____

_____

LIFE IS WORTH LIVING
Does money define happiness? If yes,
to what point?

_____

_____

You are unique.
Nobody else is you.

Doing away with your narrow vision in favor of your panoramic vision is not always easy to do when we are caught up in the mundane rituals of daily life.

We spend so many hours working, dreaming of the day that we can finally be our own boss.

Why? Because autonomy is important to us. We are all entrepreneurs, but we don't realize that some of us only have one client, and that's the employer we work for right now.

If our current job is our job because it pays the bills and nothing more, then we have already lost. That should be a wake-up call to what else is important in our lives, like our core values. I have spent my entire life reverse-engineering from them. This has led me to varying careers, from professional athletics to finance, and finally, to serving others through writing—I actually decided to be an author during one of my own "YOU Matter" workshops. That's when I am really in the zone and benefiting from the momentum I create. That is when I lose track of time and place and do nothing but focus. That is when I am most fulfilled. You can experience this too.

Fulfillment awaits all of us.

The horizon calls and is waiting. Let's set sail at dawn.

Thinking About Thinking

What we need to be good at for career masterminding is metacognition.

What is that, you might ask? Put simply, metacognition is "thinking about thinking." It is something we as humans are both gifted and cursed with. In order to translate this idea to the workspace, we have to become aware of what we are feeling whenever it happens and how our bodies react. Metacognition allows us (in real-time) to see how we and our bodies are reacting to the world. It is fundamental to separate our perceptions of what is happening in any given event (subjective) to analyze what is really happening (objective). Later, this "thinking about thinking" becomes "thinking without thinking" as you program your mind, and thinking effectively becomes second nature.

I was aware of metacognition during my freshman year at the University of California, San Diego, before I transferred to the University of California, Los Angeles (UCLA). I got very good at it, because I was very confident, but I knew not to be arrogant. I blocked out the negativity and doubt from others because I believed in myself. I was able to go up to anyone, even the prettiest girl on campus, and introduce myself. My philosophy being that *if I was positive, positive things would happen to me, and that if I was negative, then negative things would happen.* This was effective, especially when I was going against the grain.

I pushed against the will of my parents, who wanted me to be a doctor in order to realize my dream to be a professional tennis player. So many people told me that I couldn't do it, but before I knew it, I was recruited by UCLA, which had the number one men's tennis team (Division I) in the whole country.

CAREER AND LIFE HACK #5
Optimism and positivity are not delusional. They're practical.

With metacognition, you must be innovative and design your own life. You are in control. You are building your way forward. You are not merely finding your true ambition or purpose, you are creating it. It is important to remember these ideas in "pause moments" as you push forward into the future.

Metacognition is the first step to becoming a Career Mastermind™.

Nuggets of Wisdom

Look inside your career and life prisms—you will find them in your heart. Your career and life are like diamonds; they have many facets. Each facet of the diamond has its own reflection and clarity. It comes from within. You must find the right lens, the right clarity, and the right light to see the uniqueness and beauty of each angle, because each represents a different perspective.

"In the gap between thoughts, non-conceptual wisdom shines continuously."

—*Milarepa*

Be Your Own Inspiration

Nelson Mandela was born in Umtata, part of South Africa's Cape Province, in 1918. He was initially given the name Rolihlahla, a Xhosa term which means "troublemaker." He was later referred to by his clan name, Madiba. Alongside President de Klerk, Mandela was awarded the Nobel Peace Prize for his service in taking down apartheid in South Africa.

After the death of his father in 1927, the nine-year-old Mandela was adopted by a high-ranking Thembu regent called Jongintaba Dalindyebo, who entered him into a mastermind group. He was essentially being groomed for a role in tribal leadership.

Following his 27-year imprisonment for living by his ideology and subsequent election as President of South Africa, Mandela faced the task of unifying a country divided by race.

Career Masterminds™ align their own careers. They fight for what they love and do what it takes to survive to live the life they have chosen and embraced. This poem helped Nelson endure that test of time and become a Master of Perseverance:

INVICTUS

Out of the night that covers me,
Black as the pit from pole to pole,
I thank whatever gods may be
For my unconquerable soul.

In the fell clutch of circumstance
I have not winced nor cried aloud.
Under the bludgeonings of chance
My head is bloody, but unbowed.

Beyond this place of wrath and tears
Looms but the Horror of the shade,
And yet the menace of the years

Finds and shall find me unafraid.
It matters not how strait the gate,
How charged with punishments the scroll,
I am the master of my fate,
I am the captain of my soul.

—William Ernest Henley

HOW TO BE A
CAREER
MASTERMIND™

Be in the driver seat of your own life,
otherwise—life will drive you.

PART 2: THE AUTHOR'S EXPERIENCE AND YOUR 7 "YOU MATTER" LENSES

MIDTOWN, NY: New Year's Eve in Times Square

CHAPTER 1 (LENS 1): POSITIVE MINDSET — PERCEPTION IS EVERYTHING

"When you change the way you look at things, the things you look at change."

—*Wayne Dyer*

Every New Year's Eve, at exactly 11:59pm, the Times Square Ball, on the roof of New York's One Times Square, descends 141 feet (43 m) in 60 seconds—along a specially designed flagpole.

MARINA DEL REY, CA: Hourglass

Much like watching the sand of an hourglass slowly trickle down, one second at a time, one grain at a time, New Yorkers and countless tourists from all over the world gaze at the lighted crystal-paneled ball as if looking into the future—and they are mesmerized.

Perspectives change over time, just like careers. They evolve, and each year, we evolve.

In 1920, a 400-pound wrought iron ball replaced the original ball made of wood. In 1955, an aluminum ball, weighing only 150 pounds, replaced the iron one. In the 1980s, new neon lights, rhinestones, and strobes were added. The ball went through another revision in 2000, and then in 2007, it became the magnificent work of art the world sees now: a crystal ball (like the lens ball I hold in my hand), made up of 2,688 crystal triangles illuminated by 32,256 LED lights. In each triangle lives a story of heartbreak and hope, chased away by the lights of a new horizon.

NEW YORK, NY: Times Square Ball

Beneath that resplendent ball, we make our New Year's resolutions and promises to loved ones, but above all to ourselves. It's where some stories end, and others begin.

NEW YORK, NY: New Year's Eve Wishing Wall

There below, close by, is a magical place, where the manifestations of these resolutions are realized. These seeds are given birth—people enter with hopes and dreams, with embers of fear, but leave with aspirations of self-reinvention.

Our students love this place. They can be themselves and aspire to be anything they wish to be. Once they enter, their lives are never the same. It's called the *Career Design Lab.*

MIDTOWN, NY: The Career Design Lab

Outside its tall doors—once upon a time, I watched the clock hit midnight on New Year's Eve, knowing my life had changed forever. It was time to design my career with no end in sight, no restrictions, no borders: the *designing of my life.*

My story of *storytelling* begins here.

The Mind of a Leader

My journey to becoming a Career Mastermind™ began when I was just a child. Unbeknownst to me at the time, my childhood memories would become a rock-solid foundation for both my success and career. However, it's these often-forgotten moments that, when remembered, allow us to truly reflect on the meaning of life and alter our often negative mindsets.

When I was a child, I was very impressionable and followed my father's ideological convictions. It was not until later on that I began to realize that this was my foundation for becoming successful in both my career and personal life. He taught me to be ethically sound and to aspire to improve my character every day. He wanted me to reach for the stars and to be bold. The sky was not the limit. This is something my grandmother would later reinforce.

"To understand the heart and mind of a person, look not at what he has already achieved, but at what he aspires to."

—Khalil Gibran

The Experience That Molded my Perception

It all started when I was seven years old. My father used to call all the kids that were outside playing tag—as if our lives depended on it—to quickly come into his bedroom and sit in a circle. It was the last thing we wanted to do. We were just kids wanting to mess around and have fun. But this was my father, and he always wore this serious expression, challenging anyone to defy him. We would sit on the floor looking up at him. I swear his gaze was almost a threat, his forehead wrinkling into a scowl. He never had to tell us to sit still and look into his eyes. We did it anyway.

CLOVIS, CA: Fresh dates

The room was tense. Between us and my father, on the bright sunlit carpet, there was a large bowl of crystal date seeds. As we stared in awe, he gently poured them into the large bowl on the carpet. For what seemed like an infinite moment, the seeds streamed down, echoing a noise reminiscent of heavy rain hitting the shutters outside.

Whenever my new friends were around to sit in the circle, they would have this puzzled, almost frightened look on their faces. My father would say, "Repeat after me." The pupils of our eyes doubled in size, fearing that we were in trouble for shuffling too loud. But we weren't in trouble. It was important for my father to look at us and see the sincerity in our eyes. He wanted us to focus on one thing.

Purpose.

Under the watchful eyes of my father, we would recite God's 99+ Attributes as if we were meditating. When I look back, I realize we were programming our minds in a spiritual mastermind ritual or focus group. My father knew it would somehow stay with us until the end of days. Was it weird or was it genius? Only time would tell.

Once we finished about 300 date seeds, moving them one by one with each recitation from the big pile onto the empty pile, he would say, "Again"—and we would start over. Thirty minutes felt like three hours. All we wanted to do was go back outside and play.

Somehow, even in our early youth, we knew this task had a purpose.

CLOVIS, CA: At the age of seven

During these brief sessions, I recall my dad emphasizing the brevity of life and how Purpose was everything. Over time, these spiritual enlightenment sessions got more intense (and fun) as he would declaim "Zor-say," which meant "louder" in our native tongue. Each time we said it, my father wanted us to say it with more passion, more meaning, more understanding, and more sincerity. We did, and it resonated.

Finding Your Own Experience

Finding a successful career begins with a solid foundation. Through my own journey, I've based most of my life on this core story and principle. My father has become a rock in my life, and his guidance has left a lasting impression that has helped me develop a positive mindset.

The purpose of sharing my story isn't necessarily to inspire and fuel you. While this memory resonates with me, it won't necessarily motivate everyone to become a Career Mastermind™. It's the personal connection that makes this story my building block. Thinking back on those days, I am overtaken with nostalgia and can appreciate those lessons more readily as an adult. It's important for you to find that same building block in your own life—what made you into who you are today.

Take a moment to think back on situations in your own life, from childhood to where you are now, especially those moments that seemed mundane or completely negative but helped you navigate through your career and life. This will help you develop a more positive mindset, preparing you for both the best and worst times you'll face in your career.

While this may seem relatively easy, changing your perception doesn't always come as readily as you might expect. It is a constant uphill battle to keep a positive mindset during the worst times. You have likely conditioned yourself over the course of your lifetime to have a certain reaction and perception when you encounter an obstacle or failure. So, it's only natural that it will take time and constant effort to completely change the way you look at things.

The Art of Evolving: Why Your Mindset Matters in Your Career

Developing a healthier, more positive mindset gives you the opportunity to grow both personally and professionally. Once you clear away the negativity, you'll gain insight into possibilities and opportunities that you were once ignorant to. While it's almost cliché to say, a positive mindset is influential and paramount to your success in any chosen field.

This, in particular, helps you open your eyes to how all seven lenses in this book work together to develop your Career Mastermind™ mindset. As you work through each lens and identify each core principle, you'll have more awareness and a forward-thinking, positive mindset. The more clearly you can understand and relate to each lens, the easier it is to achieve your status as a Career Mastermind™.

CAREER AND LIFE HACK #6

Do you have perspective? Your creative and design space has no borders.

Unwillingness to change your perception will likely stall you both in your career and in your everyday life. Opportunities usually come when you are flexible and prudent with your decisions and time. If you constantly dwell on things with a negative mindset, you often lose sight of other ways to achieve your goals. So instead of looking at things in a planned way, open your mind to a spontaneity that will allow you to target and seize opportunities that come along.

Change Your Perspective, Change Your Life

As you read each chapter, you will see how I have built my career on this exact foundation and core principle, and this will serve to complement the guidance I am giving you. Even during the most tumultuous times, I've managed to not just survive, but thrive because of my positive perspective and outlook on life. My purpose in this book is to help you also use a positive mindset to influence and benefit your own career.

I have outlined a few steps that have been helpful to me and, in turn, should be helpful to you:

- Be confident, but never arrogant. People are drawn to confident people, but shy away from arrogant people.

- Masterminding your mindset is the foundation to mastering your career.

- Metacognition and your mind's map will broaden your future, and this will fill your heart with gratitude. Make sure you appreciate it.

- Clear your vision, be grateful, and focus.

- Block out negative thoughts, no matter whom they come from. Believe in yourself and if necessary, go against the grain.

Are you ready to truly make a change?

Our Past is a Mirror of Reflections

When my father was with us, he and my mother had a side hustle. We all need side hustles. Not just for times like this, but in general. Mine are keynote speaking, writing, advisory roles in startups, and investing in various businesses completely unrelated to higher education. For my father, it was selling backpacks and school supplies, and for my mother, it was leveraging her artistic talent. She loved flowers—all kinds, from daisies to roses. She also loved arranging them uniquely and would later sell them. Our entire garage looked like a rose garden thanks to her. People loved them, and it generated supplemental income. She did it because she loved doing it.

We used to wake up at 4:30 a.m. in the morning on Saturdays and Sundays to make it early to the Sunnyside Drive-In Theatre Swap Meet. Like a flea market, a Swap Meet is a place where people come to buy, sell, and/or trade various goods, including electronics, clothes, organic vegetables, herbs, and furniture. Yes, my parents worked seven days a week! In fact, they invested in a huge white cargo truck to carry it all in, costing them $20,000! They weren't playing.

CLOVIS, CA: Sunnyside Drive-In Theatre (Swap Meet venue)

As for my older brother, Shiraz, and my younger sister, Sara, they hated it. These meets began so early in the morning, and it was freezing cold. Aside from helping our parents, we weren't committed, especially on weekends. Occasionally, we would wander around and just shop, which was fun (even though we hardly ever bought anything), but that was about it. I actually had a crush on one of our fellow vendors, a girl from Nicaragua who helped her dad sell; she would also wander—I loved her smile. She made those mornings bearable.

CLOVIS, CA: Inside the Swap Meet

Destiny in Motion

My tennis career actually started after a hard day's work at the swap meet. For my 10th birthday, my father bought me my first tennis racquet. It was *destiny in motion*—I had recently begun playing paddle tennis in elementary school! I won the first tournament I ever entered, a doubles tournament with my best friend at the time, Oskar Choynowski. We used to ask our parents to drop us off an hour early at school, just to play tennis. That was the beginning of my commitment to something I loved.

Reality is Not Kind

Unfortunately my father didn't live to see it, but life had to go on. When I turned eleven, my father suffered an unexpected stroke and passed away, *peacefully.* This compounded my family's need for a side hustle. We thought our swap meet days would soon be over, but this changed everything.

Life got even harder. It was just too much work, and school was intense—we needed a day off. But then it happened. My mother walked into our room before the sunrise on a Saturday morning. We all pretended we were asleep. Believe it or not, she left without us. Bless her soul! We never let her do that again, as unloading the truck was not a one-person job. It takes a team. It would take us at least an hour to load and another hour to unload. That should give you an idea of how big the truck was. That's also why we got there early. I was convinced I just needed a chai tea in the morning. If it was made right, it gave me power. My mother fulfilled that promise daily.

You Are Your Only Limit

Losing a family member is traumatic. Talk about being outside of your comfort zone and a feeling of uncertainty. It was scary. As our economic status quickly declined, I remember having just 50 cents in my pocket: one quarter for a cookie and the other for a chocolate milk. That was all I could afford at the time. I began losing weight and was the thinnest I had ever been. But our family didn't give up. My mother would scold us when we complained about "limited" choices in the fridge: "Your daddy always said, 'Never say there is nothing in the fridge.'" We did what any other family would have done in those situations: we prayed. My mother used to say, "Hope is life."

Changing Your Meaning of Life

There were times when I almost gave up, especially on an empty stomach. I had to get through three hours of sprints and tennis training! I had to tell myself that I could do it, and that hunger was of no consequence. I had to block out the negative thoughts in order to keep moving. I had my doubts, of course. Others did not have faith in me. Patience is a virtue, and it tested me.

"Perspective is not a science, but a hope."

—*John Berger*

I've realized that this is what the word "career" is all about: competing *with yourself.*

Do you have a game plan?

Are you in it to win it?

There's nothing better than winning and proving everyone wrong in the process. But to me, that's not enough; we shouldn't be doing it for those reasons.

I knew my life was not terrible, but I still felt a void. I discovered, during my trials, that what was missing was giving back and being thankful. We all need Purpose. We just need to know how to *find and guard it.*

Freedom to Live

The day we sold the truck meant more than getting our weekends back. It meant freedom from debt and from the need to kill ourselves with this side hustle. It also meant no more embarrassing mornings being dropped off at school! We used to plead with our mom to drop us off around the block so we wouldn't get bullied because of our truck. She frustratingly complied.

We all need to define freedom for ourselves. I believe the freedom to be able to do what you want each day is powerful: freedom from debt, and the freedom to be your own boss at work.

What does freedom mean to you?

Immerse Yourself in What You Love

Everyone needs the right people around them to support them. My mother was always in my corner before I went out on the tennis court daring to be myself—and fight like a champion—no matter how high my opponent's ranking was. I will never take that for granted. Each one of us can benefit from a "Team Career Mastermind™" (entourage) always cheering for you in your corner.

My mother surprised me with one of the most meaningful *just because* gifts ever: a membership to Sierra Sport & Racquet Club. It was the most prestigious club in the valley, home to all the top players. A short time later, I won the Boy's 18 & Under Club Championships and defeated the number three-ranked men's player, securing my place in the top five players of the entire club. I was making waves, all thanks to my mother. She would drop me off at 6:00 in the morning on her way to work and pick me up at 6:00 in the evening on her way back. The club became my life. It was where I studied, played, trained, and socialized. It was there I grew up and immersed myself in my aspiration to be great.

Be an Overachiever

Work ethic matters. You can't be a Career Mastermind™ without mastering your work effort. You should aim to be an overachiever.

My entire family was ambitious. My older brother, my younger sister, and I, shared our dreams with each other. We were also troopers. One of those dreams was to be young scientists! When we were young, and science fair season rolled around, we barely slept. Long nights drinking ridiculous amounts of caffeine became a normal routine, with only one goal in mind: winning!

We were clearly a scientific family from the get-go. Our success at the science fairs was especially significant because our father witnessed our victories. My brother won first place in California, I came in second (which he likes to remind me of to this day), and my sister was recognized for outstanding achievement.

Our victories made us famous in our community as future scientists and nerds. (You'll hear more about what became of my siblings in Chapter Five.) As for me, I was what they called a "nerd-jock." That meant I was really good at both sports and academics. For one year, I was undefeated as a junior in tennis for boys 14 and under. I also won the regional Best Sportsmanship Award the same year and was awarded Rookie of the Year. I became a celebrity on campus practically overnight and was dating the most popular girl in school, Sheri. She was a cheerleader, and for a nerd, this was almost unheard of. I tutored psychology and got high fives from all the jocks on campus.

I went from my honors courses straight to tennis practice, with no break in between. Later, I went on to be the high school's MVP three years in a row, finishing the year ranked #1 in both singles and doubles. Balancing my studies and athletics was mental training for me, not only in high school but in college—it would later help me balance my career and life vision.

Without an action plan, I would never have been able to achieve success as a student-athlete. Balancing these is no easy task and it takes discipline, something every Career Mastermind™ takes very seriously.

If you keep pushing, eventually you get in a rhythm. Then, it's like dancing to intellectual jazz in your mind. It gets easier as you find rhythm. My trick was to stay on top of things. I anticipate and stay ahead of the flow—*always*. This is what you must do, too.

Tienes Flow?

Flow is a concept coined by author and psychology professor, Mihaly Csikszentmihalyi. It is a fundamental aspect of our personality that links to value. When we "flow," we feel connected to a greater purpose and a more fulfilled state of mind. It can happen to you anytime, and when it does, you're in the "zone." This does not need to happen at the beginning or at the end of your career. It can happen throughout.

Flow can happen during activities we love, like when a basketball player loses track of time, and suddenly everything flows seamlessly, leading to the best game of his life. It happens to artists and poets who sit at their desks or in their workshops for hours upon hours until they exhaust themselves at the end of the project. Flow happens to business owners, too, when they feel the universe pouring into them and out of them.

Have you ever achieved this state? How did it make you feel?

Flow is a state that can lead us to live happier, more fulfilled lives. Csikszentmihalyi said that happiness "is not a rigid state that can't be changed. On the contrary, happiness takes a committed effort to be manifested. After the baseline set point, there is a percentage of happiness that every individual has the responsibility to take control of. He believes that flow is crucial to creating genuine happiness."

Csikszentmihalyi outlined eight characteristics of flow in his book, *Flow: The Psychology of Optimal Experience:*

1. Complete concentration on the task

2. Clarity of goals and reward in mind and immediate feedback

3. Transformation of time (speeding up/slowing down of time)

4. The experience is intrinsically rewarding

5. Effortlessness and ease

6. Balance between challenge and skills

7. Actions and awareness are merged, losing self-conscious rumination

8. A feeling of control over the task

I experienced this flow state during my tennis training and often in the midst of games. I loved the training, the risks, and the possibilities. It all fascinated and intrigued me.

MANHATTAN BEACH, CA: At the Sand Dune Park, 1997

Your Personal Mantra

One of my personal mantras is:

> *"I believe that if I work hard enough, I can create opportunities that didn't exist before."*

Combining flow with a personal mantra is a winning combination. A personal mantra is an affirmation that motivates and inspires you. It's a positive phrase that you can use to build your self-confidence. It helps focus your mind.

I trained at the dune in Southern California, a huge mountain of sand that you had to climb. Each step felt like ten steps. You sink, you fall, and you keep climbing. I would keep pushing and repeat my personal mantra, "Believe and be brave." At the top, I could see my world below me. Careers and life are much like this dune: they have peaks and valleys.

I too experienced that "loss of time" and felt completely rewarded. This had something to do with my intrinsic and extrinsic motivation. I wanted to be fit and hone my skills as a tennis player, but I also wanted to win games and tournaments. The marriage of these concepts led to more frequent flow states (an important reminder when you are searching for ways to increase your chances of flow). Of the two, intrinsic motivation is more important than extrinsic flow because you have more control over it. Both may work together, but intrinsic motivation should be your default consideration, as this will strengthen your pursuit of purpose. This is especially important when you are pursuing a career.

"Career" means much more than a job—it's life.

Ikigai

Ikigai is a Japanese term that means "Reason for Being." It is a philosophical idea illustrating not *how to live*, but *why we live*. It is what gets us up in the morning. Ikigai is a convergence of Four Primary Elements:

1. What you love (your passion)

2. What the world needs (your mission)

3. What you are good at (your vocation)

4. What you can get paid for (your profession)

The Ikigai exists at the crossroads of what you are passionate about and where your talents lie. Many people desire material wealth, while many others have found a different route to a meaningful life. Although

this concept has been described in many ways, it always comes to the same
conclusion: Meaningfulness.

Ikigai

A JAPANESE CONCEPT MEANING "A REASON FOR BEING"

Satisfaction, but feeling of uselessness

What you LOVE

Delight and fullness, but no wealth

PASSION

MISSION

What you are GOOD AT

Ikigai

What the world NEEDS

PROFESSION

VOCATION

Comfortable, but feeling of emptiness

What you can be PAID FOR

Excitement and complacency, but sense of uncertainty

OKINAWA: Ikigai, JPN

Leading a Meaningful Life Means
You Are a "Giver"

Dan Buettner, the author of *Blue Zones: Lessons on Living Longer from the
People Who've Lived the Longest,* has written extensively on Ikigai. He said that
everyone should make three lists: things that you value, things that you

like to do, and things you do well. The crossover in these three lists is your core, your Ikigai. Take a moment to list some of them now.

1. *Things you value:*

2. *Things you do well:*

3. *Things you like to do:*

I discovered my Ikigai in this way, as well as by creating my career and life bucket lists, which I will walk you through later in the book.

When you find your Ikigai and work towards it, you will reap the rewards of fulfillment, happiness, and longevity.

If you want to find your Ikigai, you should ask yourself four fundamental questions:

1. *What do I love?*

2. *What am I good at?*

3. *What can I be paid for?*

4. *What does the world need?*

In their book, *Ikigai: The Japanese Secret to a Long and Happy Life*, authors Héctor García and Francesc Miralles provide ten rules that will help anyone discover their Ikigai—creating life balance and purpose:

1. Stay active and don't retire.

2. Leave urgency behind and adopt a slower pace of life.

3. Only eat until you are 80 percent full.

4. Surround yourself with good friends.

5. Get in shape through daily, gentle exercise.

6. Smile and acknowledge people around you.

7. Reconnect with nature.

8. Give thanks to anything that brightens your day and makes you feel alive.

9. Live in the moment.

10. Follow your Ikigai.

Trust the Timing of Your Life

We all have Ikigai. I call mine my "sweet spot." I compare my Ikigai to the sweet spot on my tennis racquet—when I hear that loud and satisfying "pop" as I ace my opponent. When I hear it, I know that the ball is traveling as fast as it can (sometimes over 130 miles per hour) and that my opponent will not be able to return it—not even the best of them. That's perfect timing!

That's what also helped me *almost* win the fastest serve contest at the Infiniti Open with a speed of 140 miles per hour. I lost to Andy Roddick who hit a serve speed of 143 miles per hour, fair play!

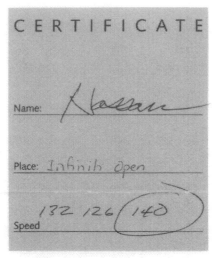

CERTIFICATE

Name:

Place: Infinih Open

Speed 132 /26 /40

Service Speed Test

Awareness of why timing matters in life is important in life design. We need to understand that sometimes it's the timing that saves you (not robs you) when it comes to careers. I see this often: many people are doomed from the beginning if they insist on wanting something to happen on *their time.*

Life doesn't work that way, and understanding timing is important in developing patience and resiliency.

Timing is what makes or breaks Ikigai.

What You Care About Deeply Will Unlock Your Ikigai

Philosopher and civil rights leader Howard W. Thurman once said, "Don't ask what the world needs. Ask what makes you come alive and go do it. Because what the world needs is people who have come alive."

These words are particularly poignant to me, and I have followed them throughout my journey of becoming a Career Mastermind™. I know that, if I do what makes me come alive, then I will produce something the world needs. People respond to those who are successful, passionate, driven, confident, and friendly.

So ask yourself: What makes YOU come alive?

Hold Your Breath, Make a Wish, Count to Three

Having a positive mindset is integral to success. When you are positive, people around you will respond accordingly. This will make you feel good. When you are feeling good, you are more opportunistic. When you are opportunistic, you are more likely to take chances.

Go ahead, make a wish...

Taking chances leads to results. Results lead to fulfilment.

Understanding—Understanding

Richard Saul Wurman, the creator of TED, gave me his book, *Understanding Understanding*. I felt honored to read it. This is the man that mastered the art of subtracting things. For example, he created the 18-minute speech and took out the intros.

"In the pursuit of knowledge, something is added every day. In the pursuit of enlightenment, something is dropped every day."

—Lao- tzu

Wurman believed that, in order to understand something, we must first know that we do not know something. There is something within us, a mixture of not-knowing and the desire to know. We must fill this void. The void is a surprise which deepens knowledge.

It is well known that questions tend to provide us with more answers. The more we learn, the more we realize what we do not know. True knowledge comes from asking questions and, once those questions are answered, asking more questions. This is the perpetual process of understanding.

"No matter what people tell you, words and ideas can change the world."

—*Robin Williams*

I considered Wurman one of my first members of my Career Mastermind™ Group. He taught me to embrace ignorance, to embrace a little bit of not knowing, because it makes you *feel* things. He has always had *that* edge and also lives on the edge. I respect that about him. He described it as "really willing to be the moth going to the flame on a daily basis."

Now, it's your turn to begin the journey to a new perspective. To find it, you must first unlock it.

CHECKLIST ITEM 1

POSITIVE MINDSET
ALMOST EVERYTHING IS PERSPECTIVE

TURN TO CLEAR VISION

▶ **Define where you are now:** (check one)

○ Positive ○ Unsure ○ Negative

▶ **Follow Up Date:**

☐ / ☐ / ☐

▶ *Why do you feel this way?*

▶ **Action Item:**

I will _____

by the Date ☐ / ☐ / ☐

▶ **Completed:** (circle one)

○ Yes ○ No

▶ *What is the 'IMPACT' action you will take within one week to make a positive change?*

▶ **Ikigai is seen as the convergence of 4 primary elements:**

• What you love (your passion)?

• What the world needs (your mission)?

• What you are good at (your vocation)?

• What you can get paid for (your profession)?

Discovering your own Ikigai is said to bring fulfilment, happiness and make you live longer.

▶ **Want to find your Ikigai?**
Ask yourself the following 4 questions:

1. What do I love?

2. What am I good at?

3. What can I be paid for now — or something that I could transform into my future hustle?

4. What does the world need?

Circle where you are now in your life:
(your "STANDING MOMENT") ▶

Venn diagram: What you LOVE, PASSION, MISSION, What you are GOOD AT, Ikigai, What the world NEEDS, PROFESSION, VOCATION, What you can be PAID FOR

"Next Steps" and Notes:

Workbook available for download at www.CareerMastermind.org/Resources

"It is not the critic who counts; not the man who points out how the strong man stumbles, or where the doer of deeds could have done them better. The credit belongs to the man who is actually in the arena, whose face is marred by dust and sweat and blood; who strives valiantly; who errs, who comes short again and again, because there is no effort without error and shortcoming; but who does actually strive to do the deeds; who knows great enthusiasms, the great devotions; who spends himself in a worthy cause; who at the best knows in the end the triumph of high achievement, and who at the worst, if he fails, at least fails while daring greatly, so that his place shall never be with those cold and timid souls who neither know victory nor defeat."

—Theodore Roosevelt

CHAPTER 2 (LENS 2):
THE UNLOCK —
CAREER AND LIFE VISION

"Your vision will become clear only when you look in your own heart. Who looks outside, dreams; who looks inside, awakes."

—*Carl Jung*

When I was in high school, I had what I called a "Champion's Scoreboard." Essentially, it was a huge goal sheet that took up the largest wall of my bedroom. Within it were my *life* goals, everything from whom I was going to marry to the year I would become the number one-ranked tennis player in the world! This helped keep me focused, helped me visualize my future, and take active steps to realize it. In order to forecast the rate I had to improve each year to break into the top ten, I noted each ranking. I also did annual self-assessments.

Seeing how personal this document was and how liable to be found by my mother, I folded it carefully in order not to tear any pages and to keep the creases straight, then hid it in the closet. All of these *little details* helped me stay focused over the years, and this focus laid the foundation for an ambitious and rewarding future.

Do you implement any systems to keep you focused? If so, what are they? If not, I recommend you do.

When I entered college, I surrounded myself with sources of inspiration. I suppose this is what drew me closer to big metropolitan cities. On my wall were photos of people who inspired me, quotes, art, and everything in between. I would look at my scoreboard at least once a month and ensure that my goals grew every year. When I fell short in an area, I added post-it notes. I had three huge (poster size) post-it notes at first. Very quickly, three became five, then five became six. If what I had written was significantly off, which often happens with any business plan, I adjusted it and often gave it a complete makeover. Sooner or later, it came together.

"If the plan doesn't work, change the plan, but never the goal."

—*Author unknown*

When I was 18, I moved away from home for the first time to pursue a double degree in biology and neuroscience with a minor in cognitive science at the University of California, San Diego (UCSD). Little did I know, I would be on my own for the next 25 years.

I never moved back, and so I had to support myself. I knew that to survive and to live my idea of freedom, I had to master metacognition in order to do my best. Before aligning a positive mindset, I had to use my own "self-determination life formula" to force out detrimental thought patterns.

Many people, including prominent members of my community, criticized me for pursuing a career in tennis. "So, you're not going to be a doctor, but you're going to go play tennis?!" they'd say. And their words echoed in my mind as I ran laps on the UCSD track each day after class. I taunted myself by choosing to listen to the negativity. But I knew I had to overcome these thoughts. I knew that battling them was going to help me be what I wanted to be and achieve what I wanted to achieve. Although I still wore my heart on my sleeve, I became resilient and humble, sound, and impenetrable.

In 1994, I became the most confident freshman on campus. I accepted a job as a barista at Espresso Roma at UCSD, which put me in the center of campus. I met everyone, from professors to the provost. I became one of the most popular students on campus.

Receiving so much love from all levels of the university, I was able to program my mind to move forward and block out the noise of negative thoughts, especially by surrounding myself with positive people. I would recommend the same to you. *Surround yourself with people who encourage you, believe in you, and who support you when you need it most.* These types of people help you connect the dots that Steve Jobs talked about.

Willpower is Life Changing

As a college student, I chose to go on a journey of self-discovery and I *chose* to find my true ambition. It was much more than just wanting to be a professional athlete. It was the fact that I could do whatever I applied my mind to—it was willpower. You can do this too. If you want it badly enough, don't search for it. Create it.

At 20, I created my own image map to visualize who I was and where I was going. This is what it looked like:

LA JOLLA, CA: Image Mind Map

Take a moment and imagine what yours might look like. There are no rules to this exercise; as long as you are true to yourself, you pass. You can also create a *Vision Board*, which is a collage of images, pictures, and affirmations of your dreams, goals, and things that make you happy.

Some of my fondest memories were making these visualizations at La Jolla Shores in San Diego, a captivating mile-long crescent of beach where active beachgoers of all interests, from all over the world, converge.

CAREER AND LIFE HACK #7
Find that special place, a "go-to" spot; make it your own.

What many of my closest friends didn't even know is that La Jolla Shores was my "go-to" spot, my special place. There was also a tennis court nearby overlooking the beach that I called my "office." It was accessible 24 hours per day, an escape when I needed it. In 1995, it was there, under the moon and facing the bioluminescent waves, that I decided to turn pro as a tennis player.

Life Moves in Waves

The way people illustrate waves is misleading. We use the wavy shape of the water's surface to visualize waves, but they actually travel in a straight line.

Light is also a wave. More specifically, it is an electromagnetic wave which does not travel in a medium. When an electromagnetic wave travels through space, it causes the electric and magnetic fields to change (or oscillate) at corresponding locations. Let's take a look at a classic diagram of how light propagates:

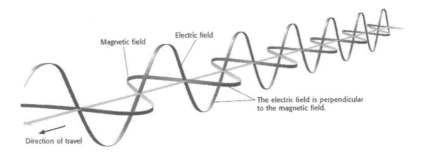

Magnetic field

Electric field

The electric field is perpendicular to the magnetic field.

Direction of travel

Electromagnetic Wave

The light travels along the central line (which is straight). It looks a lot like the double helix structure of DNA. At each point where the light passes through, there are vectors, which means that they have values and directions at each location. Therefore, everything in this diagram is telling us what's going on at the center.

As I saw the light illuminate the waves, I thought of how the path to our careers oscillates. Was there a way for career to parallel life, and vice versa? If only I could reduce the standard deviation of my life, perhaps I could get there sooner.

I had just finished my freshman year of college and had gained enough courage to take a leave of absence from the university to pursue my dream. I trained my mind over the years to stop listening to the naysayers, and I only brought my closest friends to that spot. It was there that I found real clarity. My thoughts stopped racing there. I could think clearly, and that was what I needed in order to make some of the most important decisions of my life.

No matter where you move to or travel, you must always have a place. I have lived in several cities in the United States, and in each of them, I've had a "getaway" that serves as my refuge of reflection. It's a place where I explore the wonders of the world, and even when I travel to unchartered territory, I find new "places." This process never ends. We must nurture that wonder and never lose it. If we do, we must find it again.

If you don't design your life, someone else will design it for you.

I want to encourage you to think of yourself as your life designer. *You must be the CEO of your own career.*

Don't try to do it alone. I always draw inspiration from others. I did this by seeking positive reinforcement from mastermind groups, quotes, poems, books, movies, songs, you name it. Sometimes, when you look outside of your comfort zone or world of expertise, you discover so much more. I recommend that you do the same.

INSTAGRAM: @SIAVASHSHAMS

Look in places you haven't looked before and tread the waters of uncertainty. For me, there was one particular song that kept me going, a song called "Sahneh" by the charismatic Persian singer, Siavash. After discovering his music, I sent him a message. And he replied! Siavash and I would communicate about life, humanity, art, and business. At one point, I even had a chance encounter with him at a restaurant in downtown San Diego. Talk about the stars aligning!

Siavash's song was about battling a negative frame of mind and returning to mental equilibrium, "the place we call home." For him, this was the space or "the stage" that he needed in order to feel fulfilled.

But this was an internal place, another way to articulate the phrase, "Home is where the heart is."

I often listened to Siavah's music that helped inspire me. He told me: "You are the voice of your future." Siavash's song helped me get through so many difficult times. It goes like this:

Mikhastam ke ba tanhaayi e khod sar konam man
I wanted to be alone with my own loneliness

gole khaaterate sahneh haa ro parpar konam
Pull off the petals of the flower of stage memories

raha sham tooye daste taghdir faramoosh konam
Be free in the hands of fate and forget things

eshghe khoondan o ba too boodan o khamoosh konam
Forget the love of singing and being with you

yadame yek shab vaghti tooye asemoon
I remember when one night in the sky

ye setaareh tanhaa mehmoon bood tooye kahkeshoon
There was only one star guest in the galaxy

delam tapid o faryad zanoon
My heart beat and screamed

goft bebin bebin avazeh khoon
Said, "Look, look, you chanter

boro rooye sahneh nashin tooye khooneh nasho setareye bi neshoon
Go on stage and don't sit at home, don't become the lost star"

sahneh eeeeee baaz mano seda kard
The stage called me again

eshghe oon dobareh
It's love again

maa ro hamseda kard
Made us sing together

sedaaye naaleye saaz darmoone roohame
The moaning of the musical instrument is the cure of my soul

Over the years, I would see him at concerts and he would recognize me in the audience instantly, walk over, and give me a huge high five in front of everyone. I became quite popular those evenings. The women would be screaming for him, but he would make it a point to greet me instead. After one such evening, we headed to a restaurant afterwards and chatted with his manager. We talked about my pro tennis career, and he asked me if I had the confidence I needed to make it. He reiterated that confidence was what made the difference in his life. I believe that myself, and I know confidence, especially if you are lacking it, will make a difference to your life also. It was something he had to develop, and he told me how he ran away from home once, and someone heard him sing. He said Luciano Pavarotti inspired him! From that day onward, his confidence grew. Now he is giving back by helping other artists as a producer.

To this day, each time I drive through the California Grapevine, I listen to a few of his songs from his album "Sahneh." Music like that just isn't made anymore! His words helped reiterate what I've been telling you throughout this book, that you need to take control of decisions you make.

Finding a Place to Call "Home"

My "place" was on the tennis court. It didn't matter which kind of court, it could be clay, hard, grass, or an indoor court. But as long as I was there and free, I felt good. This may seem like an external place, but my body and mind felt in balance when I was playing tennis. I felt true inner and powerful physical strength, sometimes so much it almost scared me. But this was my happy place, and it allowed me the success I had.

Hold Yourself Accountable

I have always tried my best to keep myself on track and hold myself accountable, no matter what I did. Everything, even my handwriting, was important (to my parents too). So much so that I always dreamed of learning calligraphy! It's on my Career Bucket List, but we will save that for another book.

I had a habit of recreating everything. Sometimes it was moving the furniture in a different place to open up the room, and other times it was because I was a perfectionist. But through this process of destruction followed by recreation, I was able to concentrate with more understanding. Each time I repeated this iterative process, I learned more about goal planning, myself, and what was realistically attainable when it came to marketing myself to sponsors. I became my own Chief Marketing Officer! After each "Goals of Life" meeting (with myself), I resolved to work smarter, harder, and improve my work ethic.

CAREER AND LIFE HACK #8
You are the CEO of your own career.

Your Attitude is Your Picker-Upper

This is the attitude I try to instill in everyone I speak to: you are a work-in-progress, all of the time. Life is about consistent self-improvement. You may never reach the top, but you also never stop reaching for it. Make sure you are clearly mapping out what it is that you want. There will be some challenges along the way, and not everything will go exactly to plan, but it will help you move further forward. The harder you pedal on a bike, the further you'll go, even if you don't know the road. And if you fall off the bike, you'll be able to get back on. *Every bruise becomes a part of you and your momentum forward.*

Here's a picture of me diving and doing just that.

LOS ANGELES TENNIS CENTER, CA: Diving during qualifying rounds for
the Mercedes Benz Cup

*"I've missed more than 9,000 shots in my career. I've lost almost 300 games. 26
times I've been trusted to take the game winning shot and missed. I've failed over and over
and over again in my life. And that is why I succeed."*

—Michael Jordan

The Year I Turned Pro

In 1995, I turned pro while I was training under the Portuguese Tennis
Coach, Fernando Vicente-Ferreira. He was like a second father to me.
Not only did he teach me how to be a better tennis player, but he also
believed in me. This year all of my results would become public, thus the
added pressure was heavy. I faced it every morning, and I ran three miles
on the Del Mar Shores in Del Mar, San Diego. I would train with him for
three hours. He knew my dreams and stories and worked closely with me.
He even knew what girl I had a crush on for years, the same girl that later
broke my heart. Her loss, right? He coached me like it was a mastermind
group with other aspiring pros. We would meet daily, and there were few

excuses to not be there, especially on time. Fernando knew I could go pro, and I knew I had to listen to him. He was a mentor and a point of reference. He was from Lisbon, but spoke with a heavy French accent. He always believed in me and instilled in me a fighting spirit, saying: "I see the tiger in your eyes."

DEL MAR, CA: Photo of the signature backhand shot

My First Pro Clothing Contract

Coach Fernando helped me get my first pro tennis contract with Lacoste. Admittedly, it was a mini-contract, but I accepted it—it was one of the biggest and best brands in the sport, and even that level was hard to come by.

I was a hard-working tennis player. I relished training with Coach Fernando. Don't get me wrong, he was no easy coach. He used to make me run, run, and run some more. I used to run so hard I would almost throw up. He called me "the Pakistani," and I would correct him and say I was an American. It was not only the difficult training that I remembered, but also the walks after practice, the strategizing with other Davis Cup players and college players, and in general, his powerful influence. This man fought hard for my contract, especially because (as he suspected) Lacoste did not believe Pakistanis could play tennis. He was in every truly aspiring professional player's corner. Coach Fernando was the one that said, with conviction, "This guy can play."

LOS ANGELES, CA: Mercedes Benz Cup

So, the Lacoste representatives listened to him. Before I knew it, everything from my polo shirts to my shorts, from my hats to my tennis bags, had a little crocodile on it. I was delighted to have such a prestigious company sponsoring me. I quickly grew in popularity alongside some of the most famous South Asian tennis players in the world.

LOS ANGELES, CA: With Aisam Ul-Haq Qureshi and Rohan Bopanna
"backstage" in the Player Lounge

Later down the line, Fernando became the President of my "Board of Directors," because turning into a professional tennis player was no easy task on a bucket list. You will learn more about this concept in Chapter 9. His faith never let up. You see, I had someone that had my best interest at heart, someone that pushed me all the way. He was wise, too, urging me not to accept prize money so that I wouldn't compromise my eligibility to compete. Boy, did that pay off! After beating one of the top national players, I was recommended to UCLA's Men's Tennis head coach, Billy Martin, who coached the #1 ranked tennis team in the nation. He later recruited me! This opportunity spearheaded my pro debut.

DEL MAR, CA: With Fernando on our last day of training
before moving to Los Angeles

I accepted admission and my invitation to join the Bruin family at UCLA. I kept in touch with Fernando and saw him while competing with my new team at the La Jolla Beach and Tennis Club in La Jolla, San Diego. There, Coach Fernando introduced me to the late and great Pancho Segura who watched my matches. This man was a legend! He was also another person who believed in me, and that propelled my confidence to a new level. Pancho whispered to me after a tough doubles loss, "You have true talent and should focus on singles," he said. "You will rise in the singles ranks faster; focusing on both will hold you back from excelling in one of them." What he didn't know was that I was already more passionate about singles. He was completely right about my success. Lots of people told me I was gifted in singles, although my volley game was one of the best around. Singles was where I wanted to be, and singles is where I went.

The lesson I learned from this is that you must believe in yourself before anyone else. We all must continue to push ourselves forward, to take control of our thoughts, live in the present and embrace change. We have to break the negative thought habits of hesitation and doubt. We must take initiative and take the blueprint of career and life project goals, and start building.

Self-awareness is crucial to developing this blueprint. Life is about freedom of choice in your decisions. *If you make the decision to change the decisions you make, you will change your life.*

MARINA DEL REY, CA: Fasting and reflecting on my birthday

We all come to a point in life where things are not working out as we had anticipated. Nothing fully goes to plan, and there are always surprises on the way, and you have to be resilient and adaptive to change. *The truth is within you, and you each already have your own inner wisdom.* Listen to it in a moment of peace and silence!

Pacing Yourself

Think of your days as a car's gearbox. Sometimes you slow down, and you have to shift accordingly, especially if you have challenges or are going uphill. Did I mention I hate driving and trying to park in downtown San Francisco? Other times, you are in high gear, and you *manage your energy rather than your time.* Your emotional intelligence and ability to put things together sufficiently, despite how you feel, will be one of your biggest assets.

Hesitation causes stress, and all these micro-moments matter. Metacognition is useful in these moments for controlling and reframing your thoughts and adapting to new situations. You must know how to hear and listen to that voice and go with it. This helps you adapt and move forward, like evolution intended.

Don't Blink When Humanity Stares You in the Eyes

In 1999, I was invited to meet the Pakistani Davis Cup Team. While walking through one of the narrowest streets in Lahore, Pakistan, with four tennis rackets on my back, I encountered a frail street child. He looked up at me with an innocent expression and wide, pine-green eyes.

LAHORE, PK: Street child who became my friend

I held out my hand, and the boy shook it softly, saying, "Peace be upon you." I didn't know it at the time, but that small but powerful gesture would later change my life. He had nothing: no parents, no car, no house, no toys, and no bicycle. But at that moment, he looked at me with utter joy and curiosity, as if I was a rock star. I felt an instant connection with him. I then walked away to prepare for my training as a professional tennis player.

ISLAMABAD, PK: Training with Davis Cup Team members and the National Team

After my training, I proceeded to explore the capital city of the Pakistani province of Punjab. Lahore is one of the largest, oldest, and most populous cities in the world—there are people everywhere: crowded on top of buses and rickshaws, and walking in every direction through busy intersections. It is also home to the Pakistani film industry, "Lollywood." In fact, at a dinner party during my stay, a major producer saw me and wanted to cast me as one of his soap opera stars because I "had the look." I respectfully declined.

I continued on, thinking about this boy who kept surfacing all over the city. I went shopping for a well-fitted suit because I knew I could buy one there at a bargain. After purchasing a nice black one, the boy appeared again, almost magically, this time waiting outside of the shop for me. He flashed a smile of broken teeth, and we went our separate ways.

In one instance, I was ten miles away from where I had first seen him. What were the chances? Was he—or his essence—following me? I laughed at my own naïveté and decided that perhaps my mind was playing tricks on me. However, a part of me kept searching for some kind of sacred inspiration that might lead me to a greater purpose in life.

Whatever the case, this child changed my path. Here I was, a professional tennis player, my life clear before me, then suddenly it's put into fresh perspective by this one special kid.

This encounter resulted in a fundamental shift in my life. I now had a greater lens of gratitude, not just "a perspective," and I realized that there is much more in life than material things and fame. I realized that so many people do not have the same opportunities as were aligned for me by my parents' blood, sweat, and tears. The young boy had not seen the vast world, but he seemed at ease. Whatever came back to him, whether it was donations or a pat on the back, no matter what, after a hard day's work, he thanked God Almighty and was content. He was my "unlock."

Could this be a secret to happiness? The *contentment* of accepting the harsh reality of what comes back to you after giving your best? Only time would tell. In the meantime, I gave him 500 rupees, which was a little less than $5. That made his day.

Until then, I didn't really think outside the box. My mind was pretty much set on being a bigshot tennis player.

Actually, that was my second goal, my "Plan B." My first goal was to get into medical school. That was the only real and culturally acceptable career on my so-called "Career Bucket List." Where I came from, this was legitimate brag material—rumors would quickly spread about you going "from zero to hero."

Yes, just one job was all it took, one "respectable" career. But I knew that if I got into medical school, I was going to defer my admission. I wanted to follow in the footsteps of some of the greatest tennis players of all time—Ivan Lendl, Boris Becker, and Stefan Edberg—who were my idols when I was a junior tennis player. I used to record Wimbledon tournaments and watch the players in slow motion every Saturday and Sunday morning to learn their form and rhythm.

LOS ANGELES, CA: Preparing for the Davis Cup Trials, 2000

I was self-taught. I didn't come from a rich family, nor could I afford Nick Bollettieri's tennis camps like most of the top junior players, many of whom became the world's best players, including Andre Agassi. They say tennis is a rich person's sport. If you can't afford the entry fees and travel expenses, you are hard out of luck without adequate sponsors.

After witnessing the harsh reality of poverty, none of that stardom mattered anymore. My struggles paled in comparison to others'. What mattered was helping kids like the one I had met. I knew he was one of many—one of thousands, in fact. I promised myself that I would give back and do something about it one day, whether or not I made it to the top of the tennis scene.

My passion for tennis led me to travel the world as a pro athlete, not knowing that one day I would be so deeply affected by the poverty-stricken areas—full of desperate people that silently spoke—saying, "We have rights over you." They understood what social responsibility meant—directly from the undercurrents of struggle, and looked at those more fortunate than themselves with the expectation that they were supposed to help them. I didn't question it; I knew they were right. I mean, some of them would be standing in the middle of heavy and dangerous intersections from the crack of dawn until midnight. Most of them were born into poverty; it was no fault of their own. With that kind of commitment and discipline, imagine what they could do if they were given a scholarship. They needed help, and I knew that one day I would be in a position to do something about it.

As my world evolved, *they became part of my vision.*

One evening, I threw myself into tireless research. I needed to know: what major, at what university, would allow me to help such children? I discovered programs in public health. They fascinated me. Then the news came. I got accepted into medical school! The hard hours of studying and preparing for advanced placement courses had all paid off. Although I had reached the first dot on my career destination map, I still only really wanted to be a tennis player. It fit my personality. I didn't need to do a personality test or self-assessment for that. I just didn't see myself working in a hospital. My friends felt that I should be an actor! But I wanted something else.

With so many humanitarian crises in the world, I felt my duty to mankind was out there. I could see myself working in International Health with a much clearer conscience. I needed more out of life than a large paycheck. I needed a different meaning.

Who would have thought that with all of the advantages I had for achieving the American Dream, I would have been more deeply impacted by the young boy in Lahore who exuded a more peaceful energy than most of the people I knew. He was also much happier than them— imagine that. Something was missing in their lives and in mine. And that was Perspective. He had it.

Know Your Limitations, then Defy Them

I came back to Los Angeles, and life was different. I just didn't see things the same way anymore. I saw people driving fancy cars they couldn't afford with no purpose in their lives except wanting to show off. The first thing I wanted to do was visit my mom and sister up north and tell them about my experience. So I went on my way.

Just through the Grapevine and north of Los Angeles, the San Joaquin Valley community in which I grew up is dear to my heart. It stands in an ocean of agriculture where many memories are buried. What I love about it is that it's close to Yosemite, a place of adventure and exploration—where I once visited with my dad—famed for its giant, ancient sequoia trees, and for Tunnel View, the iconic vista of towering Bridalveil Fall and the granite cliffs of El Capitan and Half Dome.

I distinctly remember Yosemite's majestic waterfalls, but within its nearly 1,200 square miles, you can find deep valleys, grand meadows, ancient giant sequoias, a vast wilderness area, and much more—all of this intrigued me as a boy.

There, I felt like an explorer.

Looking back, Yosemite was like my early careers, full of new places and experiences—and adventures.

The community that I grew up in is a spiritual community, led by Dr. El Sayed Ramadan, also known as Sheikh Ramadan. I am immensely grateful to Dr. Ramadan for consistently looking after my mother and sister when I'm far away. It's a family-oriented community, where friends and extended family come first. It was also teeming with physicians. I had plenty in my family, including a few surgeons. They all told me I should become a doctor.

I originally intended to be an orthopedic surgeon so that I could work with athletes and, in particular, help them with serious injuries. Some of the doctors in our community went out of their way to volunteer their time and money for the poor, but others competed for the largest mansions with elevators, gigantic pools, and indoor squash courts. I didn't see myself like that, not even before meeting the boy. I knew I wanted to make a difference in life, I just didn't know how. I began to consider doing a medical degree, combined with a masters in public health, because the programs intrigued me. But I knew, realistically, the four years of medical school would destroy my chances of playing pro tennis. There was no way of training and going to medical school at the same time; that just wasn't practical.

I talked to my mother and sister about my feelings and *what was driving me* towards pursuing a degree in public health. They understood my experiences overseas and were very supportive; however, my mother still encouraged me to go to medical school. Deferring medical school admission was still an option, so I gravitated in that direction but kept it a secret.

Feeling good about the options I had in front of me, I headed back to Los Angeles. I remember singing Michael Jackson's "Man in the Mirror," and this song pumped me up in the morning before classes. When it's biochemistry and history, you need it—trust me! I knew that I had to be more intentional with my life, to live with more vigor and passion, and to take charge of my career. And I was doing just that. I studied very hard, sometimes all night. Eventually, life's dominos began falling in the direction I wanted.

You have to believe you can do something, despite limitations.

Ambition Rests On Your Own Virtue

Okay, so the life I had before sounds like it was decent, right? I was a professional tennis player, traveled the world, and explored new cultures and people. The problem was, I had beliefs that limited me from unlocking my true potential. Basically, I believed I had to attend medical school, otherwise I would never be happy. My ambition wasn't driving me and fueling me. The opinions of other people were. That simply didn't make sense. Worry about others whom you don't necessarily care about, yet, they are what matters when it comes to your career? No, I had to change this. The images of success were clouding my thoughts and getting in the way. I knew that it meant job security, status, and wealth, along with a label on my forehead: "Dr. Akmal." That meant I was successful.

For my mother and aunts, this also meant marriage proposals—and they were right. The phone calls started coming, people knocking on our front door, all because of hearsay after I graduated from UCLA and got into medical school. In South Asian culture, this type of thing is common, but it wasn't my cup of chai. I wasn't traditional in that sense. An arranged marriage, although it might work for some people, just wasn't for me. I was a die-hard romantic and was going to find my own love someday.

Some of the proposals that started coming my way were from female physicians whose parents were also doctors. Talk about pressure. I honestly wasn't ready to get married and to give up my dream of being on the prestigious ATP Tour. Unless the person I was considering was going to be a lifelong traveler and companion, it wasn't even an option. I wanted mutual value and mutual support of our aspirations. Otherwise, what's the point?

Long story short, my suitors weren't interested in my tennis stories; in fact, they were shocked that I saw it as anything other than a hobby. I was in desperate need of a Career Mastermind™ group, because I knew that group wouldn't bring me down. It would be a catalyst for me.

Everyone Needs a Career Catalyst

My UCLA men's tennis team became this powerhouse. It felt like nobody could beat us. Although we were college players, we were really all pros. Many of us were recruited from the pro tour, meaning we were world-ranked but didn't accept prize money so we could have the opportunity for both college scholarships and competition.

INSTAGRAM: @JULROJER

We were Finalists in the NCAA Men's Tennis Championships in 2000, and it had been a tremendous run. We were victorious in the National Indoor Championships earlier that year, but lost to Georgia in the finals after securing Championship Point. That's right, we were one point away from winning it all. Although we choked, we knew our team was incredibly talented, the best on the college scene. I remember my friend and teammate, Jean-Julien Rojer, playing number five singles after I'd earned my all-time letterwinner in 1999. Imagine that. He won Wimbledon in 2015 and is currently 19 in the world in doubles with a career high of 3. The team had incredible depth!

LOS ANGELES, CA: Former UCLA men's tennis standout Jean-Julien Rojer picked up the biggest victory of his career in 2015, teaming with Horia Tecau to hoist the men's doubles trophy at Wimbledon (it marked the 43rd Grand Slam title by a UCLA player)

These fellas weren't just team members; they were family, brothers. We were there for each other, for positive reinforcement and for emotional shelter. Our place of refuge, known as the *Team Room*, was open 24/7, and we all had a key. It was a place to study, a place to reflect, and a place to cry. We endured the loss of family members, witnessed the toll of drug use, faced personal and professional challenges, saw team members quit—you name it. That's where we would meet and get through it together. Have you ever experienced this sense of togetherness?

LOS ANGELES, CA: With teammate Jean-Julien Rojer in the Player's Lounge

FACEBOOK: @UCLAMENSTENNIS

The Team Room was my go-to place in Los Angeles. It was a place where we would motivate each other and help one another stay on track.

The room was filled with team photos from past generations and legacies. It was a place to celebrate who we were, the "Bruins." My coach at the time, Billy Martin, was always there for us, night and day. He was what I call an "Enabler." He made things happen, looked out for all of us like his own kids, and made sure we were taken care of. Yet, he wouldn't hold our hand, he expected us to put in the work. He welcomed us into his home and was very positive. He really cared, wanted the best for us, and understood the game. Coaches, managers, and leaders that encourage autonomy and responsibility are immensely helpful to our professional growth as well as our growth as human beings. You must seek out these types of people as you move forward.

LOS ANGELES, CA : UCLA Men's Tennis Team, 1997-1998

I had defined *success* for myself at the age of ten, and it had nothing to do with being a rich doctor, but rather with having a team. Other people's definition of success was nowhere near my own. I knew deep down that life was more than status and ego, more than an accumulation of wealth. Wealth cannot buy you everything, I knew that. In fact, the comments

I received at local events and gatherings, discouraging me from playing college or pro tennis, almost thwarted my efforts to succeed at them.

I felt the pressure and knew it was time for a reframe. *Reframes can change lives.*

I realized that there was something in me that I needed to unlock. That thing is in you too, you've just got to find it and surpass what you perceive as your limitations. I was always confident, but sometimes we doubt ourselves. So, mine was *endless* confidence. What's yours?

My UCLA tennis family was a catalyst to my reframe and career, and gave me the confidence to keep seeing things positively and clearly. I received this signed frame from them after landing a new contract with Adidas and finishing my classes. They were wishing me the best on the pro tour. This was the moment I was "set free" to be a full-time pro and leave college tennis behind.

My reframe was completed. What's your reframe?

LOS ANGELES, CA: *Turning pro* signed frame gifted to me by
UCLA Men's Tennis Team members and coach.

Forward Momentum

Forward Momentum is an urgent problem. Forward Momentum is strategic foresight and proactive planning, combined with positive results and energy; a consistent step-by-step process that requires movement in the right direction of stated goals; making progress and crushing goals.

State your goals. What are they? Once you have them, then what?

How do you think forward, and how do you combine that thinking with positive results?

You have to get way ahead of the competition. You do this by thinking differently. For example, if college X's career center is trying to give their students a competitive advantage by sending out their upcoming graduates' resumes a few months before graduation, you find a way to have all the resume critiquing done a year in advance. This means you have to meet students earlier to build relationships and bring them up to speed so that their resume is "readily referable." This way, you can send resumes out for upcoming graduates first! As a result, your speed to referral will make all the difference.

Easier said than done, I get it. Well, first, you need to be in the right state-of-mind. Your personal "life lenses" matter, because YOU matter. You are the master of your own destiny, but only when you are the master of your own mindset.

Think *4—ward!* With progressive Forward Momentum, here are four results:

1. The more choices you have.

2. The freer you will become.

3. The more risks you will take.

4. The more forward momentum you will build—as you *clear your path forward.*

This problem has existed for centuries. Did I ever experience a quandary? Yes, I was between a rock and a hard place with tennis versus medical school, and I had to challenge the way I thought about it.

LOS ANGELES, CA: India West Magazine

In physics, momentum is the resistance of a moving object to come to a stop and is expressed as speed times mass (velocity x mass). The greater the momentum, the harder it is to stop the object's movement.

In life, *Forward Momentum is the purposeful movement toward a goal, a vision, or a desired destination.*

You should think of momentum as a force unwilling to come to a halt.

You are that force as a Career Mastermind™. *You are the Career Unlock.*

Take a moment to think about your unlock and how it relates to your life's balance. Go ahead. Is all of this starting to make sense? Yes? Good!

Now that you understand how to unlock your career and life vision, it's time to align your purpose.

"When we record with written word what our minds have conceived, we allow others a glimpse of our inner world — the unborn universe within. It is filled with the stars of our greatest dreams, the dust of our disappointments and the gravity of all of our experience."

—*Chanti Niven*

CHECKLIST ITEM 2

THE UNLOCK:
CAREER AND LIFE VISION

▶ **Define where you are now:** (check one)
- ○ My career vision is unlocked
- ○ My life vision is unlocked

▶ **Follow Up Date:**
[ ] / [ ] / [ ]

▶ *Why do you feel this way?*

▶ **Action Item:**
I will [ ]
by the Date [ ] / [ ] / [ ]

▶ **Completed:** (circle one)
○ Yes ○ No

▶ *What is the "IMPACT" action you will take within one week to make a positive change?*

Career
Life

"Next Steps" and Notes:

Workbook available for download at www.CareerMastermind.org/Resources

Success without fulfillment is failure.

CHAPTER 3 (LENS 3):
DISCOVERY CALLS —
THE PURPOSE IN YOU

"When you photograph people in color, you photograph their clothes. But when you photograph people in black and white, you photograph their souls!"

—*Ted Grant, Canadian Photojournalist*

*I*t's time for you to explore. Don't be shy, I will go with you. Discovery is calling.

With each step, let's count our blessings. *Humble your mind by humbling your thoughts.* This is a journey you will never forget. Let me tell you more about my mine.

I decided to start taking more calculated risks to get exactly what I desired from life. I was training six hours a day split among tennis practice, the gym, and cardio training. After dinner, I was exhausted! But I still spent my nights reflecting, studying, and applying to the best international health programs all over the globe. In my statements of purpose, I wrote about the boy I met and focused on the "why" when it came to my career transition.

After embracing the hustle—I was finally accepted into the Forced Migration and Health—Master of Public Health Program in community health sciences with a focus on epidemiology and decided I was going to also be an epidemiologist!

To my surprise, I got accepted to one of the best programs in the world! I was one of 24 students selected out of thousands. What an honor!

That kid universalized my realization. After packing everything I moved across the country. One of the first things I did was go to the top of the Empire State Building, and I looked out of the coin-operated binoculars, then I focused the center knob and realized that this concrete jungle was my new home. That was my moment, and nobody could take it away from me. *Every single one of us must stop in order to clear our vision.*

That minute would stay with me forever. It is too easy to get caught up in the cut-throat lifestyle—getting lost in our own lives and lose sight of what really matters—and where it is we should be going.

The problem is that we do not all know what we want. Sometimes we discover it *after the fact*. Knowing what you want out of life is integral to becoming a Career Mastermind™, and it takes time, patience, and hard work. The potential is in us all, and this book will show you how to meet these goals and aims—both efficiently and effectively.

Steve Jobs understood this. Knowing that hindsight is 20/20, he learned to connect life's dots looking backward. As a teen, I had 20/15 vision. A person with 20/15 vision can see objects at 20 feet that a person with 20/20 vision can only see at 15 feet.

Figuratively, 20/15 vision is called foresight, and every Career Mastermind™ *has it.* With it, forward momentum comes much more naturally, and for a lucky few—it's a breeze.

Life is unpredictable. Some call it "God's timing," and others call it "luck." No matter what you call it, *you must be the one internally and externally leading yours.*

Introspection and Extrospection

So many of us invest our time, energy, and what we think makes us happy in externalities that we cannot directly control. This can make us feel powerless. Career and life balance is about harmony, balancing the external and internal by mastering "the self." Are you pursuing this mastering of *self*? No, I didn't say selfie!

Self-mastery is being in control of the internal thought processes that guide your emotions, habits, and behaviors.

Think of a blind person. Or look at a baby's expression when it first opens its eyes to the big wide world. How do you feel about this? The way you feel may shift your perspective. You will change what it is you *can* see. This process is all about self-realization and self-awareness. What life situations bring about the best in you? How can you pursue these further?

It is important at this point to understand the difference between introspection and extrospection, as well as meta-consciousness. *Understanding these terms and bringing them together will be integral to your future success.*

This will all help you know yourself. You will understand what skills you have and how to own them. You must believe that you will make a difference not only in your life, but in someone else's as well. Life is *your* race, but who do you want to run with?

Try Old Things, Prototype New Things

I explored many careers on my way to self-understanding. I rode BMX bikes, studied martial arts, wrote poetry, performed Bollywood dances at weddings, and even tested my acting skills. If I could do all this, so can you.

REMEMBER: TIME = MONEY. It doesn't matter if you have the career you've always wanted if you don't have time to enjoy it. Remember the word *balance*. Remember what it means to you. Remember how you will feel when all the elements of your life come into balance!

Do You Have the Willpower?

Willpower is severely underestimated. It must be visualized. Discovery begins with imagination. Imagine yourself in Yosemite standing on top of a huge rock, looking over treetops, past a lake, and into the sky. Contemplate how awe-inspiring it is, how much potential lies in the physical world. What is it that you see and feel?

When you are in your empowered place, start working on a life bucket list as well as a career bucket list, and make sure they are balanced. When these are 50/50, you will have what so many people want: a good work-life balance!

Don't just take my word for it. Mahatma Gandhi once put it eloquently: "Happiness is when what you think, what you say, and what you do are in harmony." Always remember that key term, *harmony*. If you are stuck in a rut, remember that you have the power to change your direction in life by changing your decisions. When you realize this and start acting on this lesson, you have the power to drastically alter the course of your life.

CAREER AND LIFE HACK #9
Ask yourself: Who is managing my career?
Make sure your answer is: "I am, always."

This is important enough to repeat. Treat it like a mantra and say it over and over to yourself: *If I change my decisions, I will change my life.*

When you have willpower, you are intentional. You must be intentional when it comes to your career.

The more choices you have, the freer you are.

There comes a time for all of us when we have to activate ourselves. Admittedly, this is easier for some than for others, but it always requires work. The key here is inspiration and the placement of value on what we are doing (value stack). Here are some quick tips on how to begin this process:

- *First of all, you have to unlock your core values. These should be timeless.*

- *Second, begin your life with a whiteboard, a blank slate.*

- *Third, start within to find out what YOU want.*

Focus on value over volume. Then surround yourself with positive people. This will lead to "mentor circles" or mastermind groups.

Implement these strategies when selecting the people you want to interact with. It is important to surround yourself with positive people you want to invest in. It is difficult to have a vision or calling if you have no idea if someone has already walked your path. Keep these people within your vision as inspiration.

For example, if you are someone who struggles with self-confidence, imagine the most confident person you know when you react to situations. Fake confidence. Do you know what happens when you fake confidence? You become confident.

You will learn more about mentor circles and mastermind groups in Chapters 9 and 10.

We All Need a Team

Life is all about discovering our purpose, so that every morning we can get up and look forward to the day ahead. However, maintaining this energy can be difficult. A way to keep us in check can be through a mastermind group. This only needs to comprise two people, though it can obviously be more. Masterminds don't give up on each other. Many mastermind groups evolve into lasting friendships, even after collective and individual goals are met.

Let's take the concept of marriage. When I worked at a bank, I asked one of our clients (who was celebrating her 50th year anniversary) her secret to a successful and happy marriage. She said, 1) You never let the other go to bed angry, 2) always keep your problems between the two of you, 3) make the home the place where you always want to be (she said she would keep it immaculately clean, light candles, have soft music playing, and dress in lingerie), and 4) always remember that it's about two imperfect people never willing to give up on the other.

Career and life mastermind groups are lifelong. It's the marriage of your career with the discovery and maintenance of your life vision. But you must make choices, and work diligently to make these choices.

Don't Stop Being Curious

The best advice I can give you in this chapter is to *follow your curiosity*. This will lead to the discovery of purpose. But don't just take my word for it; curiosity has been a driving force since the beginning of time—and for many leaders.

Curiosity allowed us to discover fire, migrate out of Africa, and invent the wheel. It led Michelangelo to paint the Sistine Chapel, and compelled Shakespeare to produce his memorable plays and sonnets. You get the idea: most successful and famous people throughout history followed their curiosity. Things didn't just happen to them.

Finding Purpose is no passive pursuit; it takes an active and engaging commitment.

Albert Einstein once said, "Imagination is more important than knowledge." Imagination leads to wonder, and wonder inspires us to get up in the morning. It's your curiosity that will take you out of your comfort zone.

Wonder Leads to Joy

I was always an imaginative boy, full of wonder. My imagination dazzled me. I knew I could dream things into reality—that my thoughts and ideas were about connecting things and innovating. I knew that the ability to do this was special. But I know everyone has this ability; it's just that some people learn how to tap into it more easily than others. You must learn to approach everything with wonder and expand on what your imagination can do. Dreaming affects reality. Use it to listen to the call of discovery, use it to find your purpose. This will lead to a wondrous life—full of joy.

Waking Up from a Dream into a Dream

Sometimes, when I was a teenager, my mother would knock on my bedroom door and find me lying on my back just staring at the ceiling. To others, it was just empty white. To me, it was a threshold to other galaxies, new dimensions, and the future. She would ask if I was alright, and I would reply, "Yes, of course," and in the calmness of my answer she would find peace of mind. She would laugh and walk away, and I would carry on, *thinking about thinking, and dreaming about dreaming.*

"All men dream: but not equally. Those who dream by night in the dusty recesses of their minds wake in the day to find that it was vanity: but the dreamers of the day are dangerous men, for they may act their dream with open eyes to make it possible."
—*T.E. Lawrence*

Imagination is a window into what can be. It's a door to the future, an escape from the past. It's an unfolding space where potential is born and ideas live and wander. It's the only place where you have control over the task of connecting the dots looking forward. What does imagination mean to you? When you close your eyes, what do you see and hear? Where do you travel?

CAREER AND LIFE HACK #10

In order to unlock your career and life vision, you must first unlock your imagination.

We must imagine the far future as vividly as we imagine it in the near term. Once we can do this, we will understand our goals and move towards them.

So, imagine living your purpose. Think *tabula rasa*, blank slate. Envision and design what it is you want, but also integrate and capitalize on it. Imagine yourself successful across all forms of being: social, financial, familial, spiritual, etc. Open the doors of imagination, and you will be rewarded with energy. *Energy allows you to live out your purpose.*

Energy is Life

My backhand and serve were by far my favorite shots as a pro tennis player. I was taught to "grip it and rip it." Energy keeps us moving. But we all move at a different pace. We all have varying frequencies: a frequency for life, and a frequency for our career. These wavelengths should be in unison. Think about what frequency you want to be on and the sound and impact of your leadership at that point.

There is a saying: *If you travel far enough, you meet yourself.*

Therefore, when you learn to travel in the mind, you will understand your vision and purpose.

We Are All Wired Differently

We function best when we are in our element. I always share one of my favorite Gandhi quotes: "You must be the change you want to see in the world." Think about that for a second, even repeat it to yourself a few times. Ghandi is calling on you to act to glean your purpose from life. Change comes from within, and this means different things to different people.

For me, that line is so important because it means giving back. As a kid, I was almost orphaned. After the loss of one parent, my mother contracted breast cancer. Fortunately, she was able to overcome it in the early stages.

As a result of an accumulation of life experiences, I became beholden to the world. It drove me forward, made me resilient, and taught me to not take life for granted.

I learned how to create purpose rather than just trying to find it. Through active and intrinsic means of motivation, I was able to overcome hardships when I was young, and I grew up more quickly as a result.

However, we all deal with the tests of life differently. We all dream, but not the same way. I've always dreamed big. From a young age, I've wanted to make a significant impact on the world—be a change agent, a visionary, not just another cog in the machine. Although I had my share of bad luck, I was never swayed by faith alone. It always took more than that. It doesn't matter how little or much you dream, what matters is that you don't give up.

Your life experiences have shaped you into who you are today. Some will be positive, and some will be negative, but all will be important. When you create change, you will prime yourself for more positivity in your life. You will make strides towards becoming who it is you want to become. Open your eyes and ears; discovery is calling your name and reaching out to you.

Same Dream, Different Day

The next step is to assume the role of chief architect for your career and lay out your life blueprint. Once you know your purpose, you have the building blocks. It's now time to build that house, and create the life you love.

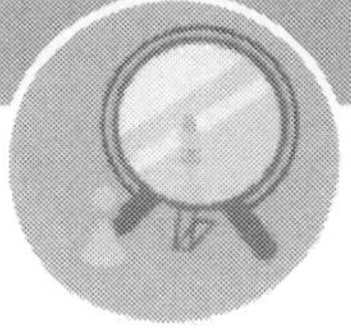

CHECKLIST ITEM 3

DISCOVERY CALLS
THE PURPOSE IN YOU

▶ **Define where you are now:** (check one)

☐ I know my purpose

☐ I don't know or understand my purpose

▶ **Follow Up Date:**

☐ / ☐ / ☐

▶ *Why do you feel this way?*

▶ **Action Item:**

I will ☐

by the Date ☐ / ☐ / ☐

▶ **Completed:** (circle one)

○ Yes   ○ No

▶ *What is the 'IMPACT' action you will take within one week to make a positive change?*

"Next Steps" and Notes:

Workbook available for download at www.CareerMastermind.org/Resources

CHAPTER 4 (LENS 4): CAREER MANIFESTO — BE AN ARCHITECT, BUILD THE LIFE YOU LOVE

"Don't downgrade your dream just to fit your reality. Upgrade your conviction to match your destiny."

—*Stuart Scott*

*E*very Career Mastermind™ experiences the reality of life. Some say, "Man proposes, God disposes." Building a life you love is integral after your find your purpose. It is one thing to dream, it is another to actualize your dreams. What does your manifesto look like?

Conceptualization leads to blueprints, which form the basis of your design. Many factors will affect the outcome, and this chapter is about the curve balls we don't expect, how to react to them, and how to use them to your best advantage.

Career and Life Design

How do you design and build your life? You begin with mindfulness. *Mindfulness is central to mastering mindset. What is mindfulness?* Mindfulness is the human ability to be fully present—aware of where we are and what we are doing—and not merely reactive to what's going on around us.

How you design your life begins with how you design each day. Start your day—today, and remember, *why* you do things matter, as the reasons collectively program your mind for what's to come—tomorrow. *How you do anything, is how you do everything.* Begin with making your bed in the morning. Look at yourself from your own human perspective. Who are you and who do you want to be? Are they the same, or are they different, and why?

So much of who we are—are states and emotions. What if the way you feel was not a reaction? It was by *design*.

Be a thermostat, not a thermometer. Don't live a reactive life. Set your standard and goals—your "to feel" list for each day. These days will turn into months and years of living in a life *you designed*.

Human-Centered Design

I've always been intrigued by human-centered design. Once, I was invited to serve as a key facilitator for a project geared towards alleviating urban food deserts using the method intended for areas such as Englewood, Illinois; this first introduced me to the concept. So what is it? Human-centered design (HCD) is a design and management framework that develops solutions to problems by involving the human perspective in all steps of the problem-solving process.

Design thinking is crucial in Career Masterminding. It is a mindset developed in Silicon Valley and based on the principles of empathetic listening, prototyping, a bias to action, and failing forward. It's a design methodology that provides a solution-based approach to solving problems. You will be using this approach to build a life you love.

There are five stages:

1) Empathize

2) Define

3) Ideate

4) Prototype

5) Test

Empathy is the centerpiece of a human-centered design process. It's a cognitive and strategic, as well as a practical process.

I applied this methodology to my own life. Once I had my ideas somewhat formalized, I created a prototype of my goals, then created a hypothesis to test them. These were my blueprints. I made sure that I could align my career ambitions alongside the passion nested in the core of my heart, otherwise known as my *calling*. My passion was to motivate people to pursue their dreams, and I reverse-engineered from this passion. I did not want to be a motivational speaker; I wanted to lead by example—to inspire by action, not just words.

Initially, I had no idea where this would take me. But before I knew it, this desire aligned itself with destiny. This came from a traumatic event, which I will discuss next.

The goal of sharing this with you is to help you understand how mindfulness plays a role in all situations—good, bad, planned, and unplanned. As you build your career, you will attempt to surround yourself with the situations that bring out the best in you. But life will test you; that's normal. That is part of the prototyping and the testing stages of design thinking. Don't let it define you if things don't go your way.

INSTAGRAM: @RIGHTTOPLAYINTL

The Turning Point: Unveiling Destiny

In 2003, I was invited to serve as an ambassador for Right To Play, an organization that harnesses one of the most powerful and fundamental forces in every child's, life: the power of play. They leverage sport for youth development, and their programs protect, educate, and empower children to heal from the harsh realities of war and abuse to create a better future for themselves.

In the United States, more than 90 professional and Olympic athletes are a part of Right To Play. They join 300 athletes from more than 40 countries around the world to make up our team of Athlete Ambassadors because they know firsthand the positive impact sport and play can have. I was honored to be one of them and to serve a five-year contract from 2003 to 2008.

Right To Play Ambassadors continue to raise awareness, promote hope, and inspire millions of supporters and children. For one of their programs, I was invited to be a spokesman on an antimalarial campaign that urged the local community to "stay in the net," a phrase meant to encourage the use of the mosquito nets.

NEW YORK, NY: Right to Play Athlete Ambassador Photoshoot, 2003

INSTAGRAM: @PLANINTERNATIONAL

I was at the end of my graduate studies, and my thesis was on the psychosocial impact of conflict on children. I found myself in a tribal area of Pakistan called Chaman, on the Kandahar border of Afghanistan to begin serving my contract with Right To Play, and I was also hired by Plan International to conduct my practicum. There, I was almost kidnapped. I was mugged at gunpoint while conducting my Columbia University internship following the war in Afghanistan.

KANDAHAR, AF: At the refugee camps in 2003, standing with Afghan refugees and my taxi driver (left)

I was in a local convenience store buying a bottle of water. Harmless enough. But this store was in a dangerous tribal area, the center of the black market, where everything from drugs to weapons were being traded. Suddenly, someone in a balaclava burst into the store and stole my wallet as I was about to pay. Pressing a machine gun against my back that felt

like a knife, this individual and his gang interrogated me to determine if
I was alone.

One of them called me the "squash player," a reference to posters
which had recently gone up around town depicting me as an International
Athlete Ambassador to the United States. My face was all over the place.
Even with 5 million refugees, there was no hiding.

Spirit Lands

As I was searching for a solution, door bells on the storefront entrance
rang. We didn't know who had walked in at first, but this startled the
men, and in a haste, they told me to leave, and I didn't hesitate. They
began yelling, angered. The thieves intended to hold me for ransom to
extort money from the Pakistan Tennis Federation (PTF). But in that
instant when the bells rang, I was free, at least for a couple of hours. They
thought whoever entered would let their secret out. We later realized it
was a just a little girl—or angel.

As I dashed towards the door, I saw the girl's face, but said nothing,
her face one that I will never forget. As I turned back, I glimpsed and saw
the men holding AK-47s. I immediately dived into a taxi and sped off.
Whoever you are, young girl, thank you and God bless you.

How this Led to a New Life Perspective

Many asked why I had my belongings with me when I was mugged. This
was Chaman, Pakistan and Kandahar, Afghanistan: no matter where we
were, it wasn't secure. Even the maids were stealing my clothes. I had to
keep my valuables with me, including the money my sponsors gave me—

there was nowhere to get a traveler's check around there. The closest bank was several hours away.

To get to the refugee camps, we traveled by taxi. Imagine desert paths, treacherous mountains with caves harboring terrorists, and windy gravel roads that would send you off the mountain if you drove too fast. I would look out my window and see no more road, only a drop. It's then that I realized I was afraid of extreme heights. Not from tall buildings or the windows of skyscrapers, but from the tops of mountains with crazy cab drivers. They were going too fast. It was on a one-way road where drivers would try to overtake each other! If that didn't kill me, I knew these men would. I had nowhere to go.

Hopeless Is the Case. Is there No Escape?

INSTAGRAM: @ BVALEJ

I lost everything, including all the money that I was going to use to cover my travel expenses. I was scheduled to compete in Pro Satellite and Futures tournaments in Europe that summer with another rising pro, Boris Vallejo, who used to train like Ivan Drago in Rocky IV. He was my greatest asset: a sounding board and practice partner. I had to break the news to him, as well as to Columbia University and my closest friends and siblings. But I didn't tell my mother, in fear she would not be able to handle the news emotionally.

The university immediately scheduled me an emergency flight. The problem was getting to the airport. Now, I had no money, not a penny. There was nowhere to wire or receive transfer money. Not a single place that would take a credit card either. I was stranded without cash for a taxi. At least I had my passport, thank God.

I immediately filed a police report with my team, and within hours, I was notified that the organization I was working for was receiving death threats targeting me, as well as the organization. I had now become a liability. I was advised to withdraw the police report, as it dishonored the criminals who were now threatening to kill me.

I walked out of the police station and was confronted with scorpions the size of frogs combing the desert. I knew I needed an exit strategy to avoid getting stung. I saw several vehicles pull up to the gates of the medical complex. I could feel the evil energy and sense that I was in the wrong place at the wrong time. I remained calm, focused, like being down a set and at break in the finals of a tournament. I knew I just had to process my emotions, one point at a time, and make things change.

The police promised that they would negotiate with the men who held me up. There was no question of whether they did or not: it was a matter of how much money they had. After a second visit to the police station, the officers told me that their efforts (beating up the thieves, as is customary there) were of no use.

The thieves had nothing. Rumor had it that they lost everything during the war.

Approximately $3,500 was missing. That may not sound like a lot, but it was integral to my pro tennis career ranking and the points I needed to accumulate to advance my career. It was gone in a flash. My sponsors believed me and wanted me to return safely. My agent felt disappointed, as he knew the loss would be difficult to recover from. If I could break into the top 200 in the world, I'd have a multi-million dollar contract waiting for me. But this experience would set me back, perhaps indefinitely.

Later, I discovered that everything was false. The police negotiated and took half the money and set the criminals free. Now they were on the loose and had one focus in mind: to murder the accuser, me.

I needed a miracle. Everyone was panicking except one person, Danish, the Director of Operations for Plan International. While we sat together, frightened at the medical office, behind the large locked gates that were the only things separating me from the perpetrators, he walked over and shook my hand, gifting me the equivalent of $100 in the palm of his hand. That was a lot of money over there, and he refused to let me pay him back. He said God would give it back to him. I will never forget him. Bless his soul.

As you can clearly see, things didn't go as planned. As a career architect, you will find this happen a lot. Your life will take a U-turn from time to time, and that's alright. We are trying things, and they don't always work. However, there is a wisdom behind what works and doesn't work. As a Career Mastermind™, you will learn when it's time to move on, and how to do it.

Looking Up at the Stars, but Still Helpless Behind These Invisible Bars

Upon my return, I met with my sponsors, and I was told that I must repay them, as the funds were not used as intended. They were also concerned my ranking would significantly drop with the loss of the European circuit, and rightly so. Was this divine intervention? A sign that my tennis career was coming to a close?

This experience taught me just how fragile (and often dangerous) life can be. Not only is it unpredictable for your career, but life is also unexpected. This is why you must be flexible and accept that not everything will play out in your favor.

My brother also told me to file a case for potential identity theft, because somebody in Afghanistan was walking around with my driver's license!

When I finally told my mother, she went pale. She was speechless, and I thought she was going to faint. Being physically back in the United States helped her deal with the shock. In all, I learned that money comes and goes—she told me not to worry about it. The larger issue was my tennis career and what would happen now.

The fear that this could be the premature end of my tennis career became my new reality. I didn't know what to do, so I consulted with other professional tennis players. The outcome seemed inevitable. After having lunch with Marin Čilić, who was competing in Indian Wells, we talked about the tennis grind on the circuit, and I watched him practice with Boris, who was coaching and training top players and the French Davis Cup team. Leaving the tour was difficult for Boris. He found peace in coaching, but we both only enjoyed coaching top juniors, not spoiled kids who were forced to play tennis by their parents.

Financially, I had little success redeeming myself with new sponsors. For me, it was almost easier to leave it all behind.

Many argued that I was one of the most talented South Asian players; even some of the legends of the game noticed my talent, although this was short-lived after what happened in Afghanistan. That experience made me evaluate what I was doing. It made me think about my purpose, and how I had to build a new life.

Needless to say, it gave me perspective, and I never wanted to be in a situation like that again. It keeps me up at night sometimes. But to change my path required me to change myself. I had to find something else to achieve and love. I had to hustle for it.

As chief architects of our own careers, we must accept the circumstances we find ourselves in, but understand that the story lives on. Remember, *we are writing our stories.*

HUSTLE: The Most Important Skill of the Future?

After watching my parents hustle in the United States, it was my turn to see what it meant to truly hustle. This time, I was alone. I had moved out of my apartment in New York City, and, for lack of a better word, I was homeless. When I got back from my trip overseas, I had nowhere to go.

Fortunately, my friend and fellow graduate student Arijit opened up his dorm room floor to me for the remainder of the summer. I was grateful. However, after a few weeks, Arijit told me his fiancé was coming to visit. Homelessness loomed over me again. What was I to do?

INSTAGRAM: @IHOUSE

My Aunt Shahnaz was kind enough to open the door for me, despite how bad I was at doing the dishes. We would sit up and have late-night chats over chai about life and our struggles. My aunt recalled picking me up on my first day of grad school and driving me to the famous International House to join about 700 grad students from all over the world. She said I couldn't stop smiling. It was a spectacular place, with a ballroom, pub, a cricket team that practices on their rooftop, and a restaurant. There were 700+ graduate residents of the building. She was right: when I got accepted, I was full of joy. This place was legendary. It was known to have the best parties in the pub downstairs on weekends, and I didn't even have to leave the building. When it was snowing outside, it was the talk of the Morningside Campus.

My aunt and I discussed the next chapter in my life, and then about family and community. We spoke about the perils of being a displaced person, separated from a community and resources. We concluded our conversation by talking about gratitude and how lucky we were. It was a special evening.

Don't Just Walk, Strut

Ralph Lauren once said, "I don't design clothes, I design dreams." This quote inspired me to design my life. Although I had always been driven by this quote, it meant more to me than ever after all my experiences of almost being kidnapped, and then having no permanent place to live.

In the period between 2003-2005, I co-hosted both the Miss India NY pageant and the Miss India USA pageant. In 2004, I was invited to the Bollywood music awards, which was spectacular in itself, but because I was invited as a professional athlete, it was even more special. While there, I was asked to audition as a model by Alia Khan, a famous South Asian designer. Out of 150 people, I was selected as one of the top models. Although I considered myself an athlete, not a model, I was open to new creative experiences.

The problem was clearly defined for me: I needed a job. I was in the ideation phase, writing down all kinds of side gigs on sticky notes and putting them all over my wall. This modeling opportunity wasn't one of them, but it still came my way from my extended network. It was a risk, but I thought to myself, "Who knows, maybe I would like it?" And I was right; it lasted for 2 to 3 years! They were also some of the best years of my life.

MANHATTAN, NY: Karamjit Bhinder Fashion Show

This modeling job was a prototype before it was a lifeline. I needed it because of all the sponsorship money I owed after my near kidnapping. I tested it, and it worked. What started as just an idea became something tangible.

MANHATTAN, NY: Karamjit Bhinder Fashion Show

Becoming one of the top South Asian models in New York City came with many perks. For example, I got to emcee at gigs, such as the Miss India pageant where I met my (now ex) girlfriend, the winner of the Miss India New York pageant. It also led me to being cast as Joey on the South Asian version of *Friends* and the host of American Desi's *Makeover Show*. In the photo below, I transform Raj into a fashion designer with a Beckham-like hairstyle!

SOHO, NY: Making the transformation

This is all well and good, but what did all these paths mean for my career? How did these experiences equip me with tools to build my life? What can you learn from my experiences?

Life's Crossings

While running across the beautiful Brooklyn Bridge one afternoon, I realized my life had passed into a new era. The next time I would go to the U.S. Open, it would be as a spectator, not as a competitor. I thought about what I was going to do next.

I was testing my life by experimenting my way forward, and I encourage you to do the same. Refine your ideas by gathering feedback from those in your mentor circles. You will learn more about how to do this in Chapter 9.

Many students I meet assume that universities will find you a job, but that doesn't necessarily translate to a career. And what if you're not a student, and there's no career center: then what do you do? Perhaps, for some, gaining an entry level position after graduation will be the foundation for building a career, but let's be honest; it will barely pay a monthly student loan bill.

Crossing the famous bridge, I realized that life's crossings are full of experiences and challenges. Each one of them is a bridge, each into the future. I needed to think about how I was going to make ends meet— although the modeling was fun, it was not going to compensate me enough to build the forward momentum I needed.

With bills piling up, I accepted the first position I was offered, as a project coordinator at Yeshiva University. This allowed me to pay my bills while doing research on HIV/AIDS. I hated research, but if it was for a good cause, I believed in it and didn't mind doing it. Besides, I learned that this was not the job for me in the long run, but I still found the experience useful. However, with the thousands I still owed, I needed another source of income.

Purpose, like connections and friend circles, helps orient people and frees people in tough times. Friends come to the rescue and remind you to take things one day at a time. Here I was gathering inspiration. I was trying to inspire new thinking by learning what people needed. Some of my friends suggested becoming a personal trainer, as so many people needed help reaching their fitness and strength goals. So I kept generating ideas, trying to push past so-called "obvious" solutions towards more breakthrough ideas. I didn't just want to be any personal trainer, I wanted to focus on a segment of the population where I thought I could add the most value: former athletes. I knew I excelled in circuit, strength, and functional training, so I studied and obtained a certificate, and was quickly hired at New York Sports Club at Rockefeller Center.

NORTH BERGEN, NJ: Wearing my personal trainer uniform after accepting the position

The design thinking approach worked! It can work for you too.

One side hustle wasn't going to cut it, so now I had two. I used to wake up at 5 a.m., since work at the Bronx clinics started just after sunrise. My day shift ended at 5 p.m., my evening shift at the gym was from 6:00 p.m. to 10 p.m., and I was lucky to find time to grab dinner in between rush hour and commuting. Then my night shift began, which entailed researching a potential third gig: starting my own nonprofit organization. It felt like three jobs because it really was. But my first two were what I needed to do to pay back money I owed. The other one was what I needed to give myself the life I desired. I needed to make more of an impact.

Accelerate Your Impact

The great thing about the design thinking approach is that it's an iterative process. I went back to the drawing board, framing a new question. *How can I make a difference?* I explored a driving question that would inspire me to search and discover a creative solution.

I started to read more positive psychology while I looked into starting my own nonprofit. This opened my eyes to the gifts I needed to appreciate, as well as to habits I needed to change to build my life and experience more happiness. My father taught me that happiness must be acquired independently. If it's not desired and worked towards, then it most definitely will not be found. Life is fragile and vulnerable. You must be motivated to search within yourself to discover it.

With graduation right around the corner, and as a soon-to-be alumnus of Mailman School of Public Health, I was invited to have breakfast with the late Dean Rosenfield and told him of my incredible experience. He motivated me to think globally, not to let this deter me, and to continue to leverage my reputation as a world-class tennis player, even if I wasn't on the circuit any longer. He felt that I had enough success under my belt to influence and help others and that I still had a lot to offer as an athlete ambassador. He was a *flash mentor*, meaning he mentored me in a single setting or occurrence. In simple terms, flash mentoring or situational mentoring allows you to quickly acquire information about a specific situation to help you move forward. That meeting was very meaningful and had a lasting impact on me despite it not being a long-term mentor relationship.

Thinking about this gave me more of life's bricks and mortar. I had started putting up the scaffolding. I was not only designing my life, but I was building it too. My father taught me to do both. You will also watch your dreams rise, culminating in the reality and fulfillment that you seek.

So, I took the dean's counsel. He was not someone I could meet with often—not many could—but I felt honored by the special invitation. Receiving his words of wisdom, I became more focused on building my social capital and meaningful relationships.

I dove into action, prototyping and testing ideas like crazy, such as joining the entrepreneurship community at Columbia and exploring how to launch my own business and enter the world of nonprofits. I also got involved in everything the university had to offer. I began volunteering with organizations like UNICEF in an effort to gain experience on the frontline of humanitarian efforts. I even auditioned and was selected for the Columbia University bhangra team, the only graduate student on the team. Talk about getting outside your comfort zone! I was shy as a kid! Well, it didn't show after a while, and I won the regional bhangra competition, and we were invited to compete at state level.

Here I am dancing during a mock wedding, called HANGAMA (meaning chaos) on College Walk:

NEW YORK, NY: Columbia University's HANGAMA

Mindfulness played a role in my success, and it will for you too. After several months, I found myself performing Bollywood dances at weddings and the International House's annual culture show. I also volunteered for various causes to help the South Asian Community in both New York and New Jersey. Just before graduation, I was awarded the Dedicated Leadership and Exceptional Community Service Award by the South Asian Community of New York City. This honor recognizes individuals' dedication and outstanding services in the fields of art, classical and folk dance, community services, and participation in organizational activities, both South Asian and mainstream.

NEW YORK, NY: Columbia University Morningside Campus Graduation

Then I graduated, the ceremony taking place just outside the doors to Low Library. With my family in the audience, I began fully creating the blueprint to launch an organization directly aligned with my degree, the first-ever with this particular niche focus. I wanted to invite the audience into this dream-while-awake experience, *an invitation to make a difference.*

FACEBOOK: @INVITATIONRELIEF

Invitation Relief was born the next day, a nonprofit dedicated to forced migration and health. It was formalized in 2006, two years after I graduated.

NEW YORK, NY: Graduating in 2004 and attending the Health Sciences
Campus celebration

Before moving out of the prestigious International House to find
non-university housing, I met the Director of the Resiliency Program
at Columbia University's Mailman School of Public Health. Her name
was Paula. She was brilliant, and we connected one night in the Pub. She
spoke tirelessly about her home in Medellin, Colombia and the need for
more humanitarian intervention there. I didn't speak a word of Spanish,
but I decided to get out of my comfort zone and research the situation.
She was right; at that time, the country had one of the highest displaced

populations worldwide. It would take a couple years to prepare such an intervention, inauguration, or to learn Spanish, but I set my mind on all three. She helped me diversify my sight and get more out of my comfort zone.

A Moment That Made All the Difference

If you change, everything around you changes.

One of my favorite memories of my dad was the time he gave me three quarters. It was very hot that day, maybe over 100 degrees. He stopped at a vending machine with a donation box next to it. The donations received went to providing basic necessities to the poor in Fresno, California. As I rushed to get out of the car, he stopped me and said, "You can put this in the vending machine, or you can donate it." I was dying of thirst and just said, "Yes, sir."

A couple minutes later, when the first quarter was halfway in the slot, I remembered his expression. Shrugging my shoulders, I gave in. As much as I wanted the coldest Coke I could find, I gave the quarters to charity. That evening, my family was invited to a dinner party, and my father bragged about what I did. It was one of the moments I had seen my father the happiest. He bought me a Coke afterwards! He taught me that there was reward in charity: that helping others is the noblest thing a person can do. This has stuck with me, and I recommend others consider charity.

Thirty years later, I use three quarters for binoculars to see over the Empire State Building. Each time I look through them, I see humanity.

What Does Humanity Mean to You?

I was invited to go to India with my friend Paula to work on telemedicine and long distance learning. There was one catch: I would have to pay half the costs, which amounted to about $2,500. I did it, and it changed my life.

For my dad, giving without expecting to receive anything in return was essential. He believed that, when you give, it comes back to you in other forms. Like karma, the universe will give back to you.

ANDAMAN AND NICOBARESE ISLANDS, IL: Greeting a young boy in a tsunami shelter

Each of us has had these *defining* moments. Take a moment to identify one or two that you have experienced and will never forget. How have these moments shaped your perspective? How might you remember other moments that further shaped your perspective?

Transience

I am telling you this because I had an experience that changed my life, and I have spoken to many others who have experienced this too—it is universal. I know that you will be able to tap into it, and it is my job to encourage you to so do. With that in mind, I have another anecdote for you.

Sense of Urgency: Responsibility to Act

Crossing the border from Pakistan into India, where I had been training, made me want these countries to transcend their generations of conflict. I was mainly responding to my calling, which was to unite humanity with my sense of social responsibility.

CAREER AND LIFE HACK #11
Compassion is underrated.

Once I got to Port Blair, India, I encountered a group of overly enthusiastic gentleman who had none but one goal in mind: to make my arrival the best it could be. Below is a picture of eight boys, who not only stepped up to take care of me and all of my luggage, but who consistently looked after over 100 children of a rehabilitation center in the Andaman and Nicobar islands. Their dedication inspired me, and I hope it inspires you too.

PORT BLAIR, IN: Eight deaf teenagers who help coordinate relief efforts for special needs
children saying "love" in sign language.

*"You give but little when you give of your possessions. It is when you give of yourself
that you truly give."*

—Khalil Gibran

The next gentle soul I met was the local teacher who was a full-
time volunteer. She immediately told me that I would be co-teaching
geography later in the week with her. Who was I to argue with her? I
thanked her with a smile and admired how she took charge and initiative.
Every person I met that day had an aura and a greater purpose than
themselves.

PORT BLAIR, IN: With the teacher in front of the doors to the rehabilitation center

Love Yourself, but not Arrogantly

It's the imperfections about a person that make them who they are. It is important to recognize your imperfections and accept them, but also to work on them. Build your self-esteem and self-confidence because you cannot be a Career Mastermind™ without them!

Leadership is humility. I remember a time when a friendly young girl with Down's syndrome asked me for my autograph. What I did in that moment was probably not what you think: I asked her if she could give me hers instead. She was thrilled and proudly signed her name. I still have that autograph in a drawer at home, and I remember how hard she pressed the pen onto the paper, and how careful she was. It had to be perfect. I look at it from time to time when I need to remind myself to be humble and thankful for where I am and what I have.

This was a way of taking responsibility and spreading kindness—simply put, it fit into my life's vision. You can spread kindness too, and it will increase your sense of self-worth.

ANDAMAN AND NICOBAR ISLANDS, IN: Asking for an autograph

Love Others

Every Career Mastermind™ has the ability to give back. You cannot be a selfish Career Mastermind™ because you would be violating the *principles* of Career Masterminding: positive collaboration, sharing with like-minded individuals, and helping others achieve their dreams. It's also built on top of the core value of being selfless. This is key to understanding the spirit of all Career Masterminds.

ANDAMAN AND NICOBAR ISLANDS, IN: Inside a tsunami shelter

People who love doing good things for other people love themselves and feel more fulfilled. Try it.

Once I returned from what was a magical experience for me, Columbia contacted me and interviewed me about my experience in India and featured me in their alumni spotlight section. I was asked to give back and serve on a panel, and I happily accepted. After all, they gave me the public health awareness and preparedness that helped me make an impact abroad. Plus, I had so many stories to tell!

Columbia University
MAILMAN SCHOOL
OF PUBLIC HEALTH

AT THE FRONTLINE

NEWSLETTER HOME | ARCHIVE

JUL 2008 | VOL3 #3

IN THIS ISSUE

- Dean.Fried@TheFrontline
- Research
- News and Events
- Faculty Updates
- Alumni News
- Student News
- News You Can Use

ALUMNI NEWS

**Hassan Akmal, MPH '04, Provides Support to
Underserved Populations in India**

Hassan Akmal, a former tennis pro and 2004 graduate of the
Mailman School, is spearheading relief and global assessment
efforts for vulnerable populations through Invitation Relief, the
NGO he founded following a trip to India in 2006.

While in India, Mr. Akmal noticed the limited resources available
to local communities, such as food, shelter, and medical
supplies, as well as basic education. Following his visit, he
founded Invitation Relief and immediately teamed with SANGHA
(Sanskrit for "community with a common goal, vision, or
purpose"), another non-profit focused on helping neglected
populations.

Together, with the support of Baptist Health Systems, the two
organizations were able to assist the Nicobar Rehabilitation
Center for Handicapped Children, where it is now possible for
Center participants to receive certificates and diplomas through
the collaboration of the University of Miami, Florida International
University, and Columbia University. Additionally, Mr. Akmal
worked with children at the Center using sign language to
communicate during the three week post-tsunami intervention
training for local health professionals and aspiring students.

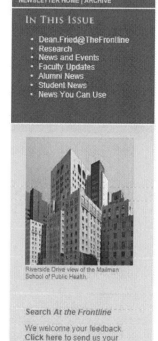

Riverside Drive view of the Mailman
School of Public Health.

Search *At the Frontline*

We welcome your feedback.
Click here to send us your
comments and suggestions.

By building a strong foundation for education at the center and
providing sustainable strategies, Mr. Akmal hopes to build on
local medical care through continuing medical education of
physicians and by improving the public health of local
communities-what he has termed "micro-macro enterprise."
Noted Mr. Akmal, "You design the bridge before you build it, so
it's appropriate and sustainable."

Back to Top
Print Article

Doing good for others is inspiring, and it motivates others to do
good as well. It's a gift to oneself, yet the giver doesn't realize this, and
shouldn't expect it.

Ay Vamos

In 2009, remembering the look in Paula's eyes and her passion about Colombia, I decided that the time had come. I was off to Medellin, to work with children displaced by the civil war. I picked up an English-Spanish dictionary along the way. *Vamos!*

Your Invitation Has Arrived

The project I launched, *Niños del Mundo*, meaning, "Kids of the World," was aimed at providing education and helping alleviate poverty in areas of forced migration. We used the chant, *"Live. Love. Hope. Believe!"* It was a series of projects about hope. We selected Colombia as the first location for the series.

When I first began the project, I knew very little about Colombia, but I was ready for a new challenge. I began to teach myself Spanish using Google Translate. A few years later, I became fluent, and I am now able to read and write in Spanish. The language was essential to know how to make it out of the roughest neighborhoods.

Niños del Mundo focused on alleviating the poverty of displaced street children in underserved areas and providing education and resources for health and well-being. This was very challenging if you didn't understand the language as well as the slang. In fact, the areas we worked in, known as the "Barrios Populares," were very dangerous. They stretch up the hills and mountains of Medellin, where access to resources and paved roads becomes scarce. Robberies, kidnapping, and theft at gunpoint are common. You actually need to take the Metro Cable to really get a glimpse of the daily life of these communities, since it's so high up in the mountains.

Wasting no time, I focused on two essential areas: value and impact.

The value: we aimed to help underserved communities through improved access to education and enterprise by using cost-effective technology and strengthening local resources: "Micro/Macro-Enterprise."

The impact: to optimize educational and medical institutions by increasing the capacity of local personnel and organizations to serve their communities. By building a stronger foundation for the education of the center and providing sustainable strategies for micro-enterprise, Invitation Relief strove to expand the medical awareness of physicians and education for the improved public health of local communities.

The Challenge

Native programs, infrastructure, and organizations have unique strengths in identifying areas of need and opportunity. By networking within communities, it was possible to set up ongoing processes that would continue to grow a community's natural resources and confidence.

Through these various experiences, I learned to use my moral compass to give myself constant direction. In Chapter Seven, we will discuss how to create this compass as a guide to your leadership as a Career Mastermind™.

"Excellence is an art won by training and habituation. We do not act rightly because we have virtue or excellence; rather, we have those because we have acted rightly. We are what we repeatedly do. Excellence, then, is not an act but a habit."

—*Aristotle*

This led me to ruminate on five aspects of charity:

1. Charity begins at home.

2. Charity begins in your own community.

3. Give without expecting anything in return.

4. At the end of each day, ask yourself what have you done to make someone's life better today?

5. Even a smile is charity.

With this anecdote in mind, I implore you to consider charity. The goodness can be life-changing not only to others, but to you as well.

MEDELLIN, CO: With one of my favorite kids during the Kids of the World Project

Deploy Empathy

I still use the design thinking approach. It starts with empathy and breakthrough ideas. Take the tsunami-stricken areas of Indonesia, for example. Unless we build and refine our ideas about sustainable solutions, such areas will never recover. This also becomes an ethical question: whether our interventions have any value to anyone. Many of those who suffer have become more resilient, but it is so important that we not abandon these moral positions by neglecting to come back to the issue.

Life is not merely about change, but also sustainability. Remember the Ikigai. Imagine putting change and sustainability in the center. These concepts go hand-in-hand.

Crafting a human story to inspire others to take action is the last step of the design thinking approach to your career. In order for anyone to be successful at this, they need a story-making and story-sharing team.

Remember, building a life you love is not going to be easy. You will need to rely on the methodology I shared in this chapter and on your ability to be intuitive. You will need to recognize patterns and form ideas that are meaningful. The ideas you construct must also be functional. Like the "YOU Matter lenses," the elements of each of the five steps of design thinking depend on one another.

You will make mistakes, and you will fail. Accept it; it's part of the process.

"I failed my way to success." —Thomas Edison

Now it's your turn. It will take time to master the design-thinking process for your career. For now, frame a question. Go ahead. Write it down. Make sure it is a driving question. You will have another opportunity at the end of Chapter 5 to practice these steps.

Next, we will talk about why you are worth the investment.

CHECKLIST ITEM 4

Career Bucket List

CAREER MANIFESTÓ
BE AN ARCHITECT, BUILD THE LIFE YOU LOVE

▶ **Define where you are now:** (check one)

☐ I am designing my life

☐ Someone else is designing my life

▶ **Follow Up Date:**

☐ / ☐ / ☐

▶ *Why do you feel this way?*

▶ **Action Item:**

I will _____

by the Date ☐ / ☐ / ☐

▶ **Completed:** (circle one)

○ Yes   ○ No

▶ *What is the 'IMPACT' action you will take within one week to make a positive change?*

Career Ladders

Life Crane

HOW DO I
WANT TO BE
REMEMBERED?

Reflecting on my
retirement speech

TEENAGE
YEARS
AND
COLLEGE

Preparing for
the life I
want to live

My
Evolving
World
View

I DON'T
WANT TO
GROW UP
YEARS

No worries in
the world!

I AM:
(click all that apply)

☐ Single

☐ Taken

☐ Building
my empire

"Next Steps" and Notes:

Workbook available for download at www.CareerMastermind.org/Resources

CHAPTER 5 (LENS 5): "YOU MATTER" — WHY YOU SHOULD INVEST IN YOURSELF

---•◆•---

"At first we will only skim the surface of the earth like young starlings, but soon, emboldened by practice and experience, we will spring into the air with the impetuousness of the eagle."

—*Jean-Jacques Rousseau*

A once in a lifetime—breathtaking moment of a murmuration of starlings taking the form of a giant eagle after they were targeted by a bird of prey, Their connection to one another is surreal and pure, yet—each one independently matters.

Starlings in Mastermind Group formation

You may be sitting there and wondering: So what is this concept of "YOU Matter" *really* all about? And I can answer you simply: It's about focus—doing what you do best, doing what makes you feel better, and doing what makes you work smarter (not harder). It's about identifying your strengths and playing to those strengths. If you play to your strengths, your job will be more rewarding, and you will get to your purpose faster. Life is about Meaning. *Discover it.* Be curious.

Create the Arch in Your Archery

You are the expert, and everyone in the audience is your cheerleader. This is the advice that was given to me by Javier R. Lewis, the former President

of Toastmasters International, explaining how not to get nervous for a
potential TEDx Talk.

"Fundamentally, the marksman aims at himself."

—*D.T. Suzuki*

The proverb above is integral to the concept of YOU Matter. The
archer pulls back the arch of the bow and is in control. You must keep
reminding yourself that you are your own life's archer. Your focus is your
focus, nobody else's. Your aim is your aim—*the string, arrow rest, pivot point,
grip, bow, handle or riser, nocking point, and draw length are up to you!*

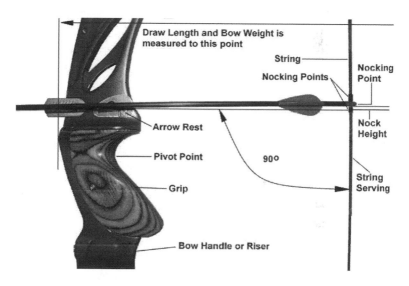

An important thing to remember, and also a central thesis of this
chapter, is that you are competing against yourself. I used to say this to
myself on the tennis court whenever I faced a top seed and when people
expected me to lose. I trained my mind, and the results surprised many
people. You can do this too.

You must believe in yourself to have true confidence in your abilities and performance. It doesn't matter what other people think. When you begin the path of self-actualization, many will seek to bring you down. Some do it maliciously, and some just don't understand your transformation. Nevertheless, stay on course. *You are on a path to your own enlightenment: take confidence in your transformation.*

You are your own competition—treat yourself that way. Constantly seek to beat and outdo yourself. When you do this, you are on the road to fulfillment. You must explore your intrinsic motivations and strive for improvement. You cannot complete life, you can only get better at living it.

Never forget:

Believe in yourself. When I tell you to take a leap of faith, I don't mean blindly. Faith is a facet of trust. Trust yourself. Life is about falling forward, getting up, and doing it all again. If you're on the ground, you can always get back up. Keep striving.

Failing Upwards

Have you ever seen kids skateboarding? Perhaps you thought they were doing something dangerous and that they should stop. But I disagree! Look deeply into what these kids are doing: they are attempting a trick, falling over, hurting themselves—and guess what? They get up and do it over again! They are *failing forward*, in search of a goal. They are investing in themselves, and competing against themselves. They all encourage each other despite skating as individuals. Much like a Career Mastermind™ Group (which you will learn more about in Chapter 10), they value hard work, commitment, failure as a learning process, and hard-earned rewards. So, when you assess yourself, channel the skateboarding kid inside you. Be adventurous, daring, and—if you fall over—get back up. It is by failing that we learn. Most of all, have fun!

In my "YOU Matter" series, I speak about how I discovered the key to human happiness and fulfillment. I know I've said this already, but it cannot be stressed enough: happiness is Meaning. Happiness is like money: it comes and goes. It's important to push yourself up in places, like the hustle and bustle of New York City, and get in the zone. When you are in the zone, you are not a lost member of a crowd, you are driven by Purpose and Meaning. Each moment you spend investing in yourself, you will reap rewards.

Also in this series, I discuss surprising data related to focusing. Did you know that 95% of the world's best archers use both eyes (to visualize depth)? This is a remarkable insight. Think about it: most of us squint when we aim. *However, with open eyes and an open mind, we keep moving toward our target.*

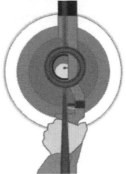

Always aim with both eyes

Everyone Has Different Paths

We all find our targets differently. My sister, Sara (I mean "Dr. Sara"), took a more traditional path than I did. She attended the University of California, San Diego (UCSD) also, but to study pharmacy and became a doctor of pharmacy. But like me, she recollected her childhood to discover what she wanted to do. She delved into the deepest part of herself and found what would give her Purpose. She believed strongly that she mattered and that only she could push herself further. I am very proud of what my sister has achieved and continues to achieve. What path(s) are you taking to invest in yourself? In what way are you reminding yourself that you matter?

CLOVIS, CA: My sweet sister Sara and my pharmacist

My parents desperately wanted one of us to become a doctor. My sister fulfilled that desire by graduating from pharmacy school. But she also loves it and the idea of being an independent woman. She loves the hours, the compensation, as well as being the friendly face of the pharmacy to the community. She looks so young for her age, so customers still ask her where the pharmacist is! Blushing, she answers, "That's me!" It also gives her the freedom to travel and explore her other interests. This linear path works for her. Freedom, for her, was and continues to be her most important incentive.

Find Your Own Freedom

My path was more roundabout. I excelled in a variety of areas, which put me on the path to being a Career Mastermind™. However, this wasn't always easy.

When there aren't clear options that you can take, you have decisions to make. Think about it. If you are at a restaurant with 100 items on the menu, you will likely take far longer to decide what you want than if there were ten. Therefore, you might be able to become competent in many areas, but you can only excel in a select few. So, how do you know what to do if you, like me, have a more roundabout journey to take? And what do you do if you want to take the linear path? The answers to both are similar, and will be discussed in the next section.

Reverse Engineer from Your Passion

LINKEDIN: WWW.LINKEDIN.COM/IN/SHIRAZ

My brother Shiraz was passionate about video games—he had the spirit of an entrepreneur. With more than 25 years of experience in virtual reality, video games, and entertainment, my brother gained deep, hands-on experience building new entertainment businesses that utilize cutting-edge technology. He led business and product development for DreamLab, which developed all of the virtual reality projects for DreamWorks Animation prior to 2016. He was also the VP of operations-product development for the video game company, THQ.

Shiraz (who, along with my father, was my primary role model) is a mentor for Boost VC, the pre-eminent accelerator for emerging technology. His career highlights include directing a string of multi-million dollar video game titles, including Disney Pixar's *The Incredibles*, Nickelodeon's *SpongeBob SquarePants* and *Scooby-Doo!*

SPACES

WWW.SPACES.COM

We all have our own spaces, both internal and externally. Considering himself a true gamer in the gamer space, Shiraz has been playing video games since he could stand. He and his co-founder, Brad Herman—both inventors of multiple patented VR technologies—recently opened a location-based virtual reality (VR) startup called SPACES. He is the CEO of the company made up of DreamWorks Animation specialists who raised millions for the startup. SPACES now counts Cinemark as one of its predominant VR partners. Cinemark is one of the world's largest movie theater chains.

In June 2018, the startup opened a new VR experience called "Terminator Salvation: Fight for the Future" to the public at the Irvine Spectrum Center in Orange County, California. "Terminator Salvation" is a high-end location-based VR experience, which means that participants get to freely roam on a stage with physical props that are incorporated into the VR experience. He opened an additional location at the Century 20 Oakridge and XD theatre in San Jose, California, at the Westfield Oakridge Shopping Center. He makes it all about you, your family, and your friends. "We make you the star," says Shiraz. "You can go see a movie. With the Spaces experience, you *become* the movie."

Shiraz also partnered with Sega's Joypolis location-based entertainment division to open the new VR attraction near the Shibuya train station in Tokyo, which is one of the busiest transit stations in the world.

After years of reverse engineering from his passion, he finally realized his dream. He was not focused on external competition, but investing in himself. Virtual reality was his way to travel, to explore the limits of cutting-edge technology. He mattered to himself. He created his own space. Now look where he is!

A Rebel with a Cause

Shiraz was also the first to rebel against going to medical school (making it easier for me). When he was in junior high, he published his first video game called "Hoverblade." He also founded a company called Micronics when he was a young teen. His spirit is inspiring to me, as he has cultivated a linear career trajectory all his life. While most paths to careers aren't linear, his was; but that is because he reverse engineered from what he was good at and loved. It was his own!

PLAYA DEL REY, CA: Shiraz, Sabah, and Ziya Akmal on Halloween

The takeaway: there are traditional and nontraditional paths, and neither one is right or wrong. It depends on you to take responsibility for yourself and make the choices about which path to travel down. You initiate it. The road to success may not even be paved for you yet. You must do this yourself. You must take yourself seriously.

View yourself from the outside in. View yourself from the inside out. All perspectives matter.

The Power of Perspective

Perspective varies from person to person. Shiraz lives in a completely different world: virtual reality. And yet, he has found perspective.

The wonder of VR is really about *teleporting* a user to a different location at any given time. The concept of presence is also central.

"Presence is a psychological state or subjective perception in which even though part or all of an individual's current experience is generated by and/or filtered through human-made technology, part of all of the individual's perception fails to accurately acknowledge the role of the technology in the experience."

—*International Society for Presence Research, 2000*

Our brains' distinct way of showing us where we are is to stimulate our motor cortex and our sensory system. You can't always see someone experience *presence*, that psychological state and perception of being present in a non-physical world, but I can assure you it happens. Imagine someone who is afraid of heights crossing a very tall bridge; you've all seen the videos. Virtual Reality can make people sweat and swear, but it can also help you achieve presence, even though this sounds counterintuitive.

My brother has been imagining the future and traveling into different worlds all his life. He has visualized it, and more importantly, he has felt it. And what did he gain from visualization? The power of Purpose. He moved towards his dreams through this process. You too can benefit from feeling your dreams. *Close your eyes, breathe, and fully consider what it is you want to do. Listen to that voice inside.* Treat that voice as important; it's part of investing in yourself.

Presence and embodiment, another term also used in virtual reality, is not something that we are always conscious of. Perspective is the same. I have learned that with our virtual reality glasses, we can put our own career and life lenses on and imagine the future. We can design our lives through our imagination, even through brief embodiment, as our brains adapt. It induces a level of empathy and understanding that is more effective. It also helps give us a better understanding of our own self-perception, thus improving our communication and self-awareness. In turn, we are propelled towards the future in a positive way.

We can apply these concepts to our lives and be more conscious of them, even though stepping outside of our self and self-image can be very difficult. However, it helps usher in change, and for Shiraz and others, VR can enable this new age of learning: what we think, what we feel, and what we feel we already know. It can give us a tangible way to accelerate new insights through the magic of perspective.

The Entrepreneur of the Future

WWW.YOUMEPLAY.COM

Entrepreneurship is clearly in my family's DNA. My ten-year old nephew, Ziya Akmal, even has his own following on YouTube after creating a video game app called "Epic Space Battles" as part of a fundraiser. He donates the app proceeds to Playa Vista Elementary School. Ziya clearly has inherited his talent from his father. He is passionate about a great deal of things. You can check him out on YouTube!

PLAYA VISTA, CA: Ziya sporting a SPACES t-shirt

YouMePlay allows two people to play collaboratively—on the same screen!

"I'm a gamer like my father before me," Ziya says. But he is also a martial artist and Curious George. He is well and truly discovering his own path! If he can do it, then so can you.

PLAYA VISTA, CA: Ziya as Curious George

Take Responsibility and Find *Your* *Place of Peace*

We must remember that we have to take responsibility for ourselves. It is up to us, rather than anyone else, to attain a work-life balance and have meaningful engagement with our friends and families. We have to take control of our own lives. The government, employers, your family and friends—nobody—will do it for you. We must take life by the horns and get on the saddle ourselves.

We are so often pacified by things like flex time, annual holiday office parties, fun committees, and casual Fridays. But there comes a moment when we have to be honest with ourselves. There are fundamental issues that need to be solved when it comes to your occupation's compatibility with life outside of work. You are complicit in your own life and how your career affects it. *You have to treat yourself how you'd want others to treat you.* You have to take responsibility to live peacefully by having peace within.

The problem for millions of people is that they give up looking for that place of "inner peace" because they stop being curious about new experiences. As they take on new responsibilities and incorporate new routines, their sense of wonder starts to escape them. When we lose our sense of wonder, our Purpose goes with it. We become robots, unassuming and unnoticed. But you can change that, especially if you are still looking for meaning and fulfillment in what you do in your day-to-day life. I looked for it every day until I found it. So can you.

CHICAGO, IL: At the coast in Lakeshore East, 2014

Is an Interesting Life Better than a Happy Life?

"We don't really want what we think we desire."

—*Slavoj Žižek*

More people quit their jobs than are laid off, as they give up their scripted life for something more meaningful.

Like Curious George, we are born curious. Our insatiable drive to learn, invent, explore, and study deserves to have the same status as every other drive in our lives, including the primal ones. As humans, we are information-gatherers. We have always looked at the stars and contemplated the vastness of the Beyond, wondering what our Purpose is and how we can make a difference.

"For my part I know nothing with any certainty, but the sight of the stars makes me dream."

—*Vincent van Gogh*

It is a fundamental problem that millions of people give up on their curiosity. Their responsibilities often lead to routine. Routines can be safe and secure, but they can also become imprisoning. When people lose their curiosity, they often spiral into apathy and depression as life loses its meaning. Don't be one of these people. Take control.

I am not saying anything particularly revolutionarily here. I borrow from famous and successful people all the time. One of my favorite physicists, Albert Einstein, encourages us to pursue our curiosities. He once said:

"Don't think about why you question, simply don't stop questioning. Don't worry about what you can't answer, and don't try to explain what you can't know. Curiosity is

its own reason. Aren't you in awe when you contemplate the mysteries of eternity, of life, of the marvelous structure behind reality? And this is the miracle of the human mind — to use its constructions, concepts, and formulas as tools to explain what man sees, feels and touches. Try to comprehend a little more each day. Have holy curiosity."

Always try to see what is behind the veil, what life is truly made up of. Look around with childlike awe. This will assist you on your quest to self-actualization. When you were a child, you mattered to yourself. Learn from your inner child. *Don't let your sense of wonder escape you.*

Your North Star

Each of us has our own North Star that we can never lose sight of.

Your North Star is your primary goal, the deep target you are seeking. Your North Star is the point where your purpose meets your faith. We will explore how this concept progressively aligns with your moral compass further in the book.

Change Your Circumstances

You can change your life circumstances, especially if you are looking for meaning and fulfillment in your daily life. Never give up. There is no better time than now.

Whenever I meet students or clients, I always ask them the same question: "Who is managing your career?" Most struggle with the answer. So many students tend to treat the career center as a placement agency, so I like to clear those misconceptions straight away. When I was in graduate school, the career services provided were minimal and mostly self-directed. No one is there to tell you how to get your dream job and live your dream life. That is up to you.

For anyone looking for what they want to do for the rest of their life, they must each take ownership and responsibility for their career development paths and understand that they are their own *life designers.* They are the architects of their own progress. For instance, I stopped seeing myself as a "career coach." I really was a "life coach!" What I really was a "life coach!" This advice, although daunting at first, is liberating.

We are all not merely looking for "a job," we are looking for a career. We are looking to align that career with our personal lives. We are looking to create, meet, and exceed our own goals. This is all about options, alignment, and freedom. Once we learn to take this responsibility and balance it with time, the world opens up for us. You will invest more time in yourself, and start treating yourself like you matter. The possibilities are endless. We must think of ourselves as students of the world. We are always learning. And again, we must always take responsibility. This attitude will put you in the driver's seat. Invest in yourself. Where will you go?

CAREER AND LIFE HACK #12
Passion is the difference between finding a job and finding a career.

Begin with the End Game, Reverse the Risk

INSTAGRAM: @THEREALOMARHAROON

After graduating from UCLA with a Bachelor's of Science in Mechanical Engineering, Omar worked for a real estate development company for a number of years. He then became a financial advisor for one of the world's largest wealth management firms. He was initially at the top of his class, but his position was eliminated during the Great Recession. He partnered with a trading analyst to start a hedge fund. However, after his partner's father died, his partner lost interest in the fund, and it was eventually shut down. Omar took a day job as a real estate appraiser to pay bills while he created a new business that would invest clients' money in the world's largest private equity firms.

Omar also had to endure a painful divorce that alienated him from friends and family. With perseverance and faith, Omar was able to grow his business, and he now manages over $100M.

CAREER AND LIFE HACK #13
Life is about transforming failure into success.

Omar's path was nothing but linear. He kept at it, and it paid off. He also helped others and referred me to the firm he was working at. He was an *enabler*, and I got an interview. You will learn more about enablers later in the book.

My end game was simple. Find a job I was good at, a job that I loved doing. I knew if I found it, I would have more longevity, and I would have an impact. Sometimes you don't know whether or not you will like something, love it, or hate it. So you have to try things.

NEXT STEPS

In 2006, I interviewed for the financial advisor position at UBS Financial Services Inc., one of the biggest banks in the world. I have to admit, it was daunting and, although I was confident, I was also nervous. I had lived in NYC for five years and had just moved back to California. It was time to get into the game.

I had no real background in finance. I did have one transferable skill, mathematics, but that was it. Maybe because of that, coupled with being jobless in Los Angeles, my friend Omar came to the rescue. Omar showed me the ropes.

I had a widowed mother to look after and a nonprofit to run. I needed a steady income, otherwise I would have crumbled. With UBS, I had to go through a rigorous seven (yes, seven!) rounds of interviews. This included hiring actors to give me a hard time over the phone, with the expectation that there was a "next step" in order to close a significant financial deal.

Coincidentally, "Next Steps" was what I called my video resume. I had just stepped down from a research position in HAART (Highly Active Antiretroviral Therapy) at Albert Einstein College of Medicine for no other reason than I was not feeling fulfilled. It was too scientific, and I wanted to use the right side of my brain. Constant research was leading me to burnout. This is why I launched my own nonprofit. Yes, it was a risk, but I was so much happier; and risks are what make life worthwhile.

Despite this, I knew I wasn't going to be able to afford living in NYC. That's why I had to go to LA. I thought to myself, if I could find a way to work with investors, perhaps I could manage their investments and do some networking for my philanthropy interests.

So, six rounds of interviews later, I found myself at the final round. Fortunately, the branch manager was a fan of athletes, because (according to him) "they are disciplined." He went on to say, "I have 100 guys that want this job. You were going to go to medical school, you were a pro tennis player, and you don't have a background in finance. You have 30 seconds. Why should I hire you?" For some reason, all my fears went away. I went into autopilot. Out of my mouth flew, "I'm a self-starter, I built a nonprofit from scratch and I know how to build a portfolio of clients." I never let my gaze break from his. He drilled me for 20 minutes.

I was convinced that I wasn't going to get the job. But then he said, "You have the discipline you need for this job and the resilience in the face of losses or rejection." He also said, "This is not a financial advising job, it's a life coaching job. You are dealing with people and problems, and you will affect the lives of many people." He was right. I feel that even my job in the career educator space is the same. We do much more than career services.

Then he walked out saying to someone on the way, "I'm gonna hire this guy; he's gonna be a star."

So, I got my break, and although it was not without a bit of luck, it was the result of my interpersonal communications and networking that got me the job. The future of careers is also about chaos and happenstance. You can increase your probability of luck. I visualized it. I invested time in myself. Can you see the end game? If not, can you come up with one? The more you know about where you want to be, the more motivation you will have. Take steps to increase chances of success and take risks. Then—bet on yourself!

The next two years were a blur as I lived the life of a stockbroker. Fast cars, money, job perks, and a 007 phone extension made me feel like James Bond. I bought a Lotus, as my 1994 Jeep Wrangler was not cutting it with all of these private bankers driving Porsches.

CULVER CITY, CA: The Lotus Esprit

As much as I liked the perks, hitting my quotas, and being known as the guy with the 007 phone extension, I knew financial services wasn't for me. Getting out of the game was a whole different story. The year 2006 was a difficult time to become a financial advisor. Little did many people know, the economy was about to crash. I knew it was, because I was closely following a few prominent economists. They helped me with my exit strategy and timing—when to "get out of the game" at the right time. First, with my mindset, second with action.

Invest Intrinsically, Invest in Gold

During my time as a financial advisor, Omar and I partnered and did quite well together. Knowing that the market was going to crash, I ended up doubling my clients' money because I got them to invest in gold before it plummeted. This helped me further down the line when I was recruited by a 5-Star, socially responsible bank as a business development manager, which allowed me to open and operate more than 100 accounts while breaking bank records beginning with $5 million university accounts. This position meant more to me because it was socially responsible. But something was still missing.

I had to leave all of this because of the economy, and because I knew my heart wasn't in finance. That's when I knew I had to go into higher education, because some of my top financial clients were from the education and nonprofit sectors.

You must discover the intersection between a job you are both good at and enjoy. Your happiness and your life matters. Remember this; it will help you achieve your goals.

Pivot to Transition Your Career

I decided that although I was going to transition careers, I didn't have to start over. I knew my worth and that I could adapt quickly to new environments. We all constantly reinvent ourselves, but we never start from the beginning. Never forget this.

I decided to start applying for jobs in higher education, but I didn't actually apply for the Director of Career Services position. I was interviewing for the role of a senior business manager. Timing is everything, and sometimes the stars align.

While interviewing me, the president of the university said to me, "Hassan, if you can motivate refugees to not give up on their lives, you can motivate students to get out of bed and interview for a job." Then he hired me for the Director of Career Services role, a completely different position, one I had never considered before. It turns out that he was a former recruiter and had laser focus when it came to transferable skills. In this case, for my benefit!

Sometimes you need a supervisor who believes in you and motivates you to believe in yourself. Thanks to him, I grew more confident, and in just my first year, I quickly transitioned from a nobody to somebody. I went from having no ranking at all to having the number one-ranked career center in the United States. I managed a near-100% employment rate in the actively-seeking graduating class category. Mine was the first location in the history of the for-profit university to hit 100% out of approximately one hundred campuses.

My former supervisor's support didn't stop there. During a performance review, he told me that if I wanted to be the National Dean of Career Services one day and I kept up my performance, he believed it was possible and I would attain it in as little as two years. This drove my ambition further.

I wasn't there to let things just tick along; none of us should ever become complacent. I wanted to completely revolutionize career services.

This came from my own negative career services experience in graduate school, where I was given a resume template and pointed towards a computer with no more suggestions outside of "Good luck with your search." I knew I needed to transform the so-called "model of a career center" in order for students to be successful. I cared. Plus, I wanted to make an impact before trying to climb the ladder. You should also try to make an impact in each career you find yourself in, before moving on.

I continued to focus and use my supervisor as a sounding board. I dove into it all head first. I sought opportunity where there was none or little. I eventually became known as the "turnaround guy." That meant exactly that: I turned all the negative news about jobs to positive news. People started getting jobs after meeting with me. The referrals kept coming.

CAREER AND LIFE HACK #14
Opportunism breeds opportunity and opportunity breeds success.

Later down the line, I was promoted to the premier location in NYC, so I moved back to the city I once called home. In fact, I never changed my New York 917 phone number because I was so loyal. This city captured what America was for me: a land of ambition. This city was a place I knew would accelerate my career. And it did. I was in that job for years, and we maintained the #1 ranked location for almost all five years, winning the Legacy of Service award in my first few. This was almost unheard of.

I've had a lot of success, and that's why I've written this book. The lessons I learned from these experiences are numbered below to help you learn from them also. These include books to read and practical advice to consider. Implementing these will put you on your way to building a life that you'll love and succeed in. All, because "YOU Matter."

Here is What I Recommend:

1. Read *The First 90 Days* by Michael D. Watkins. It will help you expedite proven strategies, including your own, and get you up to speed quickly in a new job.

2. Learn who and where your resources are. If you know each person's name and their role, you can filter needs better and delegate more effectively.

3. Transitions can be challenging. Mistakes can be career suicide. Have a plan and use this book as your trusted guide.

4. Get to know your supervisors and sit down with them. Let them know what you are interested in. It may lead to stretch projects that can set you up for upward mobility in the future.

5. Identify the most important stakeholders.

6. Build a team.

7. Develop a plan (not a five-year plan; two to three years, max).

8. Use collaborative and situational leadership to execute this plan.

9. Celebrate the little successes on the way.

10. Lead with humility.

Career and Life Bucket List

A fantastic way to invest in yourself is by having a Career and Life Bucket list. Every Career Mastermind™ has one. It's a pact to fulfill a list of goals from the moment they write the list until their last day in this world. For some, a bucket list is synonymous with identity. It gives people purpose and direction.

Most people think of a bucket list in casual terms, as if a Life Bucket List and Career Bucket List are two separate things. One of the goals of a Career Mastermind™ is to combine these lists and look at them side-by-side. This will enable you to have a more holistic view of your life and help you to map out where you are going.

Think of binoculars: they seem like simple technology. Many people pick up a pair without much thought aside from focusing their vision. However, they are much more complicated. Within are prisms that extend the light path between the front lens that you look into and that captures the light, and the eyepiece. Lengthening the prism increases the magnification without having to change the length of the binoculars.

There are all kinds of binoculars for different purposes, from astronomy to bird-watching. Each set must be appropriate for what you are trying to accomplish. Collimation is a process that refers to bringing something into line, or to make parallel. For binoculars, it's a process that refers to the optical alignment of the prisms. You also use this process for career alignment. Imagine one of the prisms representing your life and the other representing your career. They must be aligned correctly for the binoculars to work correctly. In other words, for you to see *clearly*.

Lenses come in all shapes and sizes. Some are used to concentrate light into a parallel beam so you can see it at a great distance. The lenses of binoculars, however, do the opposite. They focus light rays from far away so you can see distant things more clearly. These are the lenses we are referring to, the ones that help us see our career and life vision more clearly.

The way light bends when it travels from air to water or glass is called refraction. Refraction is the key to how lenses work—and lenses are essential to binoculars.

Because prisms are heavy, binoculars are heavy. Our life prisms are full of limiting beliefs, and our career prisms are full of extrinsic motivators. These weigh us down and sometimes get misaligned, making our vision blurry. Prisms are larger wedges of glass that rotate images. Without them, light rays that pass through a convex lens from a distance look like they're upside-down. Prisms rectify this issue and help us see correctly—not only in binoculars, but in our lives.

Knowing that we have these prisms, we must also understand that our life and career prisms are in constant conflict with each other, against time. For example, our work/life balance can be very challenging. The harder and longer you work, the less time you have for yourself or for your family, friends, significant others, or pets. On the contrary, the more time you spend on vacation or at home, the less productive you are. Our career and life visions are competing against each other.

In the preface, we explored how to combine these two visions. Now, to conclude your understanding of this chapter, I would like you to create a career and life bucket list, but one where they go hand in hand and don't compete against each other, or with time. They should both, simultaneously, be focused on you and what's important to you.

First, create your life bucket list. Then, create your career bucket list. Create this list as if time was not an issue. Prioritize the items from 1 to 15. Then do this for your career bucket list. Now look at them side by side and determine what you would change if this was only one list. Consider which life bucket items and which career bucket items mesh well together, then re-adjust your list.

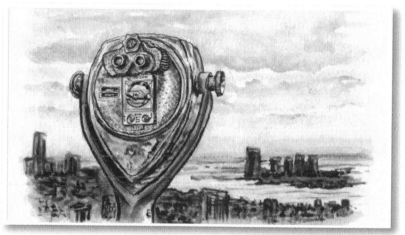

NEW YORK, NY: Illustration of Coin Operated Binoculars

Aligning Your Career and Life Prisms with Your "YOU Matter" Lenses (Eyepieces)

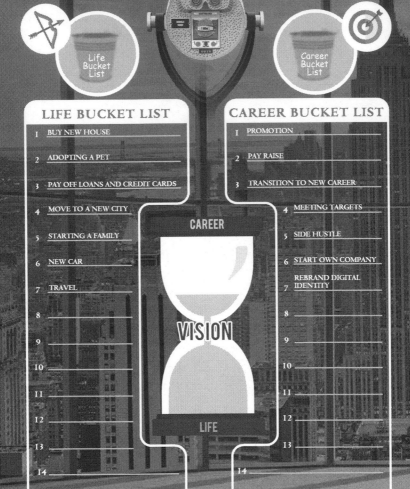

LIFE BUCKET LIST

1. BUY NEW HOUSE
2. ADOPTING A PET
3. PAY OFF LOANS AND CREDIT CARDS
4. MOVE TO A NEW CITY
5. STARTING A FAMILY
6. NEW CAR
7. TRAVEL
8.
9.
10.
11.
12.
13.
14.
15.

CAREER BUCKET LIST

1. PROMOTION
2. PAY RAISE
3. TRANSITION TO NEW CAREER
4. MEETING TARGETS
5. SIDE HUSTLE
6. START OWN COMPANY
7. REBRAND DIGITAL IDENTITY
8.
9.
10.
11.
12.
13.
14.
15.

CAREER

VISION

LIFE

Infographic available for download at www.CareerMastermind.org/Resources

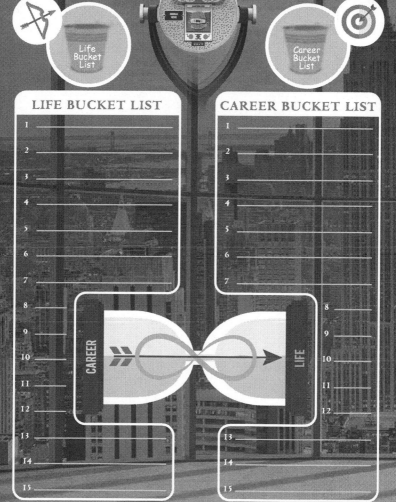

Aligning Your Career and Life Prisms with Your "YOU Matter" Lenses (Eyepieces)

Life Bucket List

Career Bucket List

LIFE BUCKET LIST

1
2
3
4
5
6
7
8
9
10
11
12
13
14
15

CAREER BUCKET LIST

1
2
3
4
5
6
7
8
9
10
11
12
13
14
15

CAREER

LIFE

Infographic available for download at www.CareerMastermind.org/Resources

On my office desk, I have an hourglass. I once waited until half of the sand seeped away, and then I turned it on its side. My vision changed horizontally and a sideways 8, or an infinity symbol, appeared across the center of the hourglass. Then it hit me. Time was no longer the focal point, and there was balance. This is what your career and life vision, as well as your career and life bucket lists, should look like.

But don't just try and get a bit further with your perceptions alone. The bigger your ambitions, the further you'll go. You have to trust yourself and work hard. You have to invest effort to see rewards over time. Practice doing this with the five design thinking steps, there is a worksheet to help you at the end of this chapter.

Change your perspective. Change your life.

After years of honing my ability, my career and life are where I need them to be, and I am still hungry. I am here to show you that you can be just where you want to be as well: a Career and Life Designer.

It's time to begin outlining how you will manage your career as a mastermind. It's time for your own Personal Business Plan.

"YOU Matter"

"YOU MATTER"
WHY YOU SHOULD INVEST IN YOURSELF

▶ **Define where you are now:** (check one)
- ☐ I am worth it
- ☐ I am not worth it

▶ **Follow Up Date:**

☐ / ☐ / ☐

▶ *Why do you feel this way?*

▶ **Action Item:**

I will _____

by the Date ☐ / ☐ / ☐

▶ **Completed:** (circle one)
- ○ Yes ○ No

▶ *What is the "IMPACT" action you will take within one week to make a positive change?*

"The formulation of a problem is often more essential than its solution."
-*Albert Einstein*

SELF - EMPATHIZE
Brainstorm potential solutions; select and develop your solution

DEFINE
Clearly articulate the problem you want to solve

IDEATE
Develop a deep understanding of the challenge

PROTOTYPE
Design a prototype (a series of prototypes) to test all part of your solution

TEST
Engage in a continuous short-cycle innovation process to continually improve your career design

"Next Steps" and Notes:

Workbook available for download at www.CareerMastermind.org/Resources

International Athlete Ambassador to Pakistan and the United States of America

CHAPTER 6 (LENS 6): YOUR OWN PERSONAL BUSINESS PLAN

"Without leaps of imagination or dreaming, we lose the excitement of possibilities. Dreaming, after all, is a form of planning."

—*Gloria Steinem*

We all know that actions speak louder than words. While it is important to dream, it is just as important to be action-oriented. It is therefore essential to not just conceptualize your business plan, but to implement it, too. For this, you will need willpower. Intentions matter. In fact, in some cases, intention is more important than outcome. *Having willpower is essential to becoming a Career Mastermind*™. Willpower drives you to climb up a mountain no matter how much you want to give up. Giving up is not part of the Career Masterminding equation, which yields a success culture. Create a personal business plan that focuses on your calling, and add to it as you climb. Keep this in mind as you go through this chapter.

Your Portfolio of Experiences = Your Portfolio of Life

The first step to building your personal business plan is doing research and networking. When you are discovering who you want to interact with, you must look at depth over breadth. It is far more important to surround yourself with people of quality over anything else. You will be picking the brains of these people in informational interviews, and they will be helping you piece together your action plan and a refined personal business plan.

The goals of your personal business plan will lay the foundation of your Career Mastermind™ Group. Later, we will explore what this structure looks like at Columbia University, looking specifically at our Career Design Lab. But for now, let's keep it simple so you understand what they are all about and how they fit into your plan.

Be careful of envious people! Your peers will always have an influence on you. If you pick them wisely, you will be influenced for the better. If you pick them lazily, they will likely make you worse. As humans, we are susceptible to our social environments. The more successful, intelligent, and encouraging the people we surround ourselves with, the more likely they will be to shape and influence us positively.

For me, one of those helpful people is Devang. He and I were students at UCLA, and we lived where many student-athletes live during their first year, at Saxon Suites. As one of the only other South Asian students near my suite, I used to greet him as we passed each other in the halls, but he used to ignore me. I heard he was the guy who aced the SATs. When I found out, I thought he probably had a big ego and that we'd never become friends. But we did! In fact, we became great friends.

We shared a love of Desi food, pizza, poetry, Bollywood, chai, women, the philosophy of life, and humanity. Although I wrote poetry in my teens and won a couple of competitions, Devang was a much more gifted poet—yet he insisted I was the better poet because my poem, "La Liaison," was featured in cafes (i.e. The Living Room) at Jolla Shores on Prospect Street in San Diego. He was just being humble. We were both pre-med, but full of doubt about whether it was what we wanted to do. We both wanted to do more than one thing, but knew it would be more challenging with the demands of medical school and residency.

Devang not only convinced me that I should explore my passion for public health, but he too decided to forego medical school. He later received his Ph.D. in biomedical engineering from UCLA, and from there developed gene therapy, stem cell, and biomaterial technologies for spinal cord injuries and chronic pain at Kyoto University and Harvard Medical School. It didn't stop there. He recently went back to school to obtain his J.D. His goal is to promote multi-level innovation and crystallize basic science to improve humanity.

Together, we were able to overcome our limiting beliefs and find what he refers to as "our nexus"—that links our different nonlinear careers together. He was the personal and professional sounding board I needed to realign my career and life bucket list priorities. Devang and I are also self-taught Japanese and Spanish speakers, respectively. Who would have thought? When you invest in and bet on yourself, it will pay dividends. Surround yourself with talent that pushes you towards what you love.

Final Destination: Your Dream Career

A successful personal business plan should help you with career and life fulfillment. However, it is not about the destination, it's about the journey. Pulin Sanghvi, the former Inaugural Executive Director of Career Services at Princeton University, described this to me when we met at Princeton for the first time. He considered and spoke of the three-part scaffolding in the book, *The Art of Happiness at Work*, developed by the Dalai Lama and Howard C. Cutler regarding our motivation to work. They list three categories. The first category is *job*, which is the work needed to obtain resources. The second is *career*, which is work aligned with the motivating factors of status, promotion, and recognition. The third, which we should all aim for, is *calling*. Calling is work combined with personal ambition and active engagement. It is our passion, and it brings out our best side.

Ask yourself: Are you working towards your calling? Is there anything you can do to help yourself achieve this in your career and life? This must be integrated into the core of your personal business plan.

We all have a sweet spot in our personal, career, and life visions. It all overlaps. Nowadays, my sweet spot is career coaching. The sweet spot is your "Reason for Being" and therefore, your calling. It's your center, and its important to expand outwards from it.

Your calling is not your only calling. You can change racquets and string tensions over time, thus your sweet spots change and evolve. You can have many labors of love over the course of your lifetime. Most people look for only one, but this is a limiting tendency. These tendencies can also change with time, as your motivations change and as life unfolds. What's important is that you recognize them, know what they are, and when they come. *You don't wait to do lifework. If you live and walk your calling every day of your life, your life will be more fulfilling.*

The Crown Global Career Passport

Career and professional development benchmarks may vary from university to university, but the qualities and skills that students or anyone needs to hone in order to enroll in competitive programs and projects to sustain their performance, to excel, and land their meaningful and purposeful career are very similar. While there is not a shortage of robust tools and career toolkits in this area, the Career Design Lab (CDL) at Columbia University decided to develop their own.

When you work towards your established goals both inside and outside of Career Mastermind™ Groups, you need to also be mindful of your career readiness. This is a hidden set of skills that helps an individual develop a number of habits and practices including professionalism, learning objectives/standards, academic and career programming, critical thinking, and job-seeking competencies.

A tool I developed to help you assess these competencies is the Crown Global Career Passport. This can help prepare you for your career. In the passport, you'll find guidance from career experts to help you on your journey into the working world and to be "career-ready."

How does the Crown Global Career Passport work? Well, for one, they're free.

You can download a copy from:
WWW.CAREERMASTERMIND.ORG/RESOURCES

Secondly, you can make the most of your passport by reviewing the career readiness competencies on page 14.

New York, NY: The Crown Global Career Passport

The *New* Career Readiness

The National Association of Colleges and Employers (NACE) defines "career readiness" as "the attainment and demonstration of requisite competencies that broadly prepare college graduates for a successful transition into the workplace." The competencies are not just important for specific students, but for you as well. We are all perpetual students of life, and must broaden our understanding.

These competencies are:

- **Critical Thinking/Problem Solving:** Exercise sound reasoning to analyze issues, make decisions, and overcome problems. The individual is able to obtain, interpret, and use knowledge, facts, and data in this process, and may demonstrate originality and inventiveness.

- **Oral/Written Communication:** Articulate thoughts and ideas clearly and effectively in written and oral forms to persons inside and outside of the organization. The individual has public speaking skills; is able to express ideas to others; and can write/edit memos, letters, and complex technical reports clearly and effectively.

- **Teamwork/Collaboration:** Build collaborative relationships with colleagues and customers representing diverse cultures, races, ages, genders, religions, lifestyles, and viewpoints. The individual is able to work within a team structure, and can negotiate and manage conflict.

- **Digital Technology:** Leverage existing digital technologies ethically and efficiently to solve problems, complete tasks, and accomplish goals. The individual demonstrates effective adaptability to new and emerging technologies.

- **Leadership:** Leverage the strengths of others to achieve common goals, and use interpersonal skills to coach and develop others. The individual is able to assess and manage their emotions and those of others; use empathetic skills to guide and motivate; and organize, prioritize, and delegate work.

- **Professionalism/Work Ethic:** Demonstrate personal accountability and effective work habits, e.g., punctuality, working productively with others, and time workload management, and understand the impact of non-verbal communication on professional work image. The individual demonstrates integrity and ethical behavior, acts responsibly with the interests of the larger community in mind, and is able to learn from their mistakes.

- **Career Management:** Identify and articulate one's skills, strengths, knowledge, and experiences relevant to the position desired and career goals, and identify areas necessary for professional growth. The individual is able to navigate and explore job options, understands and can take the steps necessary to pursue opportunities, and understands how to self-advocate for opportunities in the workplace.

- **Global/Intercultural Fluency:** Value, respect, and learn from diverse cultures, races, ages, genders, sexual orientations, and religions. The individual demonstrates openness, inclusiveness, sensitivity, and the ability to interact respectfully with all people and understand individuals' differences.

Source: NACE Career Readiness Competencies

I have so much appreciation for the work that NACE has done in this area, which has helped support my team's efforts to improve our students' *Career Readiness IQ.* You can improve yours too and make sure that the areas you feel need more attention are addressed in your personal business plan.

However, this list is by no means complete. Empathy, patience, self-awareness, compassion, and altruism are traits that are highly underestimated and should be considered in future revisions. They all have been instrumental in my journey, and they will likely be instrumental in yours. Use this section on the Crown Global Career Passport to assess your "Career Readiness IQ."

Here is the scale:

WHAT IS YOUR CAREER READINESS IQ?

Connect with an Career Design Lab (CDL) professional and assess how prepared you are to succeed.

INDEX OF SPS TRACKER

1	2	3	4	5	6	7	8	9	10

NOT PREPARED   PREPARED TO SUCCEED

SELF-RATING	CDL RATING	DATE

PREPARED TO SUCCEED
(CDL RATINGS OF 9 OR 10)

```
┌ ── ── ── ┐
|          |
|  PLACE   |
|  STAMP   |
|  HERE    |
|          |
└ ── ── ── ┘
```

This program is an innovative career readiness tool that helps students begin their career journey towards meaningful careers. It can help you, too. The passport engages students in a broad range of career-related preparedness activities and events. It also serves as a self-reflection and motivating checklist tool to help students develop their personal brand and career profile. Upon completion, students attain the CROWN stamp. This furthers them towards career readiness and gives them a chance to build up their own personal business plans.

The CROWN Global Career Passport allows you to monitor your progress with a career mentor and assess your "Career Readiness IQ" or "CDL Index" of Career Readiness at any given point. The goal is not only confidence, but self-awareness, self-reflection, and self-mastery.

Designing Your Roadmap

The earlier you learn about post-secondary pathways and careers, the sooner you can develop meaningful personal aspirations towards them. To access higher education, for example, students need a clear sense of the roadmap to their goals and the critical resources at key transition points to eventually increase entry to a well-matched career. This includes exploration, financial knowledge, leveraging internship opportunities, digital identity development, positioning and branding, and transition activities.

The passport also includes tips on how to elevate your brand and polish your pitch. This all works with keeping your personal business plan in mind. Remember to invest time in yourself, and you will get rewarded.

This section of the Crown Global Career Passport can help you get started:

PRACTICE YOUR PITCH

First impressions really do matter. Sure, you know that you need to look professional, but what will you say? Use this space to structure your 30-second "elevator pitch" that conveys your value to employers—and why they should hire you for the position. **Make sure to connect your passion to purpose!**

STAND-OUT STRENGTHS:

- Transferrable skills: _____

- Hard skills: _____

- Soft skills: _____

TELL YOUR STORY:

- Passion: _____

- Vision: _____

- Goals: _____

- Work Philosophy: _____

Global Innovator, People Motivator

Each of us needs our own global career passport. We need to be global citizens and track our engagement with organizations, cultures, places, and people. Global cultural fluency is one of NACE's Career Readiness Competencies. It's these competencies that bridge the gap between your degree and workplace, and help you hit the ground running.

MORNINGSIDE CAMPUS, NY: Get your Crown Global Career Passport stamped

Do you have your Crown Global Career Passport yet?

"Education is our passport to the future, for tomorrow belongs to the people who prepare for it today."

—Malcolm X

My Spirit Animal: The Black Stallion

For anyone building their own personal business plan, they must include key leaders that can make a positive impact in helping you execute your plan smoothly. These are people who, essentially, can open doors for you or give you the push you need on a variety of levels.

I also want to share my knowledge on the importance of getting to know people, especially if you are going to work with them. It is a philosophy of mine to communicate to individuals in a kind, caring, and honest way—and to ask them questions in order to find out what their true nature is. What is important to them? Why is it important to them?

Let me give you a little example about discovering your essence. Let's delve into ourselves. When we discover our essence, we work towards our future. With that in mind: what's your spirit animal?

The Majestic Stallion; Photo Credit—Cally Macherly

I always ask people I interview what their spirit animal is. Why? Because it throws them off. Nobody wants to hear rehearsed answers. It helps me learn about their personality and why they see themselves this way. We must know ourselves and be able to communicate this to other people. If you do not know your spirit animal, then I would advise you to discover one. For example, horses have enormous endurance, a capacity for challenging work, and are natural leaders. There is a lot to learn from the world of animals, and learning about their behaviors allows us to learn about ourselves.

Another reason knowing ourselves is important is that job descriptions have significantly changed over time. Your interests matter more than ever on your resume. This can include a love of animals or passions outside of work. Don't believe me? Take a look at Tesla's job description below for an HR Business Partner. You will see that there is a greater focus on soft skills and attitude. They want someone who isn't afraid to "roll up their sleeves." They also want to know the person behind the role.

The Role

We work hard, play hard and operate as one team. Check your ego at the door. We don't allow them on the property. We care about people, growth, excellence and results. We tend to lose sleep over them as this is not easy. Bottom line, we are in search of real people that believe in and deliver the impossible every day. An experienced HR professional who enjoys driving engagement and building organizational scalability. No day is the same and the ideal fit is someone who thrives in a dynamic organization where anything is possible and much is still being built.

You will bring with you, years of professional HR experience and positive mindset to drive engagement and building organizational scalability.

At the end of the day, hiring managers are looking for hires that won't be difficult to train, a strong fit for their team, and future leaders. Interpersonal skills are paramount for business, and there are many ways of learning and implementing new and effective techniques. So, find your

spirit animal, and embody it. Take your time. And once you know your
spirit animal, get to know other people's as well.

What's Your Superpower?

Another variation of getting to know people and yourself to help you
execute your personal business plan is knowing your superpower.

In tennis, we are taught to "play to the crowd." There are players that
can make a crowd roar like Mats Wilander did against Ivan Lendl in the
classic 1988 U.S. Open Finals. That was his superpower, and he knew
how and when to use it. The crowd can feel the emotion!

Do you have a superpower? If you do, this should be an integral part
of your personal business plan. What is it about you that would make you
stand out in a crowd? What makes you, you?

Is it self-confidence? Empathy? Creativity?

There are also some superpowers that are in your best interest
to develop. For example, as a public speaker, you have to play to your
audience. Every Career Mastermind™ needs to be a great communicator
because remember, when you're building your plan, other people are
involved in this. Take a Toastmasters course or practice in front of a
mirror. Record yourself speaking, even just the audio, and pay attention
to your breathing, pace, enunciation, and body language.

Know Your Audience

As with any business plan, you will need to present it. In order to do so
effectively, you need to know whom you are presenting to.

Fresno, CA: Speaking at my brother's wedding reception

Whether you're a client of a career center, a career coach yourself, or just here to learn, it's important to get to know someone before trying to help them or seek help from them. You have to "dig in" to the details of their life. Ask yourself: How can I honestly critique and optimize any piece of writing if I know nothing about the person behind it? How will I help individuals build up their personal business goals, or attempt to critique their resumes, if I don't know anything about them?

You might be wondering, what kinds of questions should I ask? Also, why are these questions important? Later, in Chapters 9 and 10, you will dive deeper into building your alliance and mastermind groups. It's critical that you begin identifying these folks now. You also want to understand what a potential member's goals are so that you can vet them appropriately as they enter and exit these mentor circles. Ultimately, you want the best fit to better assist you with your goals and with theirs.

Let me give you an example. My student consultations these days go something like this:

Hi Aladdin, I would like to introduce myself. My name is Hassan. I have been doing career advising for 10+ years. Before this, I was a professional tennis player. I have some pretty extensive training in resume writing, cover letter creation, job search, and career development. I am going to be your Career Coach. Now that means a few things.

1st. I'm going to learn as much about you as I can. I'm going to ask you a lot of questions, some of which may sound odd at first. Some questions you may not have been asked before, but I want to assure you that I'm not being nosy. What I want is to learn as much about you as possible so I can advocate for you as best I can. By knowing your desired salary, I can develop an understanding of what types of job leads will best meet your needs. I don't want to ever waste your time with job leads that are beneath you or temporarily out of your reach. Same with your GPA. I want to make sure I can appropriately advise you to take an offer or to try to negotiate a better offer. I want to know all about your network of friends and associates, so I can advise you on how to utilize your network to maximize your chance of finding a position and if possible, to speed that process up.

2nd. Once I get to know you better, I'm going to use my experience and give advice on how to improve your resume, cover letters, portfolio, and thank you letters. I'm going to warn you now that every person you meet will have a different opinion on what a resume should look like. Don't be surprised if I contradict what someone else has told you, even if it was another career advisor. It's your job right now to listen to these differing opinions and come up with a set of documents that you own and are responsible for. Just keep in mind that I routinely review dozens of resumes weekly and have a good feel for what works and what doesn't. I have also received specific training on aspects of cover letter and resume writing.

3ʳᵈ. I will also give you specific feedback on your interviewing skills. We may do one mock interview, we may do many mock interviews. This will be tailored to you specifically. I often meet people who believe they have really strong skills, but say or do things during a mock interview that can derail an actual interview. Again, I do this often and want nothing more than to help you realize your career goals.

4ᵗʰ: I am here to help you do these things quickly. In today's economy, every dollar of income is immensely important. I will be sourcing job leads every day. Some will apply to you, and some will apply to other graduates. But when one does fit your background, we need to move fast. So I may ask that you work on a resume tonight, call me tomorrow, or drive by an employer's office the night before the interview so you know where it is, how long it takes to get there, and won't risk being late. If an applicant doesn't move quickly, we run the risk of losing a job to someone who moved faster. I don't want to have that happen, so speed is of the essence.

Last thing, I am going to ask that every time we meet, you treat it as if it were an interview. Here's why: I sometimes have graduates who believe that dressing up means dressing like you would on a Saturday night. But that's not quite right. If you treat this as an interview, and I see evidence that you dress appropriately, are well groomed, have a professional demeanor, open the door for others, etc., then I know that you are aware and do these things in a manner that benefits you. If I don't see these things, then we have to have a discussion, and we may waste your time covering things that you already know.

Does that sound OK? Alright, let's learn more about you:

1. *What do you currently do for a living?*

2. *What is your current job? What do you like about it? What don't you like?*

3. *What is important about your next job?*

   a. *Size of company: Small, midsize, big?*

   b. *Type of position: generalist, specialized?*

  c. *Are you willing to travel? How much? Locally, regionally, nationally, internationally?*

  d. *I always look locally first, but are you willing to relocate? What would make you relocate? Salary, job type, etc.?*

  e. *How far are you willing to commute?*

  f. *Do you have reliable transportation?*

4. *What do you earn currently?*

5. *If you are not working, how are you supporting yourself? Is someone supporting you? How does that person respond to you at the moment?*

6. *If you make $_____ now, how much do you need in your next job?*

7. *What is/was your approximate GPA?*

8. *Who were your favorite professors? Will they provide you a reference?*

9. *What were your favorite classes? Why?*

10. *Tell me about your social network? Church, friends or family at different companies, volunteer activities, current promotional opportunities at work?*

11. *What else do I need to know about you?*

Once I get this information, I try to dig even deeper. They are, firstly, giving me "their representatives." In other words, they may not be opening up and telling me who they really are, only what they think I want to hear. That will do neither of us any good. I want to find out who they really are, not who they want me to think they are.

Once I open those doors, we really get started. Everything up to that point is just breaking the ice.

Get energized about relationship building, they take time!

Critiquing Your Resume

Every business plan has a section that describes the professional experience and education of the presenter/s. You are going to meet loads of people from all walks of life. Chances are that at some point they will ask for a copy of your resume or CV. You have to be prepared. It can be while you are just picking someone's brain during an informational interview, or something more formal. So, you are going to need a polished resume. I'm here to help you. This will be part of your personal business plan, and it's essential.

It's not easy to critique something. My ethos is to be kind and make positive comments, but also to provide constructive feedback. Critiquing is meant to help others who are striving to do something better. It needs to be encouraging, but also useful. Below is an example of a common critique I've given to someone who may be just like you. I believe it is helpful to anyone who is looking to improve their resume. Are you aware of these red flags? Are you guilty of any yourself?

Thank you for submitting your resume. I reviewed it with the goal of giving you an honest, straightforward assessment, not judging your skills and qualifications. I should warn you about my style: I'm direct and to the point, so I hope you won't be offended by my comments. Critiquing does not exist to make someone feel bad, it exists to help them.

Most job seekers at your stage in their career take the wrong approach when writing their resumes. Instead of touting the impact they had on their company or why they were an asset, they fill their resumes with descriptions of their current and prior jobs. They don't highlight their areas of expertise, and as a result, they do not distinguish themselves from the hundreds of other applicants seeking the same job. In other words, they may do a pretty good job talking about general aspects, but don't truly connect their passion to purpose, or demonstrate that this field is indeed their true ambition.

Having worked with many candidates at your particular career stage, I have some insight into what you are probably looking for in your next job. Most of my clients want to advance into a more senior position that will yield an increase in salary, or to advance into a role that has a career path to management in their next job. Others want to change professions or industries altogether. Either way, their goal is to "take it up a notch" or do something new that will expand the depth or breadth of their experience.

Ironically, most job seekers at your stage in their career write resumes that are targeted toward a job that is below their most recent positions. Their resumes are full of the tasks they performed and responsibilities they had, but they do not tell the recruiter or hiring manager the impact they had on the business and why they were a valuable asset to the company.

So, let's get started with a review of your resume:

Here's the good news: My first impression is that you have a wide array of skills and experiences. You have a lot to offer an employer. Now, here's the bad news: Your resume does not pass the 30-second test, and the content is not up to the standards one would expect from a candidate like you. Countless studies have proven that resume quality is the key factor in selecting a candidate for an interview. Your resume needs a boost from a visual, content, and overall writing standpoint to engage the reader. It needs to make them want to learn more about you. I didn't find it exciting, and it didn't make me want to run to the phone to call you. In short, your resume is effectively sabotaging your job search.

Your resume is missing key elements that we see on the best resumes at your level of experience. Here are the major issues I see on your resume:

The Visual Presentation of Your Resume

We've all been told that looks don't matter as much as substance, but in the case of your resume, this just isn't true. I found your design to be crowded. The appearance is not polished, and it doesn't say "high potential" or offer a statement at the top under your name such as "Driving growth through leadership, innovation, and value." What's your work philosophy? Why should they hire you and only you? Remember that your resume is your marketing tool. It's a potential employer's first impression of you. Now think about how generic brands are marketed versus the name brand. The packaging and advertising of the name brand are all carefully selected to attract attention and convince you to buy the product. Your resume should do the same thing—you want to be the brand name product. I'm concerned that your resume is selling you like a generic, and that it's not likely to get picked. The ideal resume design is airy, clean, and uncluttered, with effective and strategic use of white space.

The Content of Your Resume

As I was reading your resume, I was trying to imagine myself as a hiring executive, looking for that ideal candidate. I asked myself if I could easily pick out your key attributes, experience, skills, and accomplishments. A recruiter will do this to quickly decide if you'll be successful in their open job. When I read your resume, the answer to that question was "no."

Here is one of the reasons why:

From the way the resume is worded, you come across as a "doer," not an "achiever." Too many of your job descriptions are task-based and not results-based. This means that they tell what you did, instead of what you achieved. This is a common mistake for non-professional resume writers. To be effective and create excitement, a great resume helps hiring executives "envision" or "picture" you delivering similar achievements at the company they represent.

Employers want to know about your previous contributions, and specifically, how you've made a difference. More importantly, they want to know how you are going to make an impact at their company.

When I read your resume, I didn't find compelling language that brings your work to life. I saw many passive words and non-action verbs. Phrases like "provides" and "managed" are monotonous and add no value to your resume. Strong action verbs, used with compelling language to outline exemplary achievements, are essential parts of a well-constructed resume.

Now, let's put it all together. Here's a real-life example taken from a former client's resume. By changing the language, we helped improve the perception of the candidate.

Passive language/Doing: Negotiated contracts with vendors.

Active language/Achieving: Slashed payroll/benefits administration costs 30% by negotiating pricing and fees, while ensuring the continuation and enhancements of services.

A change like this makes a dramatic improvement. I hope you can see the difference when we implement action verbs, achievements, and results.

The Writing on the Wall

It's easy to overlook writing errors in your resume. They could be typographical errors, inconsistent verb tenses, formatting, extra spaces, bleeded text (incorrect margins), grammatical errors, punctuation problems, or misspelled words. You've rewritten the resume and proofread it multiple times, so when you read it back, you are likely to read what you meant, not actually what you wrote, but errors can be the kiss of death for your resume. Recruiters are reading your resume with fresh eyes, and they're experts at finding errors. A misspelled word or a punctuation error may not seem like a big deal, but to an employer, these errors demonstrate a lack of professionalism and attention to detail. That's not the impression you want to give.

I have spotted at least one of the above-mentioned errors on the majority of resumes I have seen. It goes something like this:

Additional Issues

- *Use of bullets to emphasize—you probably want to consider limiting them in some areas to increase the impact to the employer. If they see too many bullets, they might find it difficult to zero in on the most important information. Size and type of bullets are also a consideration. Although seemingly minor, the visual impact of a resume is the key to ensuring that an employer reads it thoroughly.*

- *Length of your resume. This doesn't include your cover letter. Employers have a limited amount of time to scan resumes in their initial search, so you want your resume to be as concise as possible. However, you want it to be keyword-enriched and pass the computer screens. Thus, you want to match your language to the job you are applying for, in addition to having the right qualifications. Don't use the same words they use. Tell your story. Every employer wants to hear a story about how you were able to manage a project from start to finish or about your leadership success.*

- *Having a References section with a list of names and contact information, or even having a note reading "References Available," is unnecessary. Employers typically assume that you'll have this on hand during interviews. Make sure this is on a separate page and don't send until requested.*

- *Make sure that the additional pages of your resume have contact information on them. That way, if a hiring manager prints your resume, but for some reason, the pages are accidentally separated, the manager will still be able to identify the additional pages. They will likely not spend time trying to place a page that has been separated and will move on to the next resume.*

- Switching jobs often. Employers refer to this as "job hopping" and may think your qualifications are great, but won't pursue you because they are afraid you won't stay for long. The good news is that there are definitely ways to present a more steady work history. We can help you address these areas and position you better.

My Recommendation

Your unique skills and experience are good, but your resume, in its current form, is not likely to get you the attention you deserve. I know it's uncomfortable to hear, but if you want to get hired or advance your career in today's super competitive job market, you must nail that first impression, and your resume is the ticket to doing it. You have to do what everyone else is doing, and more, to get noticed. It's a tough economy. Your resume needs to be an easy read, giving the reader the 3-4 things they are looking for in 7 seconds.

That's why I recommend that you rewrite your resume. You can use newer templates or just modify your existing one.

Many employers now use automated tracking systems to evaluate and screen their incoming resumes. To be "processed" properly by one of these systems, a resume must be built with the right structure, keywords, and format. This is known as keyword optimization, and most non-professionals are not well-versed in this technique.

However, my team of career and life vision consultants are continuously updated on the newest trends, keywords, and phrases. We work directly with hiring managers, recruiters, and HR personnel, so they know precisely what kind of resumes and cover letters get their attention. We don't always use templates. Your resume is written to capture your distinctive skills, personality, and industry.

Cover Letter

Think of your cover letter as the key that opens a recruiter's gates. Employers tell us that a poor cover letter will actually eliminate a candidate from any further consideration. A carefully crafted, customized cover letter distinguishes you from the crowd. It's the best way to make a memorable appeal that personally links you to the job. It also gives you an opportunity to tell your story and highlight elements that may not be on your resume. Although some people have lost faith in their use, I still recommend them if done right.

Focus on hitting the following points:

1) What was your most recent job? What did you do there? What did you improve? Did you positively impact the culture and how?

2) What are you an expert in? Or, what do you excel in?

3) How were you innovative in your most recent or relevant role? Did you pioneer anything?

4) What value are you bringing to the table for the employer?

5) How do your personal and professional goals align with the mission of the organization?

Here is a sample:

Ms. Mary Brown
Public Health Advisor
National Safety Council
1725 K Street, NW
Washington, DC, 20006

01-05-2019

Dear Ms. Brown

Please find enclosed my resume and writing sample for the position of Public Health Coordinator, Announcement 99-875, at the National Safety Council.

My relevant experience includes:

· Public Health Intern at the National Institute of Health, Centers for Disease Control and Prevention for 1 year. I helped coordinate projects and provided assistance to private organizations and educational institutions. Through social media outlets, I improved information on physical activity and nutrition.

· Excelling in physical activity and nutrition issues including editing websites, press releases, newsletters, and training materials.

· Helping organize the first public policy conference for public health students and national forums on the importance of physical education on health and well-being.

I would be an asset to your organization because of the following qualifications:

· Currently pursuing a BS degree in Exercise Science with a concentration in Health Education from The University of Virginia.

I am seeking new opportunities where I can use my knowledge of physical activity and nutrition issues gained from my years volunteering at the National Institute of Health. I am aware that disseminating environmental and health information in the school systems is vital and challenging. I would like to get closer to the students and teachers in schools by writing, creating, and managing educational programs that will have an impact on environmental health through education.

Thank you for your time and consideration. I can be reached at 212-xxx-xxxx at your convenience. I look forward to your response.

Sincerely,
Roar-ee the Lion
Roaree@columbia.edu

Many people ask me how long the resume and cover letter should be. For the resume, one or two pages is usually safe (one page is recommended for a cover letter), but it depends on the amount of experience you have and the quality of content. It can be longer, especially if it's a CV (and in that case will be probably much longer), so the answer, is—it depends! Don't shrink the font just to make it fit and let the font go into the margins.

Try not to use an objective (use a summary instead) and always highlight your core competencies. Don't get caught up in details like where the education section should go. Again, there is no right answer. It depends on what you are trying to showcase first. Someone who went to Harvard may want to put that at the top, whereas someone who worked at Google may lead with that experience.

Now, about the future of resumes and cover letters. Platforms like LinkedIn have taken over virtual recruiting spaces and are what some hiring managers prefer to use when looking for candidates. What else is coming? It's simple: video business cards. Begin thinking about what yours would say and what story it will tell. More about this in Chapter 8!

Thinking Forward

Times are changing, so we have to adapt our thinking. I always shift my clients' focus towards their brands, specifically their digital brands. Resumes and cover letters will soon be a thing of the past, so I focus on value propositions, elevator pitches, and the importance of the LinkedIn summary. Do you have a branding statement on your profile?

Below is an example of a well-written LinkedIn summary:

*Audience Strategy Editor (at a major American newspaper with worldwide influence and
readership)*

*I come to digital media and journalism by my drive to understand information and
how it travels. Good journalism is a three-step process: the gathering of information, the
molding of a truthful narrative, and the careful dissemination of that story. While I am
fully trained as a multimedia journalist, the oft-neglected step three of distribution and
reach is where my passion in journalism truly lies.*

*Previously, I worked as a Social Content Editor and Digital Strategist. In this
role, I liaised between editorial teams, audience development, and social media platforms
to ensure that content reached the right audiences with the most depth and in the greatest
volume. I worked primarily on YouTube Strategy (I'm certified by YouTube in content
strategy).*

Here is another example from one of my current staff members,
Greg Costanzo, who is the Associate Director of Industry Relations for
the Career Design Lab. It reads:

*I believe that hands-on experience, trial and error, and reflection allows one to clarify
a vision, piece together personal and professional goals, and build forward-momentum
in the pursuit of their ambitions. This "strategy" has led me professionally to career
services where I'm motivated to connect students to methods of self-discovery and career
opportunities.*

*Between my first career in finance and now working in higher education, I chased
down interests to see what would emerge as true passions and what could be labeled as
hobbies, interesting projects, or creative stints. After creating short films at the New York
Film Academy, coaching my old middle school boys' basketball team, and teaching SAT
prep courses in South Korea, I discovered that stepping outside my comfort zone to follow
passions isn't easy, but essential for growth.*

While I still have diverse interests, the vocational drive that I found sustainable was in education. Today I am happy to simply connect students to employers, and vice versa through a variety of means.

Embracing change and the unknown has proven to move me forward in my career, and now is a message I get to share with students every day.

Once you have a strong summary, ask yourself: do you have a branding statement? Think about what it is that you really do and why it's important to you. Here's mine:

"For a living, I help build dreams and witness their impact."

Then reflect on whether you are building and expanding your networks organically. Are you creating and producing quality content online in the forms of blogs, videos or vlogs, and podcasts? If not, why?

This section was written to give you a better idea of how to write your resume, cover letter, and build a great LinkedIn summary. I also wanted to show you the importance of getting to know someone. Life is a race, but you can be better at it if you understand how to communicate effectively, leading to more productive collaboration between individuals.

These examples will provide more ammunition in your networking arsenal. Furthermore, you can ask yourself if you have ticked all the boxes of the recommendations I have given you. Don't rush these tools; put the necessary time into them. It is important to get these right, as they are your first impressions.

"We are CEOs of our own companies: Me Inc. To be in business today, our most important job is to be head marketer for the brand called You."

—*Tom Peters*

On Your Mark, Get Set... Go!

Who will you run life's marathon with? First, you have to train with the right people! But then—your race is your race alone.

Let's continue your personal business plan formation with the deep consideration of your social capital. You have to choose your mastermind members like you choose good fruit. You can't depend solely on them, though; you have to be self-motivating and be in dialogue with yourself.

Also, don't forget to revisit the five life design strategies. You may review them at the end of the chapter in the worksheet. These should be your motifs to keep you moving and working to complete the plan.

The personal business plan can be as formal or as informal as you like. For example, let's assume your career goal is to find a mentor, and you decide to create a personal business plan to execute this. With this plan will come a Mentorship Mastermind Group, so you will need to outline your goals. I have worked with thousands of individuals looking to align mentors, and our plan looked something like this:

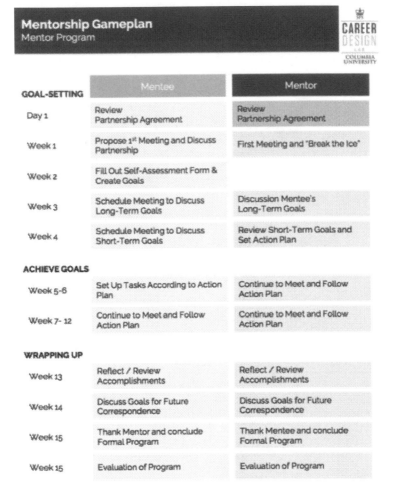

	Mentee	Mentor
GOAL-SETTING		
Day 1	Review Partnership Agreement	Review Partnership Agreement
Week 1	Propose 1st Meeting and Discuss Partnership	First Meeting and "Break the Ice"
Week 2	Fill Out Self-Assessment Form & Create Goals	
Week 3	Schedule Meeting to Discuss Long-Term Goals	Discussion Mentee's Long-Term Goals
Week 4	Schedule Meeting to Discuss Short-Term Goals	Review Short-Term Goals and Set Action Plan
ACHIEVE GOALS		
Week 5-6	Set Up Tasks According to Action Plan	Continue to Meet and Follow Action Plan
Week 7- 12	Continue to Meet and Follow Action Plan	Continue to Meet and Follow Action Plan
WRAPPING UP		
Week 13	Reflect / Review Accomplishments	Reflect / Review Accomplishments
Week 14	Discuss Goals for Future Correspondence	Discuss Goals for Future Correspondence
Week 15	Thank Mentor and conclude Formal Program	Thank Mentee and conclude Formal Program
Week 15	Evaluation of Program	Evaluation of Program

Workbook available for download at www.CareerMastermind.org/Resources

Look into it more and see how it can help develop you. As you think about that, I want you to meet an old friend of mine.

Introducing Dr. Pedro Manrique

WWW.LINKEDIN.COM/IN/PEDROMANRIQUE

Pedro Manrique is my former boss. He gave me my first job as an adjunct professor. He further taught me the value of having a clear business and life plan. He, too, was someone that worked in a variety of jobs, starting in the field of audio engineering. He worked as a Director of Engineering in a modest loudspeaker company in Montreal, followed by VLSI Design at CIDTEC in Syracuse, and at Photobit in Pasadena for NASA and CMOS image sensor applications, respectively.

Returning to audio, Pedro transitioned to Harman International as the Global Engineering Program Manager, where he obtained nine patents, one of which was for Infinity Systems, JBL, and Harman Kardon. His contributions there included managing development of several dozen loudspeakers and consumer electronics products for the same companies.

He formed DRP Systems Inc., an Organizational Development consulting company with clients that included Belkin, Innovative Dimmers, and Columbia University.

While at Belkin as Global Engineering Program Manager overseeing several hundred products, Pedro completed his tenth patent, this one for electronic surge devices in residential settings. He served as Chief Technology Officer (CTO) at Innovative Dimmers, a lighting control company that supports TV and film productions throughout the country. His duties there included strategic roadmapping, engineering management, operations, project management, manufacturing, contract manufacturing, procurement, and IT administration. Moreover, while consulting for Columbia University, his contributions included keynote speaking, panel moderation, career development workshops, and podcasts.

Pedro transitioned to education at DeVry University as Dean for the College of Engineering and Information Sciences. As an author as well as administrator and professor, he's written on game programing and curriculum design for engineering students.

He assigned me to "Critical Thinking and Problem Solving," "Career Strategies," and a couple of other courses. He was an incredible mentor, going that extra mile to make sure I was prepared. I kid you not, for the next ten years, every time I saw him, he would buy me a coffee and refused to let me pay. This consistent kindness taught me that interpersonal skills and the little things can go a long way in your life. Here he was, helping me execute my personal business plan, and I was getting a free latte too!

Pedro was an incredibly busy man, but he found time for those that he cared about, and he respected their time. This also taught me the importance of being on time and not wasting someone else's time.

In addition to his other responsibilities, he volunteered as President of the Sherman Oaks Chamber of Commerce after Los Angeles Mayor Garcetti's office reached out to join their Blue-Ribbon Commission on Employment Equity. His contributions there included the first job employment fair featuring mock interviews to help formerly incarcerated people prepare for on-the-spot hiring opportunities.

Almost ten years later, Pedro is one of our most popular speakers for the Career Design Lab at Columbia University and is a co-facilitator for the "YOU Matter" Design Your Career Workshop.

COLUMBIA MORNINGSIDE CAMPUS, NY: Pedro Manrique co-facilitating the
"YOU Matter" Design Your Career Workshop

Pedro's academic history includes a bachelor of engineering degree in electrical engineering, followed by a M.A.Sc. in electrical engineering. As a PhD candidate in business administration, he specialized in organizational leadership, and his dissertation focused on organizational dysfunction in the manufacturing sector of Southern California. Today, he serves as an adjunct professor at Phillips Graduate University where he teaches doctoral students in the Organizational Management and Consulting program and serves as dissertation chair. Ever grateful and optimistic, Pedro embraces undercurrents of opportunities, sharing knowledge and crediting others with helping him throughout this journey.

As a member of my "Personal Board of Directors," Pedro imparts nuggets of wisdom such as, "Business cards come and go, but relationships last a lifetime." He is living proof that you can be anything you want at almost any point in your career by focusing on transferable skills. He has been an enduring and invaluable mentor.

Include your mentors in your personal business plan. They are critical. Align multiple figures in this list. More on mentors in Chapter 9.

Ten Talks

I invited Pedro to participate in a custom professional development series for my Career Design Lab team. You see, once you identify members in your network that can help you, you're broadening your impact and "sharing the love." I aligned ten consecutive coaching sessions guided by career educators. I called them "Ten Talks." (Shout-out to my former colleague, Julie Sells, at Loyola University for suggesting the name!) Pedro assisted us with three of these incremental phases focused on the following:

Part I: Effective Ownership

- Roles, responsibilities, and priorities outlined per business quarter. This lends itself to one-on-one 30 minute sessions.

Part II: Performance Management Matrix

- Individual development plan (IDP) for the next two years, career aspirations and how to integrate them in our current framework. The IDP is "driven" by the employee and "facilitated" by the employer.

- Integrate individual contributions as a quarterly roadmap into group outcomes for the coming year.

- Develop and implement a plan to operationalize performance management.

Part III: Workplace legacy

- Mission, Vision of the group, and the long-term outcomes sought under the Executive Director's leadership.

- Establish individual contributor outcomes, how they see themselves helping to move the group forward.

- Map out the elements of the workplace legacy that represent collective wisdom, the vision of the CDL brand, and what that means outside our group.

- Develop and implement a plan to operationalize the workplace legacy.

These phases not only worked, but they helped us build strength and autonomy.

Outside-In

After working with thousands of undergraduate and graduate students on their personal business plans, one pain point is climbing the ladder.

One of Pedro's recommended approaches that stands out for those trying to climb the traditional career ladder (advance their position within their current organization), is called "Outside In." It focuses on mastering your position and simultaneously assisting in areas outside of your direct responsibilities.

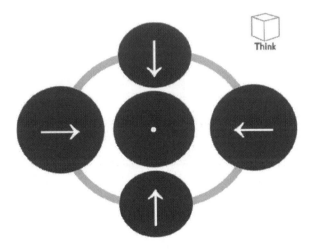

Working from the outside—in has the advantage of leveraging timing, resources, and momentum to generate desired outcomes. For example, politicians leverage constituents in the community to generate change in the government. In the workplace, we use judicious timing, resources, and even departments to generate change upstream in organizations. Initiatives include healthcare and retirement plans, employee benefits, and even free holiday staff parties. The key, and perhaps the challenge in many instances, is to pace ourselves to set these elements in motion.

Pedro is now one of my Principal Career and Life Consultants. You too can benefit from his guidance and warm approach.

Learn more here:
WWW.CAREERMASTERMIND.ORG/CONSULTANTS

Is the Job Proposal Underrated?

The question is, what if you are trying to land a position that doesn't exist in your current company but does in your dream company? Or, what if it doesn't exist at all?

The modern economy has, in many ways, limited the scope of new opportunities. In our current political climate, this is especially true for international students! You have to be persuasive and have a story that sells. If it doesn't sell, people won't remember your elevator pitch when looking at a pile of resumes after a career fair, nor will you get noticed among the thousands of resumes that organizations receive. Feeling discouraged? There are other ways to stand out against your competition.

Climbing the Career Ladder

In my first few years as Director of Career Services, I remember finding an area of improvement when it came to career services training for the university. Our leadership meetings had approximately 50-60 associate level and director level attendees—all trying to learn (over the phone) how to integrate new systems or adopt best practices (on a national conference call that happened once a month, at best). In fact, all of the training was over the phone on conference calls. I thought to myself, *what if there was to be an Associate Dean of Career Services that would handle different regions and would physically travel to coach and observe them? Wouldn't that be much more useful and valuable?*

Build a Proposition

When it came to career outcomes, achieving a 90% employed-in-field rate was a difficult but worthwhile accomplishment. At the time, we had the number one-ranked career services department in the nation, but I had my eyes set on being the National Dean of Career Services. Thus, I decided to write my first job proposal. However, I didn't call it a "job proposal" because that's not what it really was. It was a business proposition for the company, and a "career proposition" for me, personally and professionally.

Many innovative companies aren't afraid to take risks to be leaders in a tough economy. They understand they must be creative and embrace a competitive position. As companies grow, they create additional positions, some entirely new. For example, the position of Chief Diversity Officer is the direct result of a job proposal in modern society. Sure, I know many of you may be afraid that your job proposal (whether you work for the company or not) may not be accepted. In fact, after writing mine, I wasn't even sure if I would get a response.

But I did, and I was told: "Great idea, but we simply don't have the budget for something like that." As they walked away, they chuckled. This was frustrating, as I was the only director who had earned a place on the national advisory board and was a member of their U.S. pilot committee. However, I didn't let it sway my belief in the value of my proposal. I told myself to be patient. It was a "win-win" in my eyes, and I was going to keep my eyes on the career horizon.

I was confident and knew that I had written a persuasive job proposal. My patience finally paid off. I knew that if I could demonstrate a problem or need, it could lead to a discussion, even if it took a while. I was right.

Not only was I creating the ideal position for my background, I was offering added value. Before I knew it, I saw the position posted. Now, granted, I wasn't given credit for proposing it. I applied and was a final candidate, but I didn't receive an offer. I was told that I was still "starting out" as Director of Career Services. Although I had won more awards than anyone in the university during my first years, I wasn't considered "career ready" for the role.

I quickly realized that there were different levels of patience, so I convinced myself to stay positive and be persistent. After all, since I wrote the job description, nobody was going to understand the cost-benefit analysis or scope as well as I could. To my delight, patience proved to be a virtue. I got a call from the VP to arrange a call with the new Associate Dean of Career Services to "pick my brain" on best practices on turning around a campus. I was told, "Hassan, you have a reputation for being the turnaround guy." Yup, they wanted me to train someone on how to do the job I wrote, after not giving it to me.

Essentially, this was a customized role. So the first thing I explained to the new hire (who landed the job I proposed) was that operations will vary depending on location and demographics. There is no one-size-fits-all, especially with technology platforms (in career services). The new hire would need to learn the landscape, understand the demographics, and get to know the people in each career center first.

Macro needs may be obvious, but it's the micro details that would ultimately make the difference. Since I knew the position's budget allocation, which I included in the proposal, I had an idea of how much wiggle room the new hire had in terms of support, travel, and training. I was direct, showing support and illustrating what I would do if I was in their shoes.

In order to justify the position, I had to encourage the new hire to demonstrate how the role could help solve some of the underlying issues different locations were facing. For example, conducting a formal evaluation on events. I suggested the Plus/Delta Assessment technique that gives you the opportunity to look at what worked well, and to celebrate your success, and also what can be improved to make your product or team more effective. Also, by forming focus groups with both staff and students, I found it easy to persuade the new hire to follow my recommended steps of action—and to report to the executive leadership of the university on progress. Why? During my career pitch, I was marketing my career profile for the specific tasks and responsibilities that the new position would entail. Not only is it important to demonstrate the benefit of adding the position, but you also have to show that you are the best candidate for the job. That means qualifying and quantifying your achievements, highlighting your transferable skills, and communicating your vision. So, they decided they wanted me to provide the onboarding and training.

CAREER AND LIFE HACK #15
If you can't influence the decision makers, who will?

So what's the overall lesson? It's simple. Be patient and don't be afraid to take informed risks. You are building your personal brand and putting together a life plan. Risks pay off, so don't be afraid if you don't get instant results. Although your proposal may not be accepted, it can still impress an employer. If there is no current budget for such a "bridge opportunity," they might reallocate funds. What they want are your critical thinking skills and ability to assess areas of opportunity while aligning readily available solutions. Not only could the company hire you, they may end up hiring you for an entirely different position based on your career readiness skills. This is also a great "entry point" into a new organization. Impress them by showing them you know where you can add value and where you can fill gaps.

Writing a winning career proposal is not easy, but the payoff can launch your career in a new and exciting direction. You don't want to come across overconfident and aware of all the hidden issues in an organization. But you do want to offer yourself as a problem solver, providing evidence of your competence and detailing next steps. Career Masterminds are experts at this in their respective areas. Reinforce both the concept and timing of the proposal to optimize your chances of being heard.

If you are currently employed at the organization, it's also helpful to include a clear transition plan. With any employer negotiation, you must include financial terms, such as cost savings and a timeline for the new implementation. The proposal shouldn't be too vague, nor should it be too lengthy, but make sure you are thorough. For example, I not only included succession planning but also professional development so my staff would be ready for additional responsibilities. Timing is critical; consider what's the most reasonable time to implement.

Remember that a career proposal is a statement with a goal in mind. Make a strong entrance with persuasive opening statements. Try anticipating questions and answering them in your summary, and make sure to thank them for their time. I can't emphasize this enough. After all, you don't want to waste their time. Make it worthwhile.

In my third year as Director of Career Services, I was finally asked to step in as Acting Associate Dean of Career Services to oversee their West

Coast operations. I earned my way. This not only elevated my brand, but it made it all worth it! Later, I was also selected as the Audit Mentor for Canada, thus I was placed in the most premier location in New York City. I was being considered for several regional center dean positions via a catalyst committee. How's that for a return on investment?

Here is a question you may be asking yourself: Is a job proposal worth it? Well yes, if it's done right. Make things happen! How do you do that, and more importantly, how do you know that it's done right? How do you make it a winning career proposition, based on your compelling career profile?

There are many elements to your personal business plan, and they are important to remember as you continue to build. To summarize, it's all about strengthening your position and story—showing that have already demonstrated success in the roles you are aspiring towards. You have to demonstrate an ability to grow the next generation of leaders.

But before you can do all of that, you need a career and life compass.

CAREER AND LIFE HACK #16
Mentor the mentors.

YOUR OWN PERSONAL BUSINESS PLAN

▶ **Define where you are now:** (check one)

☐ I have one ready-to-go

☐ Don't have one or I am struggling

▶ **Follow Up Date:**

☐ / ☐ / ☐

▶ *Why do you feel this way?*

▶ **Action Item:**

I will _____

by the Date ☐ / ☐ / ☐

▶ **Completed:** (circle one)

○ Yes ○ No

▶ *What is the "IMPACT" action you will take within one week to make a positive change?*

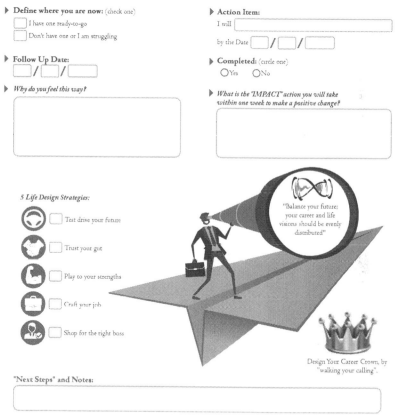

5 Life Design Strategies:

☐ Test drive your future

☐ Trust your gut

☐ Play to your strengths

☐ Craft your job

☐ Shop for the right boss

"Balance your future; your career and life visions should be evenly distributed"

Design Your Career Crown, by "walking your calling".

"Next Steps" and Notes:

Workbook available for download at www.CareerMastermind.org/Resources

"The service you do for others is the rent you pay for the room here on earth."

—*Muhammad Ali*

CHAPTER 7 (LENS 7): A NOBLE
CAREER AND MORAL COMPASS

◆◗◆

"Character is the real foundation of all worthwhile success. Try not to become a man of success, but rather a man of value. Character cannot be developed in ease and quiet. Only through experience of trial and suffering can the soul be strengthened, vision cleared, ambition inspired, and success achieved. If a man is self-controlled, truthful, wise, and resolute, is there aught that can stay out of reach of such a man?"

—*John Hays Hammond*

*T*he soul of a true mastermind is on a journey toward purity. The light of the soul, its wisdom, is built upon pillars of honesty and gratitude. All masterminds are in a constant struggle to be truthful with themselves. We strive to be better people. You too will join our struggle.

Authenticity is absolutely essential to being. Things you say and do become parts of who you are. *First, you must think authentically. Then, you must speak authentically. Finally, you must act authentically.* Being in conflict with yourself will hinder you in the long-run. Do not put out false symbols, and always stay true to yourself. People recognize authenticity because it is not a mask that will eventually be taken off. It's the soul shining through the exterior.

When I was younger, my father allowed me to make my own choices. As a result, I was able to develop my own moral compass. He granted me a measure of freedom, and this put me on the path to success. There are many ways in which this can be achieved. I have outlined this below.

Self-Discipline, Your Edge

Fasting was a way for me to develop patience, self-restraint, and self-control. I learned that, once you can refrain from food and water, you can refrain from most things in life, at will. The temptation to eat or drink during a fast is *always* there. But when you persist, you develop self-mastery. This was a way for me to program my mind, to be more driven as I stepped boldly into the future. Consider how you can cultivate your own patience, self-restraint, and self-control, too. This all plays a part in your moral compass.

When I needed new ideas for my next book, I would travel to clear my mind. I would surround myself with natural beauty to get a grander perspective. To meditate, I would pray. This was the same for my parents and my grandparents, and they passed it down to me. As a result of my deeply introspective process, I have learned to give back and be selfless.

Motivating yourself is hard, but friends, family, and mastermind groups can help you get the motivation you need. We all exist in relation to other people, and sometimes it is they that motivate us when we need it most.

Thinking back to when my mother was searching for a job immediately after my father passed away, I can only imagine how desperate and vulnerable she must have felt. She filed for bankruptcy. We experienced poverty and suffering first-hand. Because it happened suddenly, we almost lost the house. My mother didn't have a job. She was a housewife, and English wasn't her first language. It completely took us off track, reducing our middle class family to struggling, lower-income status.

I remember one time during a hail storm when one of our neighbors walked over and informed my mother that there was a chemist position available in Visalia, CA, about an hour's drive from where we lived. Our neighbor, drenched by the harsh rain, stood there in our doorway with a cheerful smile. I couldn't believe it; sure enough, she convinced my mother to drive my dad's huge old truck (one she hated and had difficulty driving) and make the drive. My mother's car was in the shop. Not only did my mother land this job; it became her career for almost the next twenty years. When I asked my mother what motivated her to stay in a position for that long, she explained that, for her, life was her children. That meant she was happy only if we were all happy, and united. She had one wish, and that was also her purpose, and this was it. She had essentially created a family mastermind group that had no expiration date. She had a noble career, one in which she helped people—her own family. Her moral compass was shaped by her care for her family. What an inspiration my mother is to me.

"I understand now that boundaries between noise and sound are conventions. All boundaries are conventions, waiting to be transcended. One may transcend any convention if only one can first conceive of doing so."

—*David Mitchell*

My mother's ability to raise three children on a modest salary was hugely motivating. She had an unwritten contract: that if she provided a lifetime of service, her employer, in return, would provide a lifetime of security. She did just that, and worked until she was let go. Imagine that: she didn't even voluntarily retire. And she would have kept working if we hadn't urged her to stop; she finally needed a break. It took her some time to adjust to retirement, but she eventually embraced it, and my nephew became the apple of her eye.

Career longevity is no longer twenty years; it's now three or four years, at best. Our generation and the next generation will likely not stay in a career for that long. Some will climb the ladder, but most will change careers and align multiple opportunities. The goal is not how high you get or how many jobs you have; the goal of a Career Mastermind™ is impact. Can you make a significant impact?

Seek Wisdom Wherever You Go

"The superior man is modest in his speech, but exceeds in his actions."

—Confucius

My nani (grandmother) was a God-fearing woman. A mother of six, she had a powerful aura. People would stop where they were and watch her gracefully pass by with her walking cane. She entered, and everyone rushed to her side or stood up in respect. She prayed consistently each day (I never saw her miss a prayer) and was always thankful. She taught me some valuable life skills, including how to read and write Arabic. She would say, "It's the language of the angels." She taught me to be noble, and how to be a storyteller. She was always modest and humble. I am forever thankful to her for teaching me and my siblings these skills. I make an effort to implement them as much as I possibly can. You will find similar life skills based on your life experiences.

"So, listen, to yourself and to those with whom you are speaking. Your wisdom then consists not of the knowledge you already have, but the continual search for knowledge, which is the highest form of wisdom."

—*Jordan Peterson*

DIAMOND BAR, CA: My grandmother congratulating my brother on his wedding

When we were growing up, my grandmother lived with us, and my mother looked after her. She also taught me something fundamental to universal Being: gratitude. It's so important for your compass. Gratitude is a skill, as well as a form of self-awareness and perception. It is extremely important to career excellence. *In order to be a Career Mastermind™, you have*

to be career-ready. To be career-ready, you must be self-aware. And self-awareness is
essential for life readiness. But how do you achieve self-awareness?

Life Readiness and Life Masterminding

My nani's actions spoke louder than words. She lived by example. She taught me to be life-ready, not just career-ready. She helped me develop a global mindset, to be patient, and to have deep faith in life, not just in myself. We lost her a couple years ago, but she always said she was ready to meet her Creator. It was a peaceful passing, and she went with dignity. I found her attitude inspiring.

My nani was not just a storyteller, she was a story-changer. Her stories were both timeless and built upon core values. She would tell stories about my mother being a role model to her peers as well as a perfectionist. She also made mention of when my father came to ask for my mother's hand. She had a story for every holiday occasion, and we all gathered in a circle anxiously awaiting a story we had never heard about them. Each story was followed by a moral lesson about values. The anticipation was exciting. She explained to us that these values can endure for a lifetime, so we should never let them go. And if we do, we must return to them. These values include things like honesty, loyalty, faith in the Creator, respect, and love.

She would say, "Love is the foundation of our existence," and made reference to the following poetic verses in our long chats over my homemade chai:

> *"Meditation in Allah is my capital.*
> *Contemplation of Allah is my companion.*
> *Reason is the root of my religion.*
> *Love is the foundation of my existence.*

Truth is my salvation.
Submission to the Divine Will is my pride.
Knowledge is my garb and virtue.
Worship is my habit.
Grief is my friend.
Enthusiasm is the vehicle of my life.
And my utmost happiness lies in prayer."

—*Prophet Muhammad (Peace be upon him)*

My nani believed passionately in prayer and meditation. She said that we had to stop and just pivot. She told me to fear Allah (meaning God Almighty) but described the fear as a *fear with love.* For her, it helped morally guide her. The "All" or *Allah*—where all praise was due, demonstrating to me her point on humility. Humility was her North Star.

HOUSTON, TX: My grandmother at age 90

My grandmother taught and showed me how we must humble ourselves by humbling our mind and bodies. She did this in prayer, putting the highest part of her body, her forehead, to the ground. We must ground ourselves like the root of a flower. Similar to grounding a metal wire—our frontal lobe—the center of activity such as motor function, problem solving, spontaneity, memory, language, initiation, judgement, impulse control, and social and sexual behavior, continually collect electrostatic from the atmosphere. This may cause headaches and can be eliminated when the forehead touches the ground. It has to be grounded time to time to optimally function. There, she would recite "God is the Most Great." When we do this, we are still in motion, but we are not sidetracked; we are headed in the right direction—as she said, a *straight path*. We are following our moral compass. You must find yours.

With each cup of chai, my grandmother's stories intensified. I couldn't help but recall my father's date seeds and the lessons they represented. My grandmother, just as strict as my father, if not stricter, would always advise me to seal the cardamom to keep the "khushboo" *or fragrance* fresh. Just as each cardamom had its own center, my grandmother was the center (the soul) of the family.

Career Mastermind™ = Life Mastermind

To be a Career Mastermind™, you must also be a Life Mastermind. Career and life overlap and intersect, just like a noble career and your moral compass—they are not in competition with each other. The goal is to have them mirror one another in order to see them as one. Think of it as the double helix of DNA. Their motion is balanced and unified, although they are different and run in different directions. They are parallel and collimated like the prisms of binoculars.

CAREER AND LIFE MASTERMIND

To be a Career Mastermind™, you must also be a Life Mastermind. Career and Life are parallel to each other, not competing to each other. Your career and life overlap, intersect, and superimpose one another. The goal is to have them mirror one another so they are seen as one. Think of it as DNA double helix. Their motion is in balance and is the same, although they are different and run in different directions.

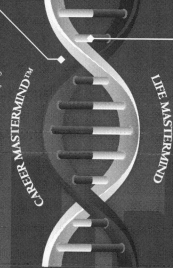

DNA contains the instructions needed for an organism to develop, survive and reproduce. To carry out these functions, DNA sequences must be converted into messages that can be used to produce proteins, which are the complex molecules that do most of the work in our bodies. A Career Mastermind™ has these instructions, as does a Life Mastermind, and they partner in harmony.

The horizontal lines you see in the image represent base pairs. They come together by an "H" bond, or "Hassan" bond for the purpose of this book. It's the catalyst that unites these two distinct paths. As I mentioned in my Author Note, it's the base and purpose, stabilizing the DNA. These pairs are complementary and interact with each other as our work and life do in our daily lives. It's "in our DNA".

MAJOR GROOVE

MINOR GROOVE

The double helix is right-handed (meaning your life lens leads it) with about 10–10.5 base pairs per turn. Think of these as steps in your career and life. They can be days, weeks, or years, even seconds. They are measured by the intensity and outcome. Each set of 10-01.5 base pairs represents years, or stages in your life. The double helix structure of DNA contains a major groove and minor groove. These represent setbacks and shortcomings. We all have them and they happen to everyone. But we bounce back, and never lose faith. The major groove occurs where the backbones are far apart, the minor groove occurs where they are close together. The more aligned they are, the better off we are.

Designed by **Hassan Akmal** and
Illustration by **Ahmed Zaeem**

Infographic available for download at www.CareerMastermind.org/Resources

DNA contains the instructions needed for an organism to develop, survive, and reproduce. To carry out these functions, DNA sequences must be converted into messages that can be used to produce proteins, which are the complex molecules doing most of the work in our bodies. A Career Mastermind™ has similar instructions, as does a Life Mastermind, and they partner with each other in harmony.

The double helix is right-handed (meaning your life lens leads it) and has about 10 to 10.5 base pairs per turn. Think of these as steps in your career and life. They can be days, weeks, or years, even seconds. They are measured by intensity and outcome. Each set of 10-10.5 base pairs—per Career Mastermind™ code, represents years, or stages in your life. The double helix structure of DNA contains a major groove and minor groove. These represent setbacks and shortcomings. We all have them, and they happen to everyone. But we bounce back. As my Nani said, "Never lose faith." The major groove occurs where the backbones are far apart; the minor groove occurs where they are close together. The more aligned they are, the better off we are—because we are in unison.

The horizontal lines you see in the image represent base pairs. They come together by an "H" bond, or for me—a "Hassan" bond, the catalyst that unites these two distinct paths. Yours, however, is your initial as we discussed in the Author's Note. As I mentioned, the base and purpose stabilize the DNA. These pairs are complementary and interact with each other, just as our work and life coordinate with each other in our daily lives.

Life is constantly intertwining, like the helical and majestic crystal structure of DNA, against time (counterclockwise). Think about it: so many things move counterclockwise: the planets around the sun, people performing the Hajj pilgrimage at the Kaaba in Mecca, race car tracks, and electrons around atoms. We are all energies moving in unison against time. Everything except the watch!

If you can master this combined vision, you will be better able to align nobility and morality in your journey. It also requires a leap of faith.

Take Quantum Leaps of Faith

INSTAGRAM: DHOOMLI

My cousin, Babar, was a distinctive figure. He was a self-made man who used to ride motorcycles in Lahore, Pakistan, and had a tattoo of the American flag on his shoulder. My mom used to hate it when he would take me on his motorcycle, but I loved it. He dreamt of coming to America one day and making it big. When he arrived, his career evolved from moving furniture to managing parking lots, selling cell phone accessories to selling real estate, and then to opening the Dhoom Restaurant in Hicksville. All he ever cared about was his family and making sure his retired father (my father's late younger brother, also a former film director in Pakistan) would never have to work or struggle again, especially in old age. My uncle is now in his 80s, God bless him.

LONG ISLAND, NY: Babar and his wife Nargis

Define the Goal, Uncover the Barriers

Babar was an example to all of us because he never gave up. He hustled, and never complained. He was always calm, against all odds. He was also a master of his emotions. It didn't matter if he had lost a property or a million dollars—he would say, "It's alright, everything will be okay." He had a positive mindset and a stoic approach, and it served him well. He designed his life this way.

> "The best way to predict the future is to create it."
>
> —Abraham Lincoln

Babar was successful because he was confident, not arrogant. Both men and women become career masterminds. What most people don't realize is that many of the men who are successful have women masterminding their success. Nargis, his wife, was a secret of his success. She assisted with accounting and pushed him forward with faith. She was his sounding board, and took care of all the little things that would get in his way. She kept things moving for him, and could cook a killer meal. She also hosted exquisite dinner parties and kept him informed on family, relatives, friends, and where he needed to be and why. She is a giving soul, and it ran in the family. Without her, he was lost.

Babar shared his wealth and helped many people by creating employment with his businesses. He hired the right people and spread opportunities all over Long Island, where he finally settled. He eventually became a Real Estate Career Mastermind™, and he did it by surrounding himself with those that already had a track record of success. Nargis also connected him to the community through family and friends, as well as the dinner parties she would host. To this day, she has a gift of bringing people together organically, and building bridges where they are needed. She is a "Connector" and giver, and this makes a difference in her community.

What's the takeaway here? First, take inspiration from proactive and successful people; it will feed your own success and fulfill you. If you want your compass to be effective, make it an ethical one. Find a sounding board: it can be your wife, your husband, a colleague, or a friend. Make sure this person can be there when you need to bounce an idea off them—or a question about what may be right or wrong. Add them to your moral compass; they become integral to your checks and balances system. Ultimately, though, you must make your own decision and take ownership of it.

Secondly, look at successful people that you know, even those that you feel envious of. What is their story? Sure, many of them benefit from luck or circumstance, but that is only after they put in the hard work. Remember: success does not define happiness. *The happiest people are givers, not takers.*

Applying yourself the best you can will increase the likelihood of good fortune coming your way. You have to make your own luck to build a life you love. You have to remember that you are the most important variable in this construction. No matter if it's chaos or happenstance—you can impact your luck and increase the probability of good things happening by optimizing your environment and the people in your network. Let me show you how this works in a real-life example.

Be Bold, Be Vulnerable

It's important to open yourself to vulnerability. Moving out of your comfort zone allows you to grow personally and professionally. All of this assists in the building of a moral compass, and eventually, in your legacy.

WWW.REDIVY.MARKETING

I'm grateful for learning to take more risks and being more creative with my budget as a career leader and professional. As an early adopter of new technology, software, and programs while I was at Loyola University Chicago, I trained myself to try new things, be vulnerable, without sacrificing principles—which I learned from two individuals who live this vision under the name of Red Ivy Marketing.

Red Ivy Marketing

In 2015, Red Ivy was an upstart two-person marketing company in Chicago. Both the stories of CEO, Tony Arce, and CMO, Miguel Paloma, were becoming all too familiar in today's world. Miguel was a long-time Chicago ad exec who realized that 50 year-old executives were becoming rarer by the day. Tony, on the other hand, had been living with deep pain, and so found solace in inspiring others who struggle to believe that brighter days were ahead. For three years, the two seemed to be going broke while going for broke with their business. That changed, however, with the genesis of an innovative device bridging the critical gap between technology and personal branding. Tony and Miguel knew the impact video would have if it were leveraged to help students land their ideal career or internship. All they needed was a champion.

The Video Business Card Pioneers: Tony Arce (left), Miguel Paloma (right)

Become a Master Breeder

It's a rare breed of person that exemplifies creativity, drive, dedication, intelligence, resilience, kindness, sincerity, and the ability to connect deeply with people. These extraordinary people spin out some of the most innovative ideas and have the perfect combination of qualities to put those ideas into action.

Tony Arce is one of these people. From a young age, Tony has had the drive to succeed and be financially independent. He started off as a kid delivering papers and working at a bank. He went on to join the Marines, then worked his way up to director of IT at a large company, until he finally realized he wanted to venture out on his own. However, it wasn't until he was faced with the devastating blow of losing all three of his children to the capricious nature of the family court system that he truly found his purpose.

From this low point, Tony desperately began searching not just for meaning in his life, but a meaning for all of us. That's when he had the vision of the Video Business Card. He knew he wasn't the only person with a story, and he could see how telling others his story connected him to other people in a way he had never been able to before. With the power of video, he knew he could share lasting moral lessons by bringing people's stories to life while helping them promote their own personal brands in a meaningful way.

The video business card was born from the idea of using technology to forge personal connections in business. Involved in the real estate industry from a young age, Tony noticed there was something missing in the way real estate brokers and most professionals connected with clients.

If you become such a Master Catalyst like Tony, you can become a Master Breeder. A *Master Breeder* cultivates new opportunities for people that didn't exist before. These opportunities make a positive difference in the world.

How are you going to be open to your advantage? There's one thing you can do.

Be a Model of Determination

Every moral compass needs determination. When Tony sought a better pitch for how people choose products and services, he never imagined the journey it would take him on. Tony's idea, rooted in the belief that people buy from people they trust, focused on local restaurants and businesses.

Tony created a dining guide that showcased local restaurants in a cinematic format, allowing online visitors to preview restaurants in a 15 second preview and/or 60-90-second narrated mini-documentary. While the guide grew to nearly three hundred restaurants, its growth was not aggressive enough to sustain the demand for the number of restaurants in the city. However, while the idea itself would not prove successful in the immediate future, it paved the way for using video to help consumers choose the people and businesses they'd like to work with.

It was at a family party that a dean from Ivy Tech College in Indiana took interest in the dining guide for a different reason. During a conversation with Tony's new business partner, Miguel Paloma, the dean asked if the format could be applied to students. Miguel quickly demonstrated the first and only *Video Business Card*, which was a prototype Tony was using to introduce people to the dining guide concept. The dean fell in love with the concept and asked us to present a version to his school, for students to use in seeking employment.

Tony and Miguel, keeping it in the family, asked Tony's cousin and Miguel's niece to be the subject of their first video business card for students. (Apart from being business partners, Tony and Miguel are nephew and uncle by way of Miguel marrying Tony's aunt.) Once completed, they presented their idea to one of the largest colleges in the United States: Ivy Tech Community College.

Every dean from across Indiana was present when Red Ivy pitched the video business card for the higher education sector. The panel of deans' grueling questions were met with quick and concise answers. And yet, the idea seemed too novel to be put into motion right away. When the dean that championed their concept took a job in Florida, it seemed like their only opportunity in higher education would end there.

Despite this first failure, Tony and Miguel remained patient and honest in their replies. Patience is half of faith; no moral compass will work without it.

Determined to find an early adopter of the video business card, Miguel called on several smaller universities to find a suitor. As with any new idea and fledgling company, it was difficult to convince the decision-makers to give Red Ivy a chance to present their opportunity. When all hope seemed lost, Miguel contacted a friend he worked with at Leo Burnett, who was now at Loyola University Chicago, his alma mater. Red Ivy got the break they'd been hoping for.

These Individuals knocked on many higher education doors explaining their product, a "video business card," without their own physical business cards. Many doors were shut in their face, but I opened my gate. As a Career Mastermind™, you must be a moral and innovation launch pad—a safe haven for new ideas. *There is no such thing as a Career Mastermind™ that is afraid to try new things.*

So, I invited them in for a demo. What I saw and learned was much more than a product worth investing in for our students. I met two gentlemen, and I heard stories I would never forget. We put together a new career business plan that included piloting a forward-thinking video business card program. This program would later achieve a 100 percent satisfaction rate that would spark the interest of universities all over the country.

Despite having a product like the video business card, Red Ivy has evolved into a company that not only seeks to promote personal brands, but also helps develop individuals personally and professionally. By creating content and curating seminars that introduce subject matter experts in various disciplines to their clients, Red Ivy has been able to share impactful knowledge with their clients that has improved the quality of their clients' lives. These clients work with Red Ivy to extract their hidden stories and share them with the public via the video business card platform. They become part of a new digital community—and you can too. What's your untold story waiting to be revealed?

Tony's dream, like mine, is to give back. Besides his business goals, he wants to rescue abductees of human trafficking and tell their stories that aren't being told. This compels me to believe in their cause and to continue to partner in socially responsible causes. Tony already had a moral compass, so I aligned his with mine.

Be an Early Adopter, Take Risks

After the success of the pilot at Loyola University Chicago, Tony, Miguel and I formed a Digital Transformation Career Mastermind™ Group. Only winners from an elevator pitch competition would qualify. I would later expand the scope of our partnership in my future role at Columbia University to include them delivering a presentation on "How to Market Yourself in the Digital Age," in addition to serving as panelists during Social Media Day and formalizing the video business card program.

Here is what they said following their presentation in a seminar format as part of a larger event I organized, entitled, "Career Week":

"Enough cannot be said about Hassan Akmal. From the first time we met him during his tenure at Quinlan School of Business, Loyola University Chicago, he impressed us with his vision and commitment for his students. His work ethic is second only to his huge heart for each and every person that has the honor of working with him. To see the way his team holds him in such high regard is inspiring. At each and every turn, Hassan and his team made us feel like we were part of their team and family. I am blessed to know him and have the honor of working together. If more people like Hassan were leading, our world would be a better place."

—Tony Arce

"I've known Hassan for a couple of years but am still amazed at how he tirelessly goes about trying to implement change for the better. So, when he told us he wanted to re-engineer the role of Career Placement and envisioned our product playing a role in making that happen, we were immediately on board. We also know him well enough that once he gets started, look out. His team--some of the most sincere and hardest working professionals we have ever met (Greg, Titus, Jessica, Diane, Murwa)—pulled off an amazing week of panels, workshops, live and virtual career fairs, breakfast, lunch, and evening events with over 200 companies. While his path that has led him to where he is

today is truly amazing, it is his continued journey that will be something to behold. Un abrazo Akmal!"

—Miguel Paloma

This feedback came as a surprise, and if they hadn't given it directly, I wouldn't have known they felt this way. While the feelings are mutual, the point here is to have empathy. Empathy combined with self-awareness is central to every Career Mastermind™.

My path, like the real characters in this chapter, was never straight, but I tried not to lose sight of my "Z," or true direction, by using this moral compass. There were times when I truly needed it. One of those times was life or death.

As you navigate through the professional world, it's important to know that people are impressed by hard work and the successful implementation of change. Tony and Miguel's feedback gave me more tools for my storytelling toolkit and they will do the same for you. Understand that those around you will be involved in building your legacy. You must be aware of how all the characters in your life shape you, too. This is not your Scarlet letter; your legacy will continue to evolve.

"A man sooner or later discovers that he is the master-gardener of his soul, the director of his life."

—James Allen

CHECKLIST ITEM 7

A NOBLE CAREER
AND MORAL COMPASS

▶ **Define where you are now:** (check one)
☐ On the right and straight path
☐ Don't know where I'm going

▶ **Action Item:**
I will [_____]
by the Date [____] / [____] / [____]

▶ **Follow Up Date:**
[____] / [____] / [____]

▶ **Completed:** (circle one)
○ Yes ○ No

▶ *Why do you feel this way?*
[_____]

▶ *What is the 'IMPACT' action you will take within one week to make a positive change?*
[_____]

CALLING

N

JOB **W** **E** **CAREER**

S

FAILURE

It's chess, not checkers!

"Next Steps" and Notes:
[_____]

Workbook available for download at www.CareerMastermind.org/Resources

PART 3: MAKE YOUR COMMITMENT TO CHANGE

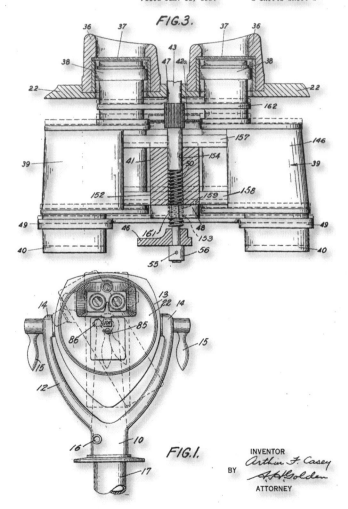

FIG.3.

FIG.1.

INVENTOR

Arthur F. Casey

BY

A.H.Golden

ATTORNEY

Coin Controlled Binoculars Patent filed January 31, 1934

CHAPTER 8:

NOT YOUR SCARLET LETTER —

BUILDING A STORYTELLING LEGACY

———————◆●◆———————

"The longer I live, the more beautiful life becomes."

———*Frank Lloyd Wright*

*S*torytelling is undergoing a significant change. New technologies enabling virtual reality, augmented reality, and artificial intelligence are changing the concept of a story. It is changing how we create and tell stories.

Most of us grew up in an age when mass media was unidirectional. You had no choice but to sit back and watch, listen or read, because that's how the technology worked. The Internet was the first example of two-way mass media. Suddenly, people had the ability to comment, share, give feedback, and create, all in real time. This has ushered in one of the most profound shifts in modern times: people are no longer as interested in being passive consumers of their media as they are in interacting with the content and its creators.

Write Your Story

Your career is not an end in itself. Like most worthwhile earthly pursuits, career development is a lifelong process. *You are not merely telling a story as a storyteller, you are a part of the ever-changing narrative.* That's something you have to be very good at and keep getting better at. Keep changing your story as you go along and be aware that you are always writing it.

According to the United States Bureau of Labor Statistics, the average worker has ten different jobs before reaching the age of forty. This number is estimated to increase. Some LinkedIn officials believe that people will change *jobs* 15 times throughout their lifetime. I argue that the actual number is higher, as some jobs and careers you will prototype and some you will quickly realize are not the best fit. Changing careers will become more frequent and some will be short lived.

Welcome to the Windy City

I had never imagined that I would live in Chicago, but I was always open to new opportunities outside of the areas I grew up in. I spent five years away from familiar surroundings, without my friends and family. But it was a good experience nonetheless, because it led me to new opportunities. It also accelerated my career in ways I could not foresee. I learned many transferable skills from various positions, in different industries, in diverse companies and organizations.

I also explored outside New York City after I felt I had made a real impact in my first organization as Director of Career Services. I moved on. I thought I had achieved everything in that position and was able to achieve more elsewhere, with new skills I had acquired.

I also prepared a succession plan, it was the right thing to do. It's important to know your job's expiration date so you know when to move on. You should constantly grow and never stagnate.

How many changes in careers will you go through in life? How will you continue to write your story for the best possible outcomes? Think of these. But first, a bit of advice.

Know Your Expiration Date

It's not enough to love our jobs. There has to be more. We must also love ourselves and want to continue growing. However, sometimes, those growth opportunities cease. You hit a brick wall or maybe there are no more positions to grow into. That's when you know to leave. And if loving well is hard, leaving well is harder. It's not just your first impression that matters, it's also your last.

Gianpiero Petriglieri, an associate professor of organizational behavior at INSEAD as well as a physician and psychiatrist, researches and practices leadership development. In a recent article in the Harvard Business Review entitled, "How to Leave a Job You Love,"he writes:

"Many people cherish their time at organizations that they left long ago, and remain loyal to them, because those places helped them discover who they were, what they could do, and where they could go next."

Gianpiero and Jennifer Petriglieri coined the term "identity workspaces" for those organizations that leave a lasting impression. Gianpiero beautifully summarizes his point:

"I don't think it's worth loving a job, or an organization. Let me repeat: they will not love you back. But if a job, or an organization helps you find work and people worth loving, then it has been good, and it is worth honoring, both while you are there and after you are gone."

This is very much the case for me. I celebrate previous employers and don't believe in burning bridges. How many times do we hear someone badmouth their last boss or organization? In many cases, it's a red flag for the new employer, even if what they are saying is true. So, make sure you don't go around bad mouthing anyone. Not only is it potentially bad for your own career progression, but it is also bad for your karma. Be positive about people; it will only help you in the long run. You're building a storytelling legacy, not a few sentences.

I noticed a position outside of the Big Apple (in my peripheral view). I applied and after several rounds of interviews (eight hours later), I got an offer. Deciding to accept a position as the Director of Career Services at Loyola University Chicago's business school, I had to leave an organization where I worked for five years, a place where I felt I had made a deep impact.

I was the top ranked director of career services, so I had the metrics and performance. This meant job security during an unstable economy. I offered two months' notice and even trained my successor, all in an effort to make the transition seamless for the organization. *In almost all cases with Career Masterminds, leaving on a high note is not an option; it's a form of gratitude for the people who helped you achieve more than you originally set out to.*

Without giving myself a break in between both positions, something I swore to myself I won't do again, I moved across the country to the beautiful city of Chicago—instantly falling in love with its skyline. I hit the ground running. Just six months later, I was asked to join the faculty as an adjunct professor of global health and to serve on the advisory roundtable of the nursing school. What an honor! I was also promoted to the Chair of Career Education at the business school. This was an important milestone for me, because I not only wanted to leverage my graduate degree, but I was still very passionate about health and making a difference.

CHICAGO, IL: First day as a new adjunct professor at Loyola University Chicago.

Little did I know, my commute to work would be just a ten minute walk to the John Hancock building where I lived on the 80th floor. The 96th floor Signature Lounge became my new reflection spot. It's where I began this particular career in Chicago, one of many careers I knew I would endure in my lifetime, and where I would complete my Chicagoland tenure.

My students were grateful for my service as their professor. One of the thank you cards received was addressed to "Jerry Maguire." On many occasions, I was like a sports agent representing these students to employers. I would go to bat for them and not take "no" for an answer. I enjoyed vouching for them and since I had met them face-to-face on several occasions, I could speak to their career readiness, professionalism, and ownership of their career developmental path. In many ways, it's a "thank you economy" and receiving the appreciation I did communicated that I had made an impact in people's lives. If one person is inspired to do something great, I've won. It only takes one, as every community needs a leader.

Here is a gift from my Health System Management students (that included many aspiring) future nurses and doctors on my last day at Loyola; it also turned out to be my birthday:

CHICAGO, IL: Last day of teaching and my birthday

Gratitude is self-reinforcing. One day, as I was standing and staring at the overcast sky with a coffee in hand, giving myself some much needed meditative time, I thought about investing in my future and how to save more money. I have always wanted to be my own boss. I resolved to continue my independent consulting and to try to save more money so I could invest in my own business. First, I realized that having an extra bedroom was unnecessary, so I put an advert out on Craigslist to rent it out.

Swipe Right

Days later, when I was halfway through my rumination process, I heard a knock on my door. I went and looked through the eyehole. Standing there was a guy, roughly 5'10", wearing a suit. He looked like a Russian spy and had deep, blue-grey eyes. He wanted to rent my place. When he came in, I showed him around. His name was Anton, and he was responding to my ad.

Anton Khlopotov

INSTAGRAM: @ANTONMEETSWORLD

Anton was a real character. He was swiping left on his phone, and I immediately thought to myself, "Is he on Tinder or browsing the Internet?" He was a model as well as a photographer, so I imagined him having parties when I wasn't there.

Well, it turned out he wasn't a Russian spy. He was a manager at Suitsupply, a Dutch men's fashion company. He inspired me. He wanted to travel, take photos, and wanted to model. He also wanted to sell suits. Well, why couldn't he do all of those things? Our career bucket lists were the focus of many of our late night chats over espresso. Even though Anton and I were so different, we could talk so deeply about life and just appreciate nature in all of its beauty. We would discuss everything.

It always began with the skyline views. We talked about careers, women, food, politics, family, God, and the future. We were good sounding boards for each other.

He would tell me how he built roads in Iraq, and regardless of our difference of opinion on the war, we always found common ground. He was very open and a good listener. He cared. We enjoyed listening to each other's different perspectives, as it helped shape our own. Anton became one of my private clients and also a close friend.

Anton went through some rough patches and dark moments. It can be difficult to troubleshoot and remain positive through challenging times. The future will never be easy, and planning for it is paramount. It is good to have a flexible plan and direction, as this will help you focus more as you get older.

From the moment of meeting Anton, whether we were meant to meet or there was a spiritual connection, one thing was clear: there was a Purpose. I picked up the lens ball he had close to the window on display and began thinking about the differing perspectives and lenses of life. So, what can all this information do for you?

CHICAGO, IL: John Hancock Building on Miracle Mile—Photo Credit: Anton Khlopotov

Stories Are Meant To Be Told

Imagine your own moment of great change. Imagine it happening, even though you didn't ask for it or pray for it. Imagine that moment finding you. Do you see your life perspective changing?

I do. Now that my moment has passed, I can remember it vividly. Sometimes we are incredulous about these moments, but we shouldn't be. We should embrace them. Mine embraced me. I was watching a time lapse through the lens ball at the top of the impeccable John Hancock Building. Suddenly, I saw life passing by and hundreds of lives changing within seconds. Everyone had a story. You have a story and moments of great change. What are your moments?

Chicago's Waterfront through a Lens Ball; Photo Credit—Anton Khlopotov

I love telling stories and listening to them. It's who we are. It helps us breathe, yet so many stories are lost and try to find their way back.

Stories are meant to be told. Anton told me his story on this day. Stories are also meant to be heard. What are some of your favorites?

More Than Meets the Eye

Anton lived an interesting life and one that inspired me. His story is important, so I want to share it with you.

Born in Kiev, Ukraine, Anton spent his early years in a small village on the outskirts of its capital. Immigrating to the United States at the age of seven with his mother and sister, felt like the opening of a door where there could only be a wall. At the age of nine, his stepfather gave him a small film camera, and soon it became apparent Anton had an eye for composition and detail, but more importantly, a curiosity for the hidden beauty in the ordinary. Throughout his teens, he traveled to Ukraine where he embarked upon two-week long expeditions into the wilderness with a band of travelers on mountain bikes, canoes, and on foot. These trips were the embodiment of embracing adventure, merriment, and the unknown. A guitar would always accompany them, and Russian bard songs about the depth of the human spirit would resonate alongside the campfire, framed by a billion stars in the mysterious and limitless night. Anton describes these escapes by saying, "I've always loved nature; it's the ultimate therapy. When you live and breathe nature and become one with it, you realize that its laws are infinitely subtle, complex, and beyond the grasp of human understanding. A serenity ensues."

At the age of 17, after unexpectedly losing his mother to cancer, Anton shifted gears. Shortly after his 18th birthday, he enlisted in the U.S. Army as an infantryman.

Arab Jabour, IQ: Anton deployed south of Baghdad

Less than a year later, he was deployed to an imminent danger zone, the province of Arab Jabour, situated just south of Baghdad. He was a machine-gunner (SAW gunner) in his unit—Alpha Company, 1-30th Infantry Regiment, 2 Brigade, and 3rd Infantry Division of the US Army. Its mission was to clear and secure an area colloquially known as "the triangle of death." For the next fourteen months, Anton's unit would experience some of the darkest and most trying times of their lives. Bradley tanks, Humvees, and boot heels would carry the frontline soldiers on their ceaseless patrols of the local villages. Night vision goggles mounted, his unit conducted night raids on houses suspected to be weapons caches and IED manufacturing labs. Temporary clinics were set up to provide hygienic and medical supplies to locals. Engineers were hired to repair irrigation systems for the farmers. A route was secured, and local school children were able to start going to school again.

Every soldier has their own way of coping and working through the pressures of war. For Anton this was photography and snail-mail letter writing. Every monotonous day of manual labor was an opportunity to capture a fleeting moment of hidden beauty. Every night was a chance to write letters to family and friends around the globe. A letter written by hand and stamped with a wax seal carries with it a piece of the author. Imagine if your handwritten thank you letter to an employer had a wax seal? What kind of message in such fine detail would that send? Perhaps that—you care?

The magic of receiving a parcel wrapped in paper and string and unfolding it in the silence and temporary safety of night amid a combat zone must be truly indescribable. One of Anton's closest friends at the time, Rosa, sent him photographs and descriptions of magnificent scenes from China that would later impact the trajectory of his life. In 2014 Anton would have a month-long photography exhibit of his photo documentary work from Iraq titled "Unopened Letter" in a popular venue in Cambridge, MA. He continued to develop his passion for photography as well as music and letter-writing into his mid and late twenties.

Upon completing his deployment and receiving an honorable discharge, Anton returned to his home in Chicago. He would have many jobs in the ensuing nine years, including barista, private armed security officer, actor, and model. It was this last, modeling, that connected him to the brand that would later serve as a stepping stone into one of the greatest chapters of his life. At the age of twenty-five, Anton landed a role as a featured extra in the blockbuster film *Divergent* and spent forty days on set, developing a relationship with the director Neil Burger. Later, he was the first male model to land on the cover of New Orleans-based fine arts magazine *Art + Design*.

At the age of twenty-seven, Anton began working for Suitsupply, an innovative and entrepreneurial men's fashion brand that had already carved a niche for itself and was now seriously impacting the international men's suiting industry. He learned and adapted quickly and soon became the top seller and performer in the Chicago branch by creating a unique series of clientele techniques.

During this period of his life, Anton and I were roommates in the iconic John Hancock Tower in the Gold Coast of Chicago. He humbly attributes much of his success in this period of his life to my guidance and mentorship. He says, "You believed in me from the start and showed me new points of view from which to view my talents and achievements, even when I didn't see them as such." In return, I got a new wardrobe!

I was able to learn the importance of having a custom suit. The difference of having a combined career and life vision is like a suit that doesn't fit your body, versus one tailored to your form. You can't compare them.

CHICAGO, IL: Anton reflecting on his career and life vision from his "go to" spot

The Savannah Cat

INSTAGRAM: @ZAKIANDMAFAZA

Anton and I had a neighbor named Kasper who owned a beautiful and wild F2 Savannah cat named Leo. Sometimes Kasper would travel for business and asked Anton to care for Leo, a beast in his own right. Inspired by the grace and beauty of this majestic creature, Anton pitched the idea of adopting a Savannah cat for our own humble abode. He described it as a life bucket item and even promised to create and manage an Instagram account for them. Two weeks later, Zaki and Mafaza were riding home from rural Illinois to the tallest residential building in the U.S.

The Savannah cat has the physique, intelligence, athleticism, and striking coat pattern of the wild African serval. Plus, they are legal in Illinois. Zaki, born on May 16, 2016, is an F4 generation Savannah, meaning he's part serval, approximately 15 percent. Mafaza, born June 8, 2016, is also an F4, and just over 10 percent serval. Both are golden spotted. Zaki looks like a bobcat and is about twice the size of a normal cat, and Mafaza looks like a cheetah and is 1.5 times larger. What can I say? I was lonely and wanted to do something for myself, so I decided to come home with them. I've never regretted it and got help from Anton caring for them. They are like dogs in a sense: they go out on leashes, they play fetch, and are absolutely loyal. They don't leave your side. They also can jump seven feet in the air!

CHICAGO, IL: Zaki (left) and Mafaza (right); Photo Credit Anton Khlopotov

Life Changers

Anton describes the experience of living in the John Hancock Tower as life changing. He described it this way:

"Often the clouds were below our window and the sun would rise, painting iridescent waves like the surface of an ocean over the top of the cloud plane. The golden rays would shimmer on the city's diverse architectural landscape and there was a sense of being in a high place, physically and spiritually."

The meaningful presence of exercise and athletic mastery throughout his life propelled him to further aspire to test his own physical and spiritual limitations.

In the winter he would casually run down to Oak Street Beach and dive into Lake Michigan, with large sheets of ice floating on the surface. "Cold water immersion has as many psychological benefits as physiological," he says. "Getting there and doing it takes willpower and determination, and practicing these is empowering and makes a person more willing to confront other tasks of life."

CHICAGO, IL: Anton being Anton

On multiple occasions Anton did a walking meditation of 50 miles, or 22 hours. In one instance, he walked all that time in subzero temperatures.

"I learned the joy of pushing myself physically from childhood, and the U.S. Army helped me to develop the discipline and routine, but only after I had completed my service did I really set out to discover my limits. Walking continuously for almost twenty-four hours in sub-zero temperature was one of my favorite parts of that winter. I got to know myself. I wanted to give up many times and was offered car rides by kind strangers along the way, but I stuck to the mission. To say something and then do it despite the pain and exorbitant effort, to me that's meaningful."

Career Masterminds breathe endurance, they are *Life Changers*.

In 2017 Anton took a quantum leap of faith and accepted a modeling contract in Cape Town, South Africa. While there he would publish his first work as a photographer, a six-page story titled "The Art of Adventure" in *Art + Design*. The head photographer of the magazine had spotted Anton's vision of Cape Town on social media and pitched the assignment, which Anton gladly accepted. At the end of this three- month journey, Anton was faced with a choice: return to Chicago or continue on his trajectory of exploration, adventure, and seeking out the hitherto unexplored. He recalled that in 2016 Suitsupply had opened a branch in Hong Kong, so he reached out and expressed interest in potentially transferring there. He purchased a one-way ticket to Shanghai where the head office for Suitsupply Asia is located. He sent a few emails and made some phone calls. Within days he had scheduled an interview with the director of sales of Suitsupply Asia and within a few months, Anton began his new life and career in Hong Kong—the gateway between East and West, Asia's World City, Pearl of the Orient.

He continues to pursue his lifelong passion of photography, music, and physical fitness as he explores the cultural, social and physical landscape of what he terms "a bucket list destination and a hidden gem of a city." He describes this most recent life change as "a major breakthrough that has unlocked a world of possibilities." Anton works at Suitsupply on Ice House Street in the Central District of Hong Kong. In addition to his usual endeavors, he's taken up hiking and surfing, and in his spare time collaborates as a model and photographer with other creatives in Hong Kong.

On the day Anton was moving to Hong Kong, we both realized how fond we had become of our barista talks. He would drink espresso, and I would make a café con leche. Besides the fact that we were once both baristas, we loved coffee. We both enjoyed contemplating life's wonders from the clouds (literally), asking questions, and proposing philosophies that made sense of our experiences.

CHICAGO, IL: 80th Floor of the John Hancock Building;
Photo Credit Anton Khlopotov

As Anton prepared for his new adventure, he said:

"By choosing a path less traveled, I simultaneously chose an intentional life. We all have our strengths and challenges but we can choose what to focus on, and we can decide our direction. By changing your environment, you can transform your life and by following your heart and having faith, you can make your dream your reality. Then it's just a matter of setting the next goal and falling in love with life all over again."

CHICAGO, IL: Fireworks over Navy Pier; Photo Credit—Anton Khlopotov

There is no such thing as the perfect career, only a well-designed and lived life.

Anton taught me that your heart is tethered to the soul of the world by a delicate string, like a spider's web. It trembles in the gale and shimmers in the sunlight. He says, "If you ever happen to glimpse its outline, whisper a word of thanks."

Self-awareness and gratitude are like a spider and its web. They can't live apart. Both are crucial for any rising Career Mastermind™.

This is not your Scarlet letter. Your legacy will continue. Keep writing your story. Your web is your safety net, your alliance.

You will need to seek *counsel*, not "advice"—as they are very different, from trailblazers and those that have walked daunting paths in various walks of life.

You will need to align a personal board of directors.

Strength in numbers

CHAPTER 9: BUILDING YOUR ALLIANCE — YOUR PERSONAL BOARD OF DIRECTORS

"Love is our true destiny. We do not find the meaning of life by ourselves alone—we find it with another."

—*Thomas Merton*

To be a Career Mastermind™, you must be a Master Connector. You must also be an Informed Connector. This chapter will explore how your personal board of directors will serve as your Career Mastermind™ Group.

Get Energized by Building Relationships

A Harvard study once found that good relationships are the foundation for happiness. Having a community and support group not only leads to a more fulfilled life, it also increases your likelihood of a longer life. Making key relationships is difficult, but it will only make you stronger. This is why it is so important to have a mastermind group. All good relationships protect our bodies, brains, and help us move forward into the world. So, get building!

Create and Circulate Compelling Content

As you begin to form your personal alliance, you will need exceptional networking skills. In the digital age, this is easier said than done. You need to be an attention grabber with great content and have a purpose in order to attract the right people to form this group. It's this group that will help you hand select your Career Mastermind™ Group that we will discuss in Chapter 10.

You've Got Mail!

I grew up during the pre-Internet period, and I remember clearly what life was like back then. We couldn't create audiences to share ideas with like we do today. There were many barriers and limited news outlets. It was highly selective and competitive. Today, however, you control whether or not you put your ideas out there. Technology has eliminated any barriers to entry. Each and every one of us has the ability to create content with a smartphone. In that sense, we are all content creators.

The Internet is free, but we are paying for it with our attention. The more information you give to Facebook or Instagram, for example, the more they can package your information and sell it to a brand. These same brands will also pay social media influencers thousands of dollars for a single post. How many people can you reach with your brand?

There are thousands of ideas surrounding the concept of mastermind groups, some pretty far-fetched. Whether or not you can test those ideas before releasing them is critical. The Internet is at scale, and we are outlandishly fortunate to be living in this era. Our parents and grandparents likely couldn't take a side hustle and translate it as easily into a career.

The algorithmic recipe is what unlocks a powerful Career Mastermind™ Group and what optimizes it. It indicates how vigorous your process is. Later in the book, we will review different forms of these groups as well as the actual vetting process. We will also explore what makes a sound mastermind group versus an existing one.

Diversity, Perspective, and Balance

Diversity, perspective, and the judicious balance of voice and contribution are deciding factors when it comes to the group's performance as a whole—and individually.

Before getting into more detail, what really matters is understanding yourself. Are you on the right path? What is the point of forming a Career Mastermind™ Group if you are in the wrong career? If that's the case, your personal board of directors should be individuals whom you can trust to help you make the transition. What if you are not experiencing life for what it's worth and there's a more significant problem at hand?

Every great career is great for that specific person, it's custom-made, and it has made that person into who they are. How do you know what career (or careers) to master?

A *"Gold Mind" is a goldmine for career masterminds.* Gold Minds understand themselves before trying to understand the world around them. They think pure, and they think sound—collecting nuggets of wisdom from their personal board of directors, but they are independent. They practice making their own purposeful decisions.

As you improve your understanding of mastermind groups, you will improve your decision-making skills, and grow your alliance —*accelerating your career in the process.*

Accelerating Your Career

Whether you take a linear or non-linear path, getting to the top of your field is very challenging. A strong support network is critical, and if you are a student, this can be a peer network. These should comprise of people you trust, who can be candid and serve as sounding boards. They should help you polish your ideas, thoughts, provide alternative perspectives, and help align solutions.

This group of people, this alliance, is your team. They will help directly and indirectly accelerate your career. It's time to pick your team members! Pick wisely.

Career Masterminds: Playing To Win

It's very easy to get complacent in our careers, but as a tennis player, I relied on a play-to-win mindset. I wouldn't enter the arena unless I had visualized winning the match. This carried over when I left the tennis world. I saw higher education constantly changing under new pressure points and developments. What I needed to do was surround myself with other players who were also "playing to win," not on the tennis court, but in the career services space. So I ventured out of my comfort zone, attending every conference I could afford relevant to career services, industry relations—and trends in the first-year experience of students and alumni relations. In a span of less than ten months, I attended several conferences and identified the "movers and shakers" in their respective areas.

Why I Needed a Personal Board of Directors for My Career

Career services have changed significantly over the years. For example, 40% of students use social media to find jobs and 80% of employers use social media to match talent with needs. The career services model has shifted from taking a transactional focus to a transformative focus. This in turn is addressing generational issues. Instead of assisting students to find jobs, career centers are helping students find themselves and how they want to engage in the world.

Initially, if we go back to the 20th century, it was faculty that were the coaches and counselors, but this slowly changed. Later, in a new paradigm, networking was born and became the dominant focus—and now it is all about specialized career centers. This whole process has and continues to decentralize.

Many graduate schools have allocated their own career centers for their own programs. For example, Loyola University Chicago, Quinlan

School of Business, aligned its own state-of-the-art career center that I opened, and schools of law, social work, public health, and engineering among others are doing the same.

The Global Community of Information Professionals define the word "collaboration" as "a working practice whereby individuals work together with a common purpose to achieve business benefit."

When I started as an executive director of an Ivy League career center, it was a proud moment. I reached the top of the career services ladder. But again, I found myself with a blank slate. I knew I needed a new and innovative strategic plan, but before I could craft one, I needed a Career Services Alliance.

With all of the changes, I needed to collaborate with my counterparts. Redesigning career centers and aligning them with optimal operations, systems, and processes with the voice of students; was the central driving force of the new decision making. I wanted to know how other top executives were doing it.

So, I aligned some of the top directors all over the U.S. and industry experts I had met at conferences. About 90% of them were receptive. Through one-on-one sessions, we shared ideas, and it became a habit. We always determined next steps and set up a follow up call to solve lingering problems, which led to the introduction of new members who brought new ideas. This group, although informal, still exists. In fact, it has broken into different groups and also categories within career services, including career education, career development, industry and employer relations, career outcomes, operations, technology, marketing, and branding.

In a quickly evolving world, you need a combination of both short-term and long-term connections to remain adaptable. Those people in your life who have seen you fail, bounce back, and succeed are priceless. Like your own family, they have seen you grow into the person you are today. Your alliance begins with these people.

The Power of a Jamaat (Group)

Mentors are so important. They should be a part of your personal board of directors and success alliances. You can also have a team of mentors that can all make up a mastermind group. Mentors help keep you in check, give you pointers, aid you in building contacts, facilitate warm introductions, and offer you practical tips that you can apply in your life quickly. You find mentors everywhere, sometimes in informal meetings.

There are also different layers of mentors and mentoring. Collectively, all of your mentors form your *Circle of Mentors*. Mentor circles might include a *promoter*, someone who puts in a good word for you. It might include an *enabler*, someone who opens a door for you. You may have *points of reference*, those that you list on job applications who can vouch positively for you.

Who do you have readily available to join your mentor circle?

Thinking Outside the Box – Mentor Circles:
The Shortcut to Growth and Confidence

	Name	Title	Organization	Linkedin Url	Location
Promoters					
Enablers					
Pts Of Reference					
Sounding Boards					
Mentors					

Are you looking to make a career change and/or transition?

Consider all possible outcomes, the pros and cons, and list potential sounding boards from your network.

THE SHORTCUT TO GROWTH AND CONFIDENCE

Let's face it, we live in a world of unlimited choices and information, so it's easy to get lost in the mix. Why not find the trailblazers and pioneers, pick their brains, and save yourself from the mistakes they may have made?

Everyone needs a personal board of directors. Mentoring circles are essentially a new spin on a timeless learning technique.

Infographic available for download at 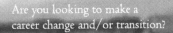www.CareerMastermind.org/Resources

You are unique. Nobody else is you.

Note, a mentor circle is part of your alliance, but is not the same as a personal board of directors—but it can evolve into one, depending on who's in it. The focus of a mentor circle—initially, is your social capital and expanding your network. Later, it's advancing your careers leveraging the insight and resources of the circle.

From your mentoring circles, you will hand-select a personal board of directors, one for each career. Typically, this is a relatively small number, 5 to 7. The number of directors depends on your needs and should align with your goals.

Both mentor circles and personal boards of directors are critical towards forming a powerful Career Mastermind™ Group.

Organic Networking

Organic networking is an important component to building your alliances. It's a byproduct of chaos and happenstance. However, this doesn't mean you just wait to have things happen. You must be proactive, collaborative, and make things happen. You want to "lure change out of hiding."

The job market is a highly competitive space. Facebook receives over 100,000 applications for an entry level position. You are just a number if you rely on applications alone. My old boss and the CEO of the bank used to say, "Every knock on the door is an opportunity waiting." You must recognize opportunities that present themselves to you, even behind clocked doors. You create the key.

Embrace Undercurrents of Opportunity

INSTAGRAM: @RAVAGHRESTAURANTS

One example of networking both strategically and organically is going to talk to someone who meets lots of people daily. Bartenders! Although, I don't drink, I met a bartender at one of my favorite restaurants in New York City, Veselina (Vessy), who worked at Ravagh Persian Cuisine. Boy did she have tact when it came to dealing with angry customers. I kid you not, this is coming from someone with the greatest customer service I have ever personally received. She could keep a smile on her face at all times. This stems from her perseverance and positive story.

Vessy is a self-published author, a Bulgarian immigrant who won an immigration lottery. She had previously worked with organizations dealing with women's rights and has a long list of credentials to boast. She let her passion drive her, and she didn't stop. She wanted to fully leverage all of the resources that were available to her. Quickly, she became a "Master Networker."

Vessy became the friendly new face wherever she went. She had a warm personality that people just gravitated too. After getting accepted to a top-ranked MBA program, her influence and leadership was easily recognizable. She became a senior advisor for the Simon Consulting Student Club. She was also selected to serve as an admissions committee ambassador and helped screen candidates for admission by looking through applications and conducting interviews. Later, she served as the Vice President of Marketing and Communications for the Simon Club Europe, and Vice President of External Affairs for the Simon Dance Club.

Rochester, NY: Vessy tackling her MBA program like a champion.

I recall first meeting Vessy 15 years ago when she was a waitress and hostess at Ravagh Persian Cuisine in Manhattan. She was also a bartender when the place got busy, which was pretty much all the time. As it was known for high quality, consistency, and delicious food, I went there regularly. At the time, Vessy worked multiple jobs, but she always kept a positive mindset and was confident, despite being exhausted. This "hustle" motivated her to constantly make new connections and also prepared her for greater responsibility.

She managed to leap from a position as a bartender to that of an intern at Tesla in San Francisco, before finishing grad school and getting a full-time job in Human Resources at Citibank in New York City.

INSTAGRAM: @CAREERSTRATEGIESNYC

Vessy is now a dear friend of mine and tells her fantastic story wherever she goes. When asked about her success, she cites "enthusiasm, hard work, and the support of my safety net" as the recipe for success. Her safety net is her alliance, and they come from all walks of life. In fact, I became a part of Vessy's alliance early on, and later—her personal board of directors, all over Persian tea! She eventually became a private client for my consulting firm, Career Strategies.

Now, Vessy helps her expanded network find jobs, mentors friends, and is a member of multiple career masterminding groups. She remains to be one of the hardest working individuals I have ever met. Nothing can stop Vessy!

Command Your Own Path

It wasn't unusual for me to receive desperate emails from students. One sent an email that said "PLEASE HELP" in the title, with no resume or text in the body. As I read it, a student named Xitlaly walked through the door. My colleague, Michael Santa Cruz, was conducting a practice interview, and she overheard. Seeing me distracted, and in an effort to help the student who was struggling with composing an answer, she said, "Why don't you say that you took initiative and spearheaded a new project that aligned with your passion and expertise?" In that moment, not only did the student smile in gratitude, but I thought to myself—how empathetic and compassionate she was! She not only had the potential to conduct practice interviews with students; she also anticipated well. Thus, without hesitating, I offered her a job on the spot, and she became our new Career Center Assistant. She accepted, although in shock!

At the time, Xitlaly was friendly but very shy, though as I got to know her, that shyness quickly vanished. From her first day working with the career services department to her last day, I noticed she would always walk through the door and immediately find a way to help, the second she put her purse down.

As I coached her over the years, she did really well. She developed the skills to do resume and cover letter critiques, and redesigned her own resume as an example to others. I asked her why she didn't run for student body president. She said she was too shy, but as she was growing out of her shell, I convinced her that she had nothing to lose. I encouraged her to take full ownership of her career. She did. She ended up running and became more confident during the six months of her campaign. Then she won and was also chosen to be the graduation speaker.

Her story of overcoming her limiting beliefs and shyness really resonated with students and my staff. Following her speech, her network instantly grew overnight, and students, faculty, staff, parents, and alumni were all moved by her words.

After graduation, I referred her to a neighboring career advisor position (one of the perks of working at a career center is warm referrals). She got it and simultaneously began her MBA while working her way up to being a Senior Career Advisor.

This story just goes to show you what an enabler and promoter can do. I simply gave her a chance and believed in her. Then I promoted her, and she took ownership of the rest. You each need to ask yourself, what's holding you back?

The Paradigm of Career Services and Alumni Relations

Amidst of a powerful paradigm shift in career services—it's a sensational time; the importance of proactively coordinating partnerships is more critical than ever. I have always argued that: *There is a goldmine waiting for the first one that finds it in higher education. It's hidden at the intersection of career services and alumni relations.*

Outside our walls is a vibrant campus community, a success culture, much of it built by alumni. They are pivotal to the success of career centers. They help bridge the gap.

Daniel Cohen is the author of *The Mentorship Revolution* and the Founder and Chief Executive Officer of Graduway, the leading provider of alumni networking and mentoring platforms with clients across 58 countries. In his book, he argues that the "Age of Mentorship" has arrived, stating, "Gone are the days when mentoring was the luxury of just the few."

"Graduate YOUR way", I tease him, about the name "Graduway." Isn't that what it's all about?

Having an excellent mentor can assist your professional development and career significantly and is a crucial part of your experience—your way. In order to align one, you must develop very strong interpersonal skills and scale your network using the latest technology. Graduway provides this to over 700 universities with impeccable support. However, what if you are not a student or alumni?

LinkedIn is a great place to build your mentor circles and network. Unfortunately, once you have them, even the most successful mentoring relationships can lose their effectiveness over time. I always ask my staff, "How are we as career professionals supporting the mentorship experience and who are we partnering with?"

The future of career services and alumni relations is one and the same—meaningful engagement. Mentorship is essential to this future, and so is scalability. Career Mastermind™ Groups provide this scale.

What the Experts Say

Once you have built your network and alliance, and have a mentor circle, then what? How do you know when you should move on to another mentor? What's the best way to end a relationship to stay on good terms? After all, you must go through several mentors before finding one worthy of joining your personal board of directors.

Jodi Glickman, the author of *Great on the Job*, once stated, "A good mentoring relationship is as long as it should be and no longer." She goes on to say that there is no use in keeping a mentor-mentee relationship if there is no chemistry or use coming out of it. If you stay in such a professional relationship even though it's not meeting your needs, then you are wasting time mutually. Kathy E. Kram, Shipley Professor in Management at the Boston University School of Management, says that we should not hesitate in breaking off our relationships if they are no longer serving us. In *Strategic Relationships at Work*, Kram encourages us to ask about our own value and what we have learned from our mentor. What is the relationship lacking? What aren't you getting from your mentor? Through inward reflection, you can see what's lacking and potentially reshape the relationship to work better. It may even be the case that your mentor's abilities are not in alignment with what you want or where your career is going. You may need a mentor with more time, for example.

Never presume that your mentor is a mind-reader. If you are not getting what you need, you have to be clear about what you want. Kram puts it eloquently: "People need to educate their mentors, too." Be as direct as possible, explain your challenges and be clear about the counsel you need. However, if you cannot go any further, it may be time to end your professional relationship.

Don't Drag it Out

If you come to the conclusion that the mentor-mentee relationship is not working, there is no point in wasting anyone's time. If this is a formal relationship, then plan a face-to-face meeting or a phone call. Or, it could just fade away. Just ensure that the interactions are not dragged out for the sake of politeness. Only be involved if you can be fully involved. This goes for both the mentees and mentors.

Disengage with Gratitude

"Gratitude is the key to leaving gracefully," says Kram. The first thing you should do is thank your mentor. Tell the person what you have gained from the relationship, including what you have learned, and how your interactions will help you in the future. Focus on what has changed about you, and why your needs are now different. Be positive. You never know what the future holds for you.

Be transparent and direct. Let your mentor know your plans for the future and why these are changing. Don't worry about offending the individual. If you prolong it, they will not be happy either. As Glickman says, "They likely have plenty of other things they can do." If your mentor reacts negatively, listen. You don't even have to agree, just listen and thank them. Then all you need to do is move on.

Play Well in the Sandbox

Connections are fundamental to the modern workplace. There is a strong likelihood that you will meet your former mentor again. Therefore, you will want to keep your professional reputation in good stead. Make sure you can offer assistance if they need it in the future. Your mentor may end up being a peer or a boss, and you might need them again. Keep that relationship intact!

Principles to Remember

Do:

- Give the relationship a chance to change; communicate with your mentor and see if they can adapt.

- Show how much you appreciate your mentor. Thank them.

- Be clear on what you have learned and how you will take this into the future.

Don't:

- Don't stay in the relationship out of obligation or because you feel bad, since this will only be harmful in the long run.

- Don't talk about what's wrong with the relationship. Be positive.

- Don't burn bridges, act as if you will see this person again. Keep the mutual respect there.

Lastly, don't live in a fairy tale where nothing needs to change. Wake up, make it change. Start building your own personal board of directors, it will take time.

How to Align Your Supervisor as a Mentor

Not all supervisors are mentors, and those that are, typically aren't good ones. When the president of a university first hired me, he told me that he was once a director of Career Services. I was in awe. I remember him specifically stating that career services professionals can go anywhere professionally, and that inspired me. I simply asked him, "Will you mentor me?" He just smiled—but he later offered to serve as an ongoing mentor once he saw I was genuine and sincere about it. What a blessing!

I wanted to be his protégé. I took full advantage of it, met with him regularly, and even included him in my 360 degree assessment, a tool that included direct feedback from my subordinates, peers (colleagues), and supervisor(s), as well as a self-evaluation.

It wasn't until a couple years later that my career services mentor told me the real reason he hired me. He said it was my audacious drive to be a visionary in the field and that overshadowed my background in health and finance. As he put it, my commitment to excellence made me stand out, and he respected that. What I didn't realize at the time was that there was a lesson to be learned, and that was self-understanding. This is the cornerstone in career education and development, a tip I'll share with others for the rest of my career. It's difficult to collaborate with others unless you understand yourself.

Having had a number of strong mentors over the years at both public and private universities, I have learned that the biggest mistake we make in our own careers is to try to do it all ourselves. I was isolated at first with all the challenges of strong career outcomes expectations in front of me. I felt the pressure of competition in higher education. Then I began to expand my circle. Collaboration is huge in the field of career development. What I hadn't realized is just how huge it was; it's the art of collaborative leadership that really is the central driving force for the future of our career ecosystem. When it came to the future of work, why didn't we start talking to each other earlier?

Well, once upon a time, career services professionals were afraid to talk to each other. This has continued to evolve with conferences such as the National Association of Colleges and Employers (NACE) and the National Career Development Association (NCDA), among others, but those two specifically have served me well. Perhaps it was the competitive side of the industry that held career development facilitators back from reaching out proactively.

I know, for example, that I didn't want to share the secret of the impressive career outcomes tool "Track-> Forward, Building Forward Momentum." Why? Well, first of all, it was working and we were competing against each other. However, I learned later that you want to share as much as you can, and you will still get your return on investment. Mentoring many other directors of career services helped me become a better mentee, as I understood the process from both ends. Helping others helped me get promoted and noticed. Not only that, but our models were applied on a regional level, and then later scaled on a national level. If they like what they see, they will come back for more, right?

Second, I was still learning the value of networking. What I didn't realize is that I was depriving myself of valuable information and that my intention to "revolutionize" the field would be largely shaped by my shared experiences with other leaders. In other words, collaboration would help me grow further into senior management.

One of the ways my career grew was largely due to my new approach, which essentially focused on building connections. In fact, it helped me build my independent consulting firm that has grown significantly over time. Many career services professionals of varying levels of experience contacted me periodically to share best practices. As aspiring career thought leaders, we need to pick each other's brains or re-think innovative angles we are utilizing. Fortunately, we have now built a career development community nationally. After all, that's what it really comes down to when if you ask the career seeker—a career network of resources and connections.

As my connections grew, my alliance grew, and soon I found myself with several personal boards of directors, each focused on a different purpose. It was from these groups I was able to organize my first formal Career Mastermind™ Group.

TEAM THEME

Moreover, connecting with new people has been fun, and each experience with each client is unique. It has taught me that career coaching is very much about the individual. With each new case, the approach should also be new, tailored for the individual's success. Every individual is different, with different challenges, and different ideas of success. Each must win their struggle as an individual. They all matter.

"Vision without a task is only a dream. A task without a vision is but drudgery. But vision with a task is a dream fulfilled. "

—*Inscription on a church wall in Sussex, England c. 1730*

BONUS: A BRIEF MENTORSHIP CASE STUDY FOR CAREER SERVICES AND ALUMNI RELATIONS

I am proud of what I have accomplished in my career. I have created mentoring programs for startups and college students. I've created mentoring mastermind groups. More specifically, I have worked with mentorship gurus like Mark J. Carter on mentorship programs at both Loyola University Chicago and at the Career Design Lab at Columbia University in New York.

WWW.MARKJCARTER.COM

Meet Mark J. Carter. Two weeks before Mark graduated college, he read *Awaken the Giant Within* by Tony Robbins. After reading it, he realized he didn't want the typical corporate career; he wanted to be in front of people, he wanted to teach and help. He was not just searching for money and success, but also meaning and purpose. So he quit his job as a sales and marketing manager at a printing company, and went back to waiting tables so he could have a flexible schedule. He also wanted a way of earning quick money for things like rent and food.

It was in his DNA to seek out people that were smarter. He knew that he would always learn and benefit from surrounding himself with smarter people. He had teachers who taught him how to build lesson plans; the University of Michigan's head basketball coach taught him how to collaborate with teams; CEOs taught him that collaboration is integral to running a successful business; and multi-platinum musicians and famous actors shared their excellent stories, too. Over the years, he has benefitted from hundreds of formal interviews and thousands of conversations on collaboration. He has spent endless hours reading biographies and autobiographies to find patterns in the behaviors of successful and intelligent people. They make up his own case study that later resulted in writing his new book *Idea Climbing*™.

During Mark's journey, he's been fortunate to collaborate on exciting projects such as:

1. Running book launches and speaking tours for bestselling business authors.

2. Working with the Founder of TED to create an event with 50 world class luminaries.

3. Creating the branding statement and heading up marketing strategy for the world's largest chapter of Meeting Professionals International (MPI).

4. Interviewing senior Dell executives and sponsors at the news desk at Dell World (now Dell EMC World).

5. Creating marketing and outreach programs for the world's largest improv festival.

6. Creating the inaugural mentoring program for the Quinlan School of Business at Loyola University Chicago.

7. Helping co-create and co-design the mentoring program for Columbia University's Career Design Lab.

Before Mark and I teamed up at Columbia University to launch a Mentorship Mastermind Group, we piloted a supplement to the Mentorship Program at Loyola University Chicago. Greg Costanzo, the Assistant Director of Career Education, wanted to take things up a notch. Together, we wanted to assess if students were "on cue" with their careers, so we called our mentorship program the "Q" Mentorship Program. For us, mentorship was about giving back, regardless of whether you were a mentor or mentee. It was about making an impact. So I called the supplement to the program: **#ImpactLives**. We teamed up with Mark and built an online mentorship crash course using innovative software.

This course was transformative—we integrated it as a pilot with our undergraduate career development course. As this was a required course, we knew that this integration would ensure that 100 percent of the undergraduate students would be aligned with a mentor before graduation!

Mark believes that this course helps avoid the mentoring challenges of, "What do we talk about?", and answers with, "How can I best help my student?" Carter further breaks it down into benefits, opportunity, and results, stressing the importance of the interactive component. According to Mark, the benefits include:

1) Saving time: Students have prep work, so they show up prepared for their meetings, knowing what to ask and how to follow up.

2) Consistent communication: *Champions* (Mentors) can log in and view students' comments and find out what they need help with before and in-between meetings.

3) Support throughout the program: Champions have direct communication with the course instructor and the person who built the training so you can ask questions, get help with any problems you encounter, and share feedback.

The importance of the interactive supplement:

4) Students crave advice and connections; alumni want to be involved with their alma mater, and career centers want to be the bridge and provide opportunities for everyone.

The problem is that there's no vehicle for everyone to accomplish those goals together, no clear strategies, and there are time restrictions for all three groups. This supplement solves those problems for everyone.

The opportunity:

Learning meaningful content through videos and podcasts, students will have access to guidance that relates to their classwork and professional life anytime from virtually anywhere. The content will feature interviews with alumni and create the final product with the team. It's important to create engaging conversations instead of just asking canned questions.

The key points about the content and each interview are:

1) Each video or podcast interview will feature a challenge that the alumni faced in their career, how they overcame it, and what projects they are currently working on. This creates an easy way for alumni to get involved without leaving their office or home because interviews are recorded remotely.

2) The content gives the students the real-world tips they need and gives listeners an opportunity to reach out to the alumni to help them with their projects, or offer connections to people they need to know.

3) Each video provides guidance for students, and the opportunity for listeners and alumni to collaborate—which will create a stronger community and consistent communication between staff, faculty, students, and alumni.

The results:

The online course supplement to the Q Mentorship Program is designed to:

1) Build communities of engaged alumni to support programs and create resources for the school.

2) Attract new students and retain current students by helping them advance their careers.

3) Get more press and community awareness about what the university is doing to help its students.

The Solution: A supplemental coaching platform that will provide a system for students and mentors:

1) Students are provided with a mentoring framework that walks them through the process from pre-meeting to follow-up.

2) Mentors obtain a framework to ask the right questions and offer actionable action items instead of just stories about their lives.

3) Faculty, staff, and stakeholders have a way to check-in online with everyone in the program, measure their progress, and offer recommendations when needed.

Once we had this very important layer added, we knew were ready to change the course of mentorship. We launched it! Sure, there were bumps in the road, but we overcame them. We realized that self-selection (with some oversight by the instructor and mentorship coordinator) was the preferable course of action based on our student culture.

Below, I describe how it works.

Mentees:

a) Submit top three choices for mentors by the second week of the semester (first week for summer session). Initiate conversation with mentor after instructor has made assignments.

Students are expected to drive this program—meaning the students take an active role in contacting mentors to plan the meeting schedules:

b) Meet at least twice with the mentor during the semester, in person (preferably), over the phone, or virtually (other contact methods with mentor are determined based on mutual agreement).

The students are asked to create a five-minute presentation with the following criteria:

a) Summarize the content of the mentorship sessions and specify the nature of your meetings, such as an informational interview or externship.

b) Reflect on the discussions you had and how these discussions will inform your own career choices.

c) Clarify the role that ethical behavior, social responsibility, and reflective practice play in your mentor's career(s).

So what makes a good mentor? Mentors that:

a) Are willing to assist with the personal and professional development of a student and provide feedback to the career center.

b) Are able to meet individually (in person, phone, or virtually) with a student at least twice during the semester.

c) Are skilled at interpersonal communication.

d) Are highly regarded within their field for their integrity and professionalism.

The mentor decides how many mentees to manage.

The Matching and Selection Process

Many higher education professionals ask me where they should focus on when it comes to mentorship. They ask about the "how," but forget about the "why." I tell them, "It's simple, focus on those individuals that want to give back." In other words, start with those that are the most excited, for example, *graduates of the last decade*. I call them the "GOLD Board." I formalized this group and they became our strongest ambassadors, our strongest promoters, and our strongest influencers. Why? They were the most engaged. As a result, they were also our strongest (and most popular) mentors.

Now, about the mentees and how to pair them. The secret is to empower mentees to choose—*the same way they should be choosing their careers.*

Students select their preferred mentors and submit a ranked list of their top three choices. The course instructor then goes through all submissions and notifies students who their mentors will be, trying his or her best to assign them their top choices. Keep in mind that the instructor must manage the mentor/student ratio in order to create a sustainable caseload for the mentors.

The Q Mentorship Program, together with Loyola's Career Preparation course (BSAD 220), provided an excellent opportunity for students to learn about the world of business from experienced professionals. Mentors are Loyola University Chicago alumni and "friends of Loyola" who are business professionals in the Chicago area.

After one semester of this pilot program, all students aligned with a mentor, and both the mentee and mentor had an overall 90% or higher satisfaction rate. 97% of students reported positive outcomes during pendency of presentations given in class and 14% of students were offered an internship as a result of the program. 50% percent of students received a tour of the mentor's place of work and/or an externship experience.

Though not a required part of the presentation, all students reported that their mentors believed Loyola's core values figured prominently into daily work and life.

Mark, Greg, and I made a good team and look forward to many more collaborations. We love telling our stories about engaging the engaged!

What's Next?

Before expanding the program at the graduate level, we explored how the program differed for undergraduate and graduate students. It was available at the graduate level, but is was largely self-directed. We explored questions such as, what about reverse-mentorship at the graduate level, where organizations choose to work with students via their capstone courses? How can alumni mentor other alumni? May alumni post career opportunities via platforms like Graduway? The answer is, "yes!" What about international students? So many questions still remained!

So this bring us to today. Loyola has now rolled it out to multiple career education sections and the program lives on.

The future of mentorship programs is exciting. One must think of mentoring not just in the short term, but long term as well. What happens beyond the program? I'd like to see these relationships continue beyond a course or program. The opportunities and return on investment are endless. Students attend universities not just for degrees, education, and experience, but for social capital. This social capital can be more worthwhile than anything else they obtain.

Networking is not supposed to be easy. Thus, everything we do to facilitate that experience is what it's all about. Demystifying the mentorship relationship is the end goal. Teaching students to manage their responsibilities and their relationships are the means.

What's your motivation?

CHAPTER 10: CAREER MASTERMIND™ GROUPS — CHAMPIONING CAREERS

◆◗◆

"The 'master mind' principle cannot obtain where perfect harmony does not prevail."
—*Napoleon Hill*

apoleon Hill defines mastermind groups as "the coordination of knowledge and effort between two or more people who work towards a definite purpose in a spirit of harmony."

Although the concept may come across as almost majestic, it has been trending for quite some time. Silicon Valley has also seen a consistent and upward rise in the popularity of the term, especially in entrepreneurial and start-up business circles.

CAREER AND LIFE HACK #17

Surround yourself with positive people who know what they are doing.

Overwhelming evidence has demonstrated the effectiveness of both research-based and informal mastermind groups. In some studies—the impact can be twice as effective. Just think of study groups, they are crucial, aren't they? They were for me back in college when it came to some of the more difficult science courses. What about you? Have you found them useful?

Benjamin Franklin passionately believed in group efficacy. He mentioned it in his autobiography as a "club of mutual improvement," which he called "The Junto." Junto, as some of us know, means "together" in Spanish. Franklin stated, *"We met on Friday evenings. The rules that I drew up required that every member, in his turn, should produce one or more queries on any point of Morals, Politics, or Natural Philosophy, to be discussed by the company."*

Do you know people whose skill sets you can bring together? A Junto where you can all help elevate each other? It is critical to remember that bringing people together is important. We are stronger as collective minds rather than just a single one. You should not undervalue the effectiveness of a collective.

"Tell me and I forget, teach me and I may remember, involve me and I learn."
—*Benjamin Franklin*

There are Two Sides to Every Bridge

A mastermind group starts with two people mentoring each other. This forms a team, with mutual benefits. They then bring others into the fold, vetting them and determining the necessary ingredients to add. A Career Mastermind™ Group can take many shapes and forms. It can be focused on creative strategies in tech, digital identity and development, social media, building your network, career transitioning, or advancement.

Brooklyn, NY: The Brooklyn Bridge

Another popular focus is entrepreneurship or intrapreneurship—something we don't talk enough about. Intrapreneurship is the practice of applying entrepreneurial skills, creativity, and approaches within an established company.

Every Career Mastermind™ is both an entrepreneur (with one or more clients) and an intrapreneur.

The list is endless. In fact, my Career Design Lab even hosts a Bioethics Student and Alumni Career Mastermind™ Group that consists of doctors, nurses, and lawyers.

Catalyst Groups

Think of a mastermind group as a catalyst group. You celebrate successes and hold one another accountable. You also help one another climb out of career ditches or challenges. We all have professional contacts on LinkedIn, but how many of those are real relationships? A mastermind group is a *focused* group with mutual support and benefits.

Members of a mastermind group are called *masterminds.* A mastermind's experience varies by a specific number of years, some with more experience, and some with less. They help each other brainstorm, solve problems, come up with new products, and deal with difficult challenges. They pick each other's brains.

Mastermind groups can be as formal and structured, or as casual and loose as the group prefers—but in general, most groups involve each person discussing a problem they're having, and the other members chiming in with ideas to help. They also hold each other accountable, which is a major theme and requirement, distinguishing it from less formal groups.

Here are some benefits to a Career Mastermind™ Group and how members may lean on one another for career and industry insight:

Accountability: Proactive participation in an exclusive like-minded group that targets specific career goals.

Social Capital: Other members and yourself—each member benefits from the network of the other members. There are lots of "warm handoffs" and/or warm introductions. Each member vouches for the other, promotes them, and introduces the other members to the right or necessary people (the decision makers).

Group Mentorship: Members don't just benefit from only one mentor at a time, but from multiple mentors—providing multiple perspectives. If one may not have insight on a particular approach, another may be more helpful and vice versa.

Success Alliance: You may encounter a new business partner through this group, or you may meet the right person. You may have similar goals, so you can collaborate on achieving them. It's like going to the gym with a training buddy. How many of us could use a spot on the bench press or use a partner when it comes to throwing medicine balls? I know I can.

Shared Learning: By being vulnerable and sharing failures, the whole group learns and supports the "bounce back." Together, the team and you will solve problems, allowing for additional creativity to overcome obstacles.

Elevating the Bar: With strong action plans, defined goal setting, and an accountability process, members execute more efficiently. In other words, you need to bring your personal business plan to the table! This leads to setting and inspiring new goals and expectations, adjusting existing ones, as well as individually and collectively pushing dreams and aspirations further.

A Career Mastermind™ Group doesn't need to last for years, although a longer-running mastermind group has a plethora of benefits and is a testament to the value of *depth over breadth*. The experience associated with these groups may be life-changing, powerful, and a driving force— propelling personal and professional growth.

The Caravan of Mastermind Travelers

In early 2018, I formed a new Career Mastermind™ Group focused on transitioning from higher education to consulting (full-time). Having been a consultant in the past, I knew that I would likely be a consultant in the future. The time was ripe to continue my journey—and there were many others interested in joining this "Master" caravan.

My Career Design Lab team was also interested in understanding how to make the same transition. They, too, had long-term goals and wanted to learn how to begin branding themselves. They also wanted to fully capture all of the skills necessary to be successful. This included understanding the lifestyle—not having a consistent paycheck, building content and frameworks for people and organizations, and the people skills needed.

As a team, we invited those that had already made the journey *home*, and learned about their struggles and their wins—as we reflected on our travels and what lay ahead.

The Mastermind Experience

I remember my structural biochemistry course at U.C.L.A.—there must have been 300 people in that auditorium! I could never get a seat, even when I was fifteen minutes early. Office hours were always booked, and there was little hope of developing a meaningful relationship with my professor. I remember thinking to myself that I could kiss my chances of having a point of reference for medical school goodbye. My experience was anything but positive.

However, my mastermind experiences were a complete 180 compared to those memories. The number of members never exceeded double digits, and the groups were full of meaningful relationships and memories. Just as small classrooms have benefits, so do small groups. I not only got to know each member beyond what they did professionally, but our relationships grew as we grew.

The Stronger the Relationships, the Stronger the Mastermind Groups

Mastermind groups are only as strong as the relationships within them. At our Career Design Lab, we open and facilitate Student and Alumni Career Mastermind™ Groups with a fact sheet. This allows for informative introductions covering interests, backgrounds, needs and goals—and what they can contribute. I highly recommend this for any mastermind group, including yours.

Relationships formed in mastermind groups tend to be very powerful and candid. There is no sugar-coating of anyone's given situation, and you see the good, the bad, and the ugly. As a result, a nondisclosure agreement is typically recommended or requested.

Mastermind groups should be welcoming and descriptive. Below is a brief example of what I send to students and alumni. You may apply a similar approach.

Thank you for your interest in joining our Student and Alumni Career Mastermind™ Group. This is a unique benefit offered to our students and alumni, and the intention is that your participation will support you in your career and/or business growth. A Mastermind Group provides a confidential, safe, constructive environment in which to examine professional activities, decisions, goals, and problems.

Each group is made up of approximately four to six like-minded individuals determined to achieve personal and professional goals, who also recognize that they can make significantly more progress when working together rather than alone.

Participating in a Mastermind Group can provide members some of the following benefits:

· Exchange of diverse ideas, creative solutions, and best practices for conducting successful job searches and modern-day business challenges

· Increase in members' professional networks

· Support and member accountability

· Progress towards career goal achievement—more so than one would have if doing it alone

There are a few rules of participation we would like to ensure you are comfortable with:

· Mastermind groups work best when everyone participates, and active participation by every member is necessary for the group's success

· Information is shared confidentially among participating members

· *Participants are expected to schedule their own meetings, no less than once a month (meetings can take place in person, over the phone, or virtually)*

We welcome you and encourage you to meet at our Times Square office!

For those members participating with less experience in mastermind groups, I provide a Goal Planner and Tracker Form. Feel free to leverage it if you are organizing a group, or use it for yourself if you are participating in one.

This is the template. Please duplicate the tab to create your own. Rename the tab with your name. Once duplicated as your own, you can remove this row.						
[Your Name]'s Goal Planner & Tracker						
* the dates are the deadlines						
** Review can be in your preferred format (i.e. rating, yes/no, etc)						
*** The timeframe follows university terms considering the nature of university operations						
2 week	9/14/18	review	9/28/18	review		review
Short-Term (< 3 months)	11/28/18	review		review		review
Long-Term (3-6 months)	12/31/18	review				

This tool will help your members keep track of their deliverables and action items *on and before* each subsequent meeting. It helps members understand the details pertaining to each individual in order to assist them better—*and* recruit new members appropriately.

Build Your Dream Team

The application process is a crucial piece of building your Career Mastermind™ Group and earning your place on a dream team of success. These groups will allocate resources you never imagined, provide accountability for your life and business goals, and enable access to ideas that can only result from the combined intelligence of a group of people committed to helping you succeed.

At the end of the day, this is a team, so you want to work with people who will cooperate and share synergies. The success of mastermind groups depends on your level of commitment and integrity.

A Mastermind Group is an Invite-Only Community

It's important to note that a mastermind group is not a club or affinity group. It's a private community with private benefits. You must be invited to the group. While I worked at UBS Financial Services Inc., I was part of a socially responsible investing affinity group. Although there are many similarities to mastermind groups, with affinity groups you could come and go as you please without any real repercussions.

An affinity group pursues a shared interest or common goal, either formally or informally. By contrast, mastermind groups are more formal in terms of attendance and accountability. Just as I've used "bridge jobs" to land next jobs, these groups may be good stepping stones to help you prepare for success in a mastermind group.

Groups like Alcoholics Anonymous have been successful because they join people with similar struggles or who feel marginalized. They need a safe space where they can be open and vulnerable, and find solutions together. Mastermind groups serve this purpose and much more.

Start Where You Are

Since I founded the Career Design Lab in summer 2017, I have been able to reimagine and reinvent not only the career center, but what it really means to be a career coach. *What we do is so much more than career services—it's really career and life design.*

In a relatively short time, I have grown an impactful team that has become a Career Mastermind™ Group in its own right. I didn't plan this mastermind group, but it happened. You too will have chaos and happenstance. Embrace it, it's all part of the process.

My team and I have a tall order in a tough economy. Career readiness is by no means easy for our students, and it too, is a process that takes time. My Director of Career Education and Development, Diane Spizzirro, helps me champion this movement to close the gap between the perception of employers and the reality of the talent of many students once they graduate. According to our surveys, they didn't match, but now we are bridging that "Career Readiness IQ" gap. Each of you must define your goals, both short-term and long-term, for each group you build or participate in.

Ask yourself: What do you believe in? I believe in bridging new lines of communication and collaboration in an opportunity arena that I call is an *ecosystem rather than place*. If I had to describe what we do on a daily basis, distilling all of the activities, coaching, events, workshops, meetings, etc., it would filter down to two things: 1) helping to build dreams, and 2) witnessing the impact. What do you really do?

You will need to be solution-oriented. You will also need to visualize the end game via your game plan. For example, by developing new best practices and providing a nimble approach to career and professional development, I am fostering a diverse, university-wide, global career culture that celebrates and breathes success.

You must understand what you are truly after, and the "why?" in it all. For example, I am deeply committed to coaching career-seekers who will strengthen our global business system. What are you committed to?

Expand Your Borders

This year, with the launch of our San Francisco location, we have become a bi-coastal career center. This is revolutionary. Don't be afraid to expand your horizons.

Our second most dense alumni population was located in San Francisco. So it only made sense for us to go there and build an innovative integrated center—right in the middle of it. Think outside the box, think differently.

My team's weekly core mastermind group focused on problem solving issues for upcoming graduates. For example, 80 percent of jobs are not listed. So that makes the search a lot harder for our students. What's the lesson here? Your connections and community will make the difference. Build yours and network.

My job is simple: I match top talent (our students and alumni) with top employers—that's it. Their job is to look for a job. What's yours?

Bicoastal Career Design Labs

The Career Design Lab is a new vision for defining and developing careers in the 21st Century. It is what I'm most proud of in my career. What is your proudest moment?

It's a brave new world for the field of career services. Let me ask: What should a Career Mastermind™ Group do for you? Well, it can take you to that next level. It can make you a champion.

Life is About Moments

During your mastermind groups, things will get personal. You will need to be vulnerable at times. You will need to be open. Share your struggles as necessary for others to understand what you are going through.

Every time I say this phrase, "Life is about moments," it resonates. Life *is* about moments, so relive them. It's in decisive moments that your destiny is shaped. Or someone else's. Moments matter. Moments pass you by. Moments bring truth, moments bring falsehood. Moments can be transformational. If you seize them, moments can make you courageous, and if not, moments can leave you in regret. Moments change people and change lives.

"Never refuse an invitation, never resist the unfamiliar, never fail to be polite, and never outstay the welcome. Just keep your mind open and suck in the experience— and if it hurts, you know what? It's probably worth it."

—Alex Garland, The Beach

For college grads, many of those moments happen during their college life cycle. Through those experiences, they begin to understand how to become career-ready for their areas of interest. "Career Readiness" is the Door to Positive Career Outcomes. What door will you unlock?

Wayfinders Must Have a Map

Every mastermind member is a wayfinder, and every wayfinder follows a map. Do you have yours? You have a compass. You might even have your "Z"—that is, if your compass is functioning properly. Imagine you are a traveler in a desert and align your moral compass with your North Star. For me, it was a little more *northeast* than north, but once I found it, I never lost sight of it.

Here are my top ten tips to help you draw your map:

1. You should first ask yourself, "Why am I pursuing this new path?" One of the biggest concerns people have when switching or trying to start their careers is fear of the unknown. As the Boy Scouts say, "Be prepared!" It's important that you fully understand what the new career path truly entails before sending résumés in every direction.

2. Many people look for jobs with resumes that are not career or major-specific for long periods of time and have little luck. Thus, they give up or get discouraged, then begin looking for alternatives. Make sure your resume and cover letter are targeted. Also, connect early on with individuals at the organization you want to work for via LinkedIn or a platform like Graduway.

3. Job shadowing, also known as externships, is underrated. Externships are similar to internships, but for a much shorter duration. These opportunities range from one day to several weeks and offer participants "a career glimpse" into what it's actually like working in a particular career field. They also provide professional contacts for future networking. Visit the organizations you are interested in.

4.   You are always more marketable to employers when you are working and have strong references. By leaving a position prematurely, not only do you jeopardize your organization with a lack of a succession plan, but you may also burn bridges. Additionally, you may create gaps in your employment. Create impact, package it, and know how to valuate and showcase it.

5.   You must discover and uncover "career readiness," the hidden skill set that helps you develop employment-seeking competencies that better prepare you for the competitive job search. This skill set of career readiness, combined with a quality degree program or the right experience, will better position you for a meaningful career outcome.

6.   We all want jobs that are meaningful but often don't have a clue where to begin. Focus on finding a career, not simply a job. There is a larger framework that must be understood. Consult the three steps of the career development process: 1) Self-assessments—"Who am I?"; 2) Career exploration—"Where am I going?"; and 3) Action plan—"How do I get there?"

7.   Success means something different to every individual. Ask yourself the question "Who is managing your career?" If the answer is that you are, then the next question is "How?" Do you have a next step in mind, and if not, why not?

For these kids, "success" is saving dolphins—when I was in the second grade, I was fascinated by them myself! In fact, I used to hide in the corner of the library (my favorite place to be before I became the King of Freeze Tag) and look at pictures of them. I loved learning about them. Then, I would hide my favorite books so nobody else could check them out!

Worldwide: Two very brave souls making a difference

8. You don't have to start at the bottom if you switch career paths. Leverage and focus on your transferable skills. Many professional skills are transferable and will entice employers because they can be leveraged in many ways.

9. It's important to understand how social media can impact your career aspirations. Consider how it relates to your career profile and brand—how it provides opportunities and challenges for you as you strive to create a personal brand that is both authentic and professional.

10. Build a consistent and effective feedback loop. A Career Mastermind™ Group that meets monthly is ideal for this and an individual self-check at the end of each day.

"I think it's very important to have a feedback loop, where you're constantly thinking about what you've done and how you could be doing it better."

—*Elon Musk, Mastermind Entrepreneur*

Collaboration, not Competition

From "side hustle" to "Life's Work," the Gig Economy is surfacing quietly. What begins as a gig or side hustle now may later bloom into a full-blown career.

It is essential to keep in mind that the careers of this emerging sharing economy are very different from the typical workday job. It is not a question of finding work, but making strides towards your life's work. Many young people are embracing the "do what you love" philosophy and are unlikely to do anything less. People are increasingly viewing work as a way to pursue meaning and explore the perimeters of their creativity, passion, and talent.

This could revolutionize how we work, reconciling secure and fulfilling employment. This is what a career is all about: working on things that are meaningful *with* like-minded people whom we respect, and finding a way to have happiness and joy even in the day-to-day.

"Alone we can do so little; together we can do so much."

—*Helen Keller*

The Career Mastermind™ Group

The next thing you need to know about a Career Mastermind™ Group is its theme—it's all about Radical Collaboration! *Radical Collaboration* is a highly interactive learning lab focused on attitudes, trust, relationship building, and transformation.

The Student and Alumni Career Mastermind™ Lens

Once you know this, the next thing you need to know is the general structure. Here's how the Career Design Lab: Career Masterminds Model works:

1) What is a Career Design Lab Mastermind Group?

- A group of like-minded individuals determined to achieve personal and professional goals, who also recognize that they can make significantly more progress when working together rather than alone

2) Why join one?

- Exchange ideas and best practices for conducting successful job searches, and possibly job leads
- Increase each other's professional networks.
- To support each other and hold each member accountable

- Serve as sounding boards

- Make substantial progress towards career goal achievement—more so than one would have if doing it alone

3) Who can join?

- Enrolled M.S. students in the School of Professional Studies and alumni

4) Who facilitates?

The Career Design Lab Managers for both NY and SF help facilitate the logistical formation of the Student and Alumni Career Mastermind™ Groups. However, we want students to take full ownership and be empowered, so we will not be at every meeting. These groups tend to consist of students and alumni that share the following characteristics:

- Self-motivation and discipline

- Enrolled in the same master's program (not required)

- Share similar career goals (e.g., seeking full-time employment vs. summer internships)

- Looking for employment in a particular industry

- Are at similar stages in their careers (e.g., entry level, senior, executive, transitioning, etc.)

5) What kind of mastermind groups will the Career Design Lab manage?

- Program-specific (i.e. Applied Analytics)

- Mentorship

- Digital-transformation

- Alumni

- Career transitioning and/or advancement

- Other: TBD

6) *Who else can be added to the group? (varying levels of experience)*

- Current grads (<6 months post-graduation)

- Alumni (>6 months post-graduation)

- Recent hires

- Employers

- Mentors

- Faculty

- Industry leaders

- Staff

7) *How many students can join?*

- Twelve persons max (initially), including facilitator(s); so ten students including facilitators (CDL staff)

- Once two people join, the group is active and the first meeting is scheduled

8) *When are applications due?*

- Applications are due at the beginning of each graduating term's month (Oct, Feb, and May) on the first of the month—members can only join following these periods if their application is approved.

- Please allow two weeks for processing and issuing a response

9) How often do members meet, and where?

- 1x/month or biweekly is recommended, however, depending on your priority analysis it may be weekly

- Meetings will take place in person at the CDL creative space, online, or through Zoom, on or off campus

- CDL welcomes and encourages all Mastermind Groups to meet at our office in Times Square

- Two no-shows for any reason disqualifies you from the group; a written excuse must be submitted in writing to the Career Mastermind™ Coordinator

10) What does the application entail?

- Students must submit an application that includes a statement of purpose (no more than one page, double-spaced)

- Students must answer the question: "What makes you a great candidate to be a CDL Student and Alumni Career Mastermind™?"

What does it cost?

- Free

What else would I be expected to do?

- A Canvas Group will be created and managed by CDL, but will be collectively owned by the group members, where resources are shared and progress/updates towards goals are recorded

- Effective ownership on creating and sharing short-term (three months or less) and long-term goals (six months+)

- Serve as an "Accountability Partner" to one other member—reminding one another, checking in, and holding one another accountable

- Share accomplishments in the first ten minutes of the meetings

- Hot Seats (participate); this will be on a rotation basis and be focused on collectively problem-solving each other's challenge

Although you may not be a student or an alumni, the goal of sharing this structure is to help you form your own group based on your own specific and desired goals. This group has been optimized for the Career Design Lab and for students in graduate programs in professional studies. However, your group will differ in context and number. The important aspect is that the group reflects on the established individuals and collective goals of its members.

Staying in the Loop

Members of mastermind groups must be informed about other members. This can be by progress updates that include news, recent results, big wins or losses, and challenges. Priorities are assessed, and in some cases, adjusted based on the expertise of the group. These are used to align new expectations. Lessons learned are also very helpful in these discussions.

MANHATTAN, NY: Focused

Are You Ready to Become a Career Mastermind™?

"Bridge jobs" and "bridge builders" can be your greatest asset.

Who you know determines your success, and this can help you take that next step. For example, when I was in financial services, we all had our "go-to" person—if not multiple. Mine was my CPA, Mr. Khan, he was excellent. Mr. Khan was a community man—someone you would see at all of the events with a good cause. He knew when people were in need and why. He was a God-fearing man, and full of empathy. He knew everyone. This was partially because he always went out of his way to greet people he didn't know. He did this because he was friendly, and also because he was a "bridge builder" in the sense that he brought people together like a mastermind facilitator would. He turned out to be my most consistent referral resource. He was a valuable go-to person, but also a friend.

One thing Mr. Khan taught me is that empathy is key to building successful relationships with clients. It will also be key in your pursuit of career masterminding.

I reaped the fruits of my networking labor when I managed to land my current Executive Director position, one of the highest positions in my field. It took three organizations to get there, including my previous and most recent position. That position or "Bridge Job" allowed me to take my career to the next level. Who would have known?

Every job helps you build new bridges. Each member of your mastermind group will be a bridge to a new opportunity and a new direction.

Create Impact

Everything has come full circle in my life to this point: from graduation on Columbia's College Walk fifteen years ago, to my speech on "greater purpose" at Low Library last year.

As Boris Becker once said, "Life moves in small circles. You win some matches and you lose some." This may seem obvious, of course, but it's a way of accepting defeat, gracefully. Tennis is a mental game against the self. It takes self-awareness, determination, and confidence.

When you are the CEO of your own career, you must make sure to add value in every role you undertake. This will improve your reputation and your skills. Once you feel that you have changed and influenced the working culture positively, you can move forward and take on other responsibilities.

What matters is creating impact everywhere you go. A Career Mastermind™ Group will help you do just that.

Accountability + Motivation Leads to Happiness

All of these lessons over the years have helped me become a *Master of my Career*. They will also help you grow similarly. They will enable you to become your own Career Mastermind™.

Remember: This is what you must do *before* you can help others champion their careers. *You must first champion your path.*

What Is the Number One Goal of a Mastermind?

Let's ask the Founder of Masterminds.org, Jullien Gordon. In the photo below, Jullien is pointing to the goal in a small, private mastermind group session he hosted for my team.

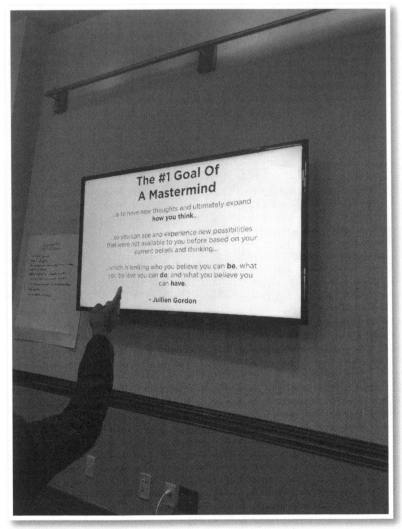

FACULTY HOUSE, COLUMBIA UNIVERSITY: Jullien Gordon
pointing to the goal of a mastermind group

Career Masterminds don't complain. They are "go-getters." They don't spend hours regretting the mistakes they made. They live each day like a new day, take risks they didn't take before, and choose to be different because it's more interesting and fun. *They build teams to achieve the unachievable.*

As a Career Mastermind™, you are able to:

- Catalyze hypothesis-driven self-reflection and the intentional, personalized exploration of the future of your meaningful work.

- Foster substantive engagement between your group members, including alumni, to support the process of career exploration and connecting.

- Use your success alliance's evolving interests to create opportunities that didn't exist before.

- Create a career culture and a transformative experience around you, wherever you go—*with grit.*

- Experience life the way it is supposed to be experienced: life is meant to be lived.

So what is the new and true definition of a Career Mastermind™? It's no different than a Life Mastermind—both are intrinsically driven if you fully have understood their essence.

It's indescribable. In each waking moment, Career and Life Masterminds know what is concealed in plain sight. Animated forces inspiring them to love each calling that they poetically walk and enjoying them all with the same level of passion and vigor.

"Poetry is an awareness of the world, a particular way of relating to reality."
—Andrei Tarkovsky

Cultivate Your Dreams

Career Masterminds are dreamers. Since the beginning of mankind, dreams have intrigued us. They have guided us or warned us. Yet we still struggle to interpret them. The philosophy of dreams explores our fears, desires, anxieties, and hopes. Some dreams are confusing and seem completely unrelated to our everyday life. But they ultimately have meaning.

Whether you dream for seconds, minutes, days, or years, dreams contain valuable information about our strengths, opportunities, and why we do the things that we do.

Today's dreams hold answers to tomorrow's obstacles. Never stop dreaming.

It's What You Do in the Dash of Life

Every time I go to the graveyard to visit my father, I look at his tombstone. The tombstone has the date the person was born, a dash, and then the date they passed away. Focus on that dash, master your life.

My hope is that this book has successfully helped you dream while being awake—helping you reflect on who you are and where you want to go, and that it will help you apply a nimble approach towards the pathways that bring you joy.

Read and share the book with your friends, family, and those that teach career development, whether it's at school, your college, or university. Share it at book clubs and social gatherings, with anyone and everyone who is interested in partaking on a path towards *a new career and life vision.*

As for now, congratulations on getting this far! My vision now is to take this concept of masterminds and build Career Mastermind™

communities—making them more powerful, loyal, diverse, and global. I would like you to join the Career Mastermind™ Community. Find out what, how, and why we do what we do here: (www.CareerMastermind.org)

Join Forces

Career Masterminds listen quietly to the seeds of sentience. Join the movement, the revolution is coming.

We are all just sculpting through time, and each journey only leads to new beginnings.

We all have a contribution to make; what will yours be?

**CAREER
DESIGN
LAB**

COLUMBIA
UNIVERSITY

BONUS: A BRIEF LEADERSHIP GUIDE FOR FUTURE CAREER SERVICES PRACTITIONERS

The model of career services is always changing. Some argue that in 10 years we won't need live career services personnel—that virtual advising via online media platforms will provide all of the career coaching information we need. I disagree, as most people lean towards an integrated model. I've learned that resourceful and informed connectors are the catalysts for change. Mastermind groups help us scale that positive change.

Why is a model like that important, one might ask? The answer is simple. Employability is larger than a career services department.

Remove the walls and open the doors to your resources. We did exactly that, inviting the National Association of Colleges and Employers (NACE) community to our Career Design Lab. That's right, we hosted their November 2018 Face2Face event. We welcomed career and industry leaders from across the country—examining trends and predictions for recruiting. We spent a half-day with college recruiting and career services colleagues from all over the U.S. to discuss what's happening, what's coming, and what we can do about it. NACE executive leadership shared trend data and insights to spur discussion, while we presented on best practices in career services during lunch.

Many directors of career services in many different kinds of universities contact me after hearing about the Career Design Lab and ask, "Hassan, how did you do it? And how did you do it so quickly"? They speak to me as if I have made history or as if what I accomplished was revolutionary. I explain to them that as they explore their current career services model, it will become clear that they need a new identity. Yes, career centers need buzz worthiness to rethink their role as a team. You are the litmus test for students. You are their hope, their life coach, and in many cases, the only one who believes in them (sometimes more than they believe in themselves).

You also need happy employees. What is success for your team, and what inspires them? After all, if people are happy, they perform better. I remember joking with other directors that a future metric to track career outcomes will soon be "happily employed." Well, meaningful work is trending, right? So we need to define *meaningful* as well as *happy*. I read an article titled "Creating Sustainable Performance" in the Jan-Feb 2012 issue of *The Harvard Business Review* that stated:

"In our research into what makes for a consistently high-performing workforce, we've found good reason to care: Happy employees produce more than unhappy ones over the long term."

Thus, what's it going to take to motivate the team of the future? That's the question that each of you must ask. What else will it take to be a state-of-the-art career center?

Here are my top ten elements:

1. Collaboration with career thought leaders.

2. You need a strong mission, shared vision, and purpose.

3. You need the right people on your team. Passion and compassion are required; a feeling of ownership and empowerment—in other words, a sense of belonging for each team member.

4. Branding statement. Just like managing your own identity and brand, your career center is a brand.

5. Re-conceptualization of your career services model from concept to delivery.

6. Career outcomes focus that builds a visible and measurable success culture.

7. Robust strategic plan that is scalable and measurable, and that also leverages the latest technology/resources.

8. High performance operations that reflect synergy. A process manual that is a living document and that invites process improvements systematically; strength and autonomy, shared responsibility, and the ability to be creative, take risks, and introduce novel concepts.

9. Tailored and innovative programs geared towards career readiness programming and results that make a lasting difference; treat each student not as a student, but as an individual with a different position than the previous or next.

10. Global or world view; aligning the right resources to help students pursue their passion and interests no matter where they are.

Finally, you need accountability. There is no point in launching a mentorship program that doesn't follow the rules—you must manage or facilitate the process to some degree. The factors that make a strong mentorship program are plentiful, and a new Pilot Career Mastermind™ Group initiative shouldn't be a substitute for what's already in place. Like mentorship, it must be also scaled to succeed.

At our Career Design Lab, we also have one-on-one mentoring. A student shouldn't wake up one day with a sense of urgency to find a mentor that is going to solve all of his or her problems. If there is one thing I have learned while rising in the ranks as a director to executive director, is that many people in different walks of life will get you out of your comfort zone and will make the strongest mentors. Individuals in very senior positions enjoy developing talent and will have keen interests in such a program. But they don't always have to be that senior. Sometimes it's someone who has recently gone through similar experiences or who has wisdom to offer for your situation. Again, this comes back to connecting to people and having meaningful conversations.

Remember also that to rise to the top, you have to make many sacrifices. It's lonely at the top, you need a team. Without the teams I've had over the years, I would have never taken the right turns.

CONCLUSION:
YOUR JOURNEY OF SELF-EVALUATION

"Dream lofty dreams, and as you dream, so shall you become. Your vision is the promise of what you shall one day be. Your Ideal is the prophecy of what you shall at last unveil."

— *James Allen*

My journey of self-evaluation helped me realize that I don't consider myself an academic anymore. Like each of you—I, too, am designing my life and career. This makes me an artist.

I wrote this book while traveling all over the world, meeting diverse people with true struggles from a plethora of cultures—who lifted themselves out of it with purpose and the intent to do good. Completing this book, the evening after the culmination of Career Week on February 8, 2019, was a natural progression in my life. Writing and *living* your story will be a natural progression in yours.

New York, NY: "That's a wrap!"—Career Week 2019

The psychologist Pierre Janet argued that underneath the layers of critical-thought functions of the conscious mind lay a powerful awareness that he called the subconscious mind. As you learn to apply the mastermind code to your career more consistently, you will improve your ability to reframe and frame more —based on enlightened self-awareness.

Tunnel vision is your enemy. If your glass is already full, mentally, you will not allow yourself to learn and tap into your inner wisdom. You only know what you do not know. The process of learning is perpetual for all career masterminds.

Reflect—try to remember what's important in your past, all of the lessons learned—and that still need to be learned. It is our conscious memory that is suspect. The function of our subconscious mind is to store and retrieve data.

Our subconscious mind makes everything we say and do fit a pattern consistent with our self-concept, our "master program." We must proactively and continually feed this program. As you progress this should feel more and more second nature.

Here's how to begin programming your subconscious mind:

- Focus on one "to feel" or "to achieve" item for a period of time of at least three weeks.

- Play it over in your mind before going to sleep and immediately when you wake up.

- Make it a habit—build a routine for it.

- Find 3-5 minutes during the day to practice getting closer to it.

Your Quest for Mastery is Continuous

We have covered several themes in this book in order to prepare you to be your own Career Mastermind™. One of them was focus.

One of the greatest things that I have ever done for myself on this Career Mastermind™ journey was to pick up a tennis racquet. From there I began the process of programming my mind to be a Career Mastermind™—*a continuous process of mastering my focus and concentrating my energy.* You too need to optimize your surroundings periodically to focus better and sharpen this skill.

From keeping my eye on the ball, to keeping my perspective—no matter where the ball goes —was the name of the game.

Lessons learned?

I have learned one profound and singular truth: that you shouldn't be forced to choose your careers, they will choose you.

The centrality of the book focused on a transformational and positive mindset, leading to a life of impact, purpose, and meaningful work. You *unfold* your perspective. You proactively shape it over time.

Like with binoculars, collimation is the alignment of all the optical elements along the binocular optical axis. This is what you are doing with your life. You are aligning your lenses. You are combining your paths in your quest for happiness. *You are living in your purpose.*

"YOU Matter" — You Will Always Matter

The "YOU Matter" Lenses are critical to your success—combining career and life vision, building on core values, helping you build a personal business plan, and crafting your own path. They will help you think with a moral compass, identify a personal board of directors, learn the art of storytelling and legacy, and custom-make a focused Career Mastermind™ group.

To help mentally prepare you for the rest of your life, let's briefly summarize how the 7 "YOU Matter" Lenses will transform your future:

1. Positive mindset: learning how to set your mind to goals and build momentum.

2. Unlock your career and life vision: this will set you free.

3. Align your career by redefining the purpose within you.

4. Don't find "a job"; build your way forward.

5. Invest in yourself because "YOU matter."

6. Learn how to create your own personal business plan.

7. Have a moral compass to guide you through life.

Regardless of whether you master one, two, or all seven of the "YOU Matter" Lenses, each lens will sharpen the next lens, cascading with each layer until you have a value stack to help you see clearer.

Other takeaways from the book include:

-Redefining the definition of purpose.

-Coining a new definition and understanding of a "Career Mastermind™."

-Giving back and character-building through adversity.

-How to anticipate the future of work, career disruption—and its impact.

Successful Attitudes

There are a couple of other factors that will play a role in whether you reach the Career Mastermind™ *apex level.*

They are the "Ten Career Masterminding Commandments":

- The first is your attitude. I once had a boss, President Brian Porter, who used to say, "Hassan, attitudes are contagious. Is yours worth catching?" Your attitude in any given set of circumstances will weigh heavily as you choose your own way. *Don't complain.*

- Secondly, your health (mental and physical); you must get enough rest, eat well, and exercise. You must take time out to take care of yourself.

- Third, be kind. Be thankful. Like people and they will like you back. Take the time to genuinely understand someone and their personality. *Be grateful.*

- Fourth (if applicable): If you manage people, get to know them. It's called Situational Leadership, and it's important. Situational Leadership refers to when leaders or managers of an organization must adjust their styles to fit the development level of the followers they are trying to influence. It will also help you be a better listener.

- Fifth: Value your time and respect the time of others. Understand that time is important to other people.

- Sixth: *Join people, not organizations.* Understand their personal and professional connection to the mission of the organization.

- Seventh: *Mind over matter.* Have strong will. A Career Mastermind™ is unshakable. Be unshakable. Be the inspiration for the youth who will be the leaders of tomorrow.

- Eighth: Learn the art of storytelling. It's a game changer.

- Ninth: "Net" + "Work" = Network; nobody ever said it was going to be easy, that's why it's called "work." Build your social, intellectual, and personal capital. This includes a personal board of directors. *One of your goals in your Career Mastermind™ group should be to become a Career Mastermind™.*

- Tenth: Personal branding: Making a name for yourself is more important than ever in this volatile economy—increasing your chances that someone who knows you will come to you with a job proposition rather than you having to look for one. Start building yours by using the characters in this book (that you may be surprised to see are not that different than you)—as springboard examples.

Bonus: Create a Video Business Card, don't hold back—*go for it*—before others beat you to the punch!

Career Masterminds Pass the Baton

FACEBOOK: @MUHAMMADBASDAQ

Like Steve Jobs, Muhammad Basdaq loved calligraphy. A calligrapher and musician from Cemberlitis, Istanbul, as a young teen he saw people playing instruments in the markets and saved money from his calligraphy work to buy an instrument. He found a qanun teacher and eventually started playing with other musicians on stage around Istanbul. The qanun is a descendent of the old Egyptian harp. It has played an integral part in Arabic music since the 10th century.

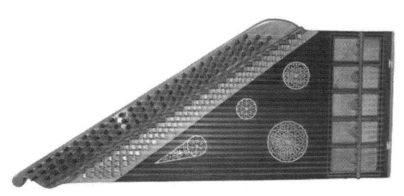

ISTANBUL, TR: Qanun, a musical instrument

ISTANBUL, TR: Muhammad Basdaq playing the Qanun

While he makes his living from calligraphy, he says, "After 5:00 p.m., I become a musician." He loves both art forms; they provide different benefits and creative outlets. However, with calligraphy he is usually drawing on commission. "With calligraphy it's more about technique

ISTANBUL, TR: MUHAMMAD BASDAQ PLAYING THE QANUN

and repetitive practice. With music, it's about allowing your heart and emotions to follow where they lead."

Career and life vision is much like music. Your life is a symphony with ups and downs. *You have to let yourself be free to feel and explore where it takes you.* Just like when you dance, but this is intellectual jazz.

ISTANBUL, TR: "In the Name of God, Most Gracious, Most Merciful" in calligraphy

For example, when you become the principal first violin, you become the concertmaster, but you are still not the conductor—you are second-in-command. Think of me as the conductor and yourself as the rising concertmaster.

If this is your career and life journey, you want to call the shots. But, you need the proper hand and tremendous power to get to the next level. You will have to adjust the strings to make the instrument speak, but at the same time, find your balance (standing tall), mastering your repertoire and place in your network or ensemble of mastermind members.

As a lifelong musician, you come together with the instrument. Once you have the baton, you are conducting your personal orchestra with your inner vision (your heart). Even with your eyes closed, you will feel the music and will know when you have achieved Career Masterminding status.

"You must be shapeless, formless, like water. When you pour water in a cup, it becomes the cup. When you pour water in a bottle, it becomes the bottle. When you pour water in a teapot, it becomes the teapot. Water can drip and it can crash. Become like water my friend."

—Bruce Lee

Reach Your C-Sharp

In music, sharp, dièse (from French), or diesis (from Greek) means higher in pitch. More specifically, in musical notation, sharp means "higher in pitch by one semitone (half step)." Sharp is the opposite of flat, which is a lowering of pitch.

You have to reach for your C-Sharp. It's not at an arm's length. It's like climbing a mountain. It's at its peak. Remember, the sky is not the limit, your "North Star" is.

This all takes practice and deep focus. Some people can hit it easier than others, but this lesson is not about vocals, it's about vision.

"What you seek is seeking you"

—Rumi

THE SKY IS NOT THE LIMIT

Find Your C-Sharp

LIFE VISION

PURPOSE

CAREER VISION

MORAL COMPASS

MINDSET

STORYTELLER +STORY-MAKER & STORY-CHANGER

LIFE BUCKET LIST

CAREER BUCKET LIST

LEGACY

Above the Trend

"See-Sharp" (C-Sharp)

Masters of Visualization

One of my favorite opera singers, Andrea Bocelli, makes a living hitting (and breaking) this tremendous note. This legend, someone who was losing his sight as a child, is a perfect example of someone who sees with his heart as he closes his eyes. He argues that musical curiosity has never abandoned him. When I listen to his voice, especially in songs like "Por ti volare"—it's almost like he's exploring his curiosity in his words. As if he's *living and telling a story*—at the same time. He stacks all of his feelings and emotions, relating them one by one to his life experiences. He says:

"Singing provides a true sense of lightheartedness. If I sing when I am alone, I feel wonderful. It's freedom."

You too are living and telling your story with each day. As you enter your future, enter with an *infinite mindset.* Enter on path to freedom.

Your "See-Sharp" is what we are really examining here. To *see-sharper* means to see with more clarity and at greater distances as you refocus your collective life lenses and clear your path forward.

The symbol of C-Sharp looks like a hashtag, only with a slight tilt. It's within the spaces of the symbol where I would like you to focus your attention.

I created this representation in an effort to help you remember *nine visionary concepts.* Think of it as your Career Masterminding cheat sheet for sharpening your vision after your vision has been cleared. They are:

Career Vision | Purpose | Life Vision

Story-teller + Story-maker & changer | Mindset | Moral Compass

Career Bucket List | Legacy | Life Bucket List

Every Career Mastermind™ sees sharp. They are *masters of visualization.*

They are at a mastery level with their craft. You too can reach this point by not just memorize these nine concepts, but understanding their applicability. Test one another. They will help you see better on rainy days.

Living in Your Purpose

When it comes to your *Master Career,* the career that aligns most directly with your purpose, be a Zen master. When you are mentally about to "turn to clear vision," wait a couple of seconds until everything around you stops moving and there is nothing stopping you from where you want to be. Keep your focus on your North Star, the direction of your true purpose.

"There is a presence, a silence, a stillness which is here by itself. There is no doer of it, no creator of this stillness. It is simply here in you, with you. It is the fragrance of your own self. There is nothing to do about this, it is naturally present. This fragrance of peace, this spaciousness, it is the fragrance of your own being."

—Mooji, *spiritual teacher and Zen master*

My father planted an almond tree in our front yard. My family didn't know it at the time, but our Master Careers were much like this tree. It was our entrepreneurial launch pad, branching into different careers over time. Depending on the kind of soil, water stress, environmental factors, as well as disease pressure, an almond orchard generally lives for 25-30 years—similar to our career runways. All of these stress and health factors also affect us as human beings. Your goal should be not to hit a plateau for your life yield, as otherwise, it starts to slowly decline. This means you are no longer emotionally connected to what you do.

My Master Career was—and still continues to be—the executive director of career services position. What will your almond tree be?

Fresno, CA: Almond Trees in Fresno County

Purposeful Storytelling and Its Irresistible Power

#DRAYESHAAHMAD

In November of 2018, my cousin Dr. Ayesha Ahmad, co-editor of the book *Humanitarian Action and Ethics*, was waiting for me at London Heathrow Airport. Let me tell you a little about my cousin. She is someone that has inspired me towards growing my almond tree. Not just that, but teaching me patience until the tree bears fruit. Almonds are the edible seeds of drupe fruits. These seeds, like the seeds of our New Year's resolutions—give birth to new careers.

Dr. Ayesha Ahmad (PhD) is a lecturer in Global Health at St. George's University of London and Honorary Lecturer at the Institute for Global Health, University College London. She specializes in transcultural psychiatry with a focus on mental health and gender-based violence during conflict and humanitarian crises with a focus on cross-cultural notions of trauma. Her almond tree doesn't stop there. She is the Co-investigator on an MRC/AHRC funded 2-year project called Story-Telling for Health: Acknowledgement, Expression, and Recovery (SHAER), bringing together collaborators from Kashmir, Afghanistan, Turkey, Tunisia, and South Africa. Her work also includes providing expert reports for asylum-seeking cases. She has published widely in academic journals and national and international media outlets as well as speaking at conference and public events worldwide. She has accomplished so much by not accepting the norm, and keeping a promise to herself that she would change the world as it is.

Ayesha's book, *Humanitarian Action and Ethics,* co-edited with James Smith was published on October 2, 2018, is what truly motivated me to finish my book. Watching her book launch at the International Committee for the Red Cross in Geneva, Switzerland, made me a believer. It made me proud and gave me the confidence to do something I had never done before.

We all need inspiration. We just need to know where to look for it. A Stanford study discovered that walking boosts creative inspiration. Sometimes it's influenced by our surroundings, and other times we must be the inspiration ourselves.

I asked Ayesha where she gets her strength from. She said, "My father and I share a deep love of books. A few days ago I sent him *A Tibetan Foothold.* In our daily phone call whilst walking home, he said 'I feel wiped out like jet lag, and it's all your fault, the books you give me are too good! I spent till 3am reading.' Then he said, 'but when you write your novel, it'll be so good I'll be awake all night reading it.' My father is my power."

I understood what Ayesha meant. My father was my power, my mother my heart, my brother, my role model, and my sister my pride. My sister always told me that I could be anything, and this is what Ayesha believed too. She would never stop fighting for what she believed in. This inner fight stemmed from her father's might.

Ayesha describes her father's determination as unmatched and that his journey from Pakistan to London on motorbike in the 1970s motivated her to travel the world to accomplish her dreams. She says:

"The journey, decades later, is still shrouded in mystery. What was he searching for, if anything at all, from the depths of the mountain hearts in Pakistan through Iran, into Turkey, and crossing the Bosphorus waters to reach European shores for the first time. In this journey, moments of lifetimes were capture, held, and mesmerized to create his future, and the family that followed. These were different times, times when concerns about conflicts and crises were abandoned far away and the acceleration of life on a motorbike took him through nature and villages and stories, living along the way from family to family and their generosities. The moments, we wish could be found again and seen in their vividness, but they remain, with admiration and inspiration. Through him, we know that journeys to anywhere can be possible, we just need to begin that first step."

The motorcycle that traveled over 3,867 miles

WWW.TYNANTSANCTUARY.ORG

My uncle, Dr. Riaz Ahmad, like my father, taught her that life is about giving back from the heart in any way you can (small or big).

His journey across the world led him to new beginnings. He is now an anesthetist and instilled purpose in Ayesha through his own leadership. He married my aunt, a nurse, and they run their own nursing home. My uncle, like me, shares a love for animals too. He created a cat sanctuary for stray cats, over one-hundred of them! The sanctuary, "Ty-Nant," means *house by the brook* in Welsh, and is located in Wales.

To me, Ayesha is the rising rockstar cousin with more initials next to her name than anyone I know. She is a poet, world traveler, and one of the warmest and most thoughtful people you will ever meet. My uncle, who never left the side of my grandmother (every chance he got) deeply inspired me too. He is one of the biggest "life rockstars" I have ever met, designing his life direction to serve humanity (and mammals), and paving the way for others to pave theirs.

Story Sharing

When I arrived, anxiously awaiting to speak on a panel at Oxford, Ayesha sent me a text saying she was there waiting for me. It said, "There is a mother who just arrived from Delhi next to me. She asked her daughter, 'Do you want a biscuit?' She replied, 'No, I want a story.'" Ayesha said that her heart felt happy after hearing that, as stories and their tellers are our hope.

#DISHOOM

After several hours of flight, Ayesha and I headed for chai and kahani (stories) at Dishoom. There, Ayesha surprised me with a writing journal that was hand-made by refugees, a signed copy of her book, and gifts for my mother and sister. I have always been a faithful supporter of her journeys. Now our paths are aligning to work on global storytelling.

"All human beings are also dream beings. Dreaming ties all mankind together."

—*Jack Kerouac*

My trip to the UK ended with a final round interview for a TEDx appearance and sitting alongside my rock star cousin at the Palace of Westminster, at the United Kingdom Parliament. I was invited to sit on a panel titled "The People of Afghanistan, Their Future." She helped lead the discussion on the mental health of Afghan refugees and trauma, commanding the room with her presence and the voice of those traumatized.

My work in global health led me to that moment. I was able to connect the dots, remembering the five million Afghan refugees on the Kandahar border who had left their former lives and stories behind. They had traveled miles and miles, their crops destroyed, but they only wanted one thing. They said, "Go and tell someone what is happening to us. Tell our stories."

Being able to share them at the UK parliament was surreal, but I thought to myself that we should be teaching them to create and tell their stories. They didn't want peanut butter dropped from helicopters; they didn't like the taste of chlorine in the water. They wanted to be enabled, to learn to prepare their own food—to be empowered, to be given another chance to live their lives. They argued that their suffering and the psychosocial issues would go away if they could get closer to *community*, closer to a "normal" life.

The value of faith and asylum has never been more important. I recalled asking an eight-year-old boy, just before I left Afghanistan years ago, what he wanted to be when he grew up. He said, "Courageous." I asked what he meant, and he said "I want to teach the corrupted Taliban the true meaning of Islam, and that it is—*peace, not violence.* I want to be humanity." This brilliant boy, like the other boy in Pakistan, left a lasting impression on me. He was wise beyond his years.

Experiences and moments in time mold our perception. They influence our growth mindset. I blinked, and the muzzle of a machine gun was pinching my back. But I didn't let that stop me or redirect my mission. You see, sometimes you have to be patient. Metacognitive beliefs are linked to both positive and negative beliefs, including limiting beliefs. There are children who have seen suffering, but have no self-limiting beliefs. They have defined their goal and uncovered the barriers. Then they have demolished the barriers.

Being a Career Mastermind™ means enabling yourself to go to your own creative and imaginative space that has no limits, no boundaries—except the ones you build for yourself. It's a path that you can confidently own and invest in over your entire life that nobody can take away.

As a thought leader, I see the youth as our future. I understand with clarity that they are the future of "We." We have to be able to develop the next generation of leaders—we have to be able to take a group of people, or an organization, and *"mentor the mentor."*

Choose Your Own Adventure

In order to look towards the future, we must first remember our past. As a kid, I used to love to play "Choose your Own Adventure" with my older brother. Every choice, from opening a door to turning around, would significantly change the course of your future. We would follow the consequences of our choices, and try to distinguish the good from the bad.

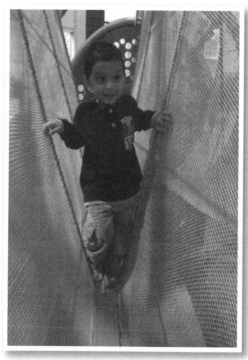

LOS ANGELES, CA: Ziya—The Explorer

We all choose our own adventures every day. But sometimes the choices that we make are based on limiting beliefs or past experiences. This can prevent us from really experiencing the things we love and aspire to do.

CAREER AND LIFE HACK #18

Wealth is not in riches, but in contentment.

Unlike a book, you can't skip ahead and check to see what would have happened if you made one choice vs. another. *Many of our stories still have to be written.*

You will meet the dawn in your descent into layers of pastels. The horizon is as broad as the promise of adventures ahead.

CAREER AND LIFE HACK #19
Life is a journey of perspective.

What Do You Want To be When You Grow Up?

So, it's time for your test. Don't worry, it's only one question to see if you have learned some of the deeper and wiser lessons in this book.

Question: What do you want to be when you grow up?

Answers:

   a) Doctor

   b) Lawyer

   c) Engineer

   d) I don't know

   e) Other _____

If you answered "d" or "e," you may have passed. It is perfectly alright to not know, and kids in their twenties shouldn't know. Those of us that are older act as if we have it all figured out, but we don't.

PLAYA VISTA, CA: Ziya on his first day of school

Once you become a Career Mastermind™, you fully embrace uncertainty. You become certain within uncertainty. For example:

This same test was posed to a kindergarten class as a project where all the kids wrote what they wanted to be when they grew up. Most said, as expected, doctor, fireman, baseball player, etc.

Chris Marshall, the president of Graduway North America, is a proud father. He said his son was different, and he was right.

Meet eight-year-old Jackson Marshall, who attends Moravian Academy in Bethlehem, PA.

Jackson said something profound: *he wanted to be everything!* He said this all on his own. His teacher, a 25-year-veteran of teaching kindergarten at Moravian Academy, has seen over 500 kids come through the school and has never had anyone respond to this question in this way. His teacher was blown away.

Jackson Marshall: Above the Trend

Jackson, who has no limiting beliefs—is a rising Career Mastermind™. God bless him!

Your Path to Discovery

The path to discovery is your own. Illuminate your own way with each unique experience and your refreshed perspective. *You do you,* be yourself, and trust the truth that's already within you.

It's free to be happy. *You may be finite, but life is infinite.*

CAREER AND LIFE HACK #20

**In a world where you can be anything—
be kind and be yourself.**

Perception Is More Powerful than Reality

Seeing with the heart, not just the mind, is a transformational mindset.

Ram Doss, the author of *Be Here Now*, says, "The way the world changes is heart to heart." He continues, "We are all just walking each other home."

Let's reinvent the ways stories are told, and share them with each other on *our way home*. Remember, your "home" is your center—your Purpose. Begin with the story of your journey towards becoming a Career Mastermind™.

We shouldn't *tell* our stories before our time is up on this earth; we have to *sing* them.

CAREER AND LIFE HACK #21

Stories from the heart are not meant to be spoken, they are meant to be sung.

This is the real end game. Don't just be a storyteller: be a story-maker, *a story-changer*.

Loyalty to the Mastermind Code

Our lives are continuously changing. Throughout this book, I have shared with you the stories of many people who have impacted me and have helped me develop the mindset of a Career Mastermind™. It has helped me to reach the top of my field, only to discover that this is not the end for me, just as it won't be for you: it is just the beginning. Be faithful to the code. Remember, the goal as an aspiring Career Mastermind™ should not be fame, but Impact.

Not everyone will have the so-called American Dream. However, those that leverage the "YOU Matter" Lenses will evolve more quickly and align their purpose more effectively. They will also learn how to master their own mindset—then create, write, and tell their stories that will endure from generation to generation.

Let us not forget that Career Masterminds are life archers. They target and transform their lives in more ways than one to impact the lives of others. This is a movement. It's also a community. They find their keys to success, open the doors to meaning, and redefine their purpose. Their lives are not happy—but joyous, because they have crafted them and because they alone have designed them. Thus they have championed their careers, and built a new life vision—a holistic perspective. Seeing with their heart, they see selflessly, and this enables them to see *clearly*.

They can see humanity. Can you? They don't blink. Will you? *Turn to change your perspectives. Turn to clear your vision.*

See your life in a new panoramic view. See far away and into the future. Find peace and love where it is waiting for you.

"Books change us. Books save us. I know this because it happened to me. Books saved me. So I do believe, through stories we can learn to change, we can learn to empathize and be more connected with the universe and with humanity."

—Elif Safak

Connecting the Dots

Who will join me on this journey to reach our "Z?" What does "Z" stand for? No, not "Ziya," my nephew—a little magnet of love that everyone loves. It stands for our *Zenith—the pinnacle of our career and life intersection.* Zenith is an Arabic word meaning "the way over one's head." Look up and embrace the truth. *Your truth.*

Go ahead, pick up a lens ball. Dare to look through it and discover new perspectives. Like the prisms in binoculars, you will be able to see new sights, new opportunities that once hid in blind spots and now surface in your peripheral vision.

Imagine an imaginary line going through the earth from your feet out the other side into the sky. Once you reach that celestial point—your career and life zenith, you will have become a Career Mastermind™.

Finding Your "Z"

Your "Z" has no end, no beginning.

My father found his "Z". For him and for my grandmother, it was in paradise. They embraced the goods and bads of real life, and were patience, always persevering. They realized that life is a stage set in its meticulous craft and design—to its finest details, only to discover they were the world's natural actors, just like you, and just like me—with the power to choose individual focus. *To live your truth is to truly live.* These choices will naturally align themselves with your North Star and "Z". For my father and grandmother, it led them back to their Master—the Master of the Day of Judgement.

"A traveller I am, and a navigator, and everyday I discover a new region within my soul."

—*Kahlil Gibran*

Your "Z" will speak to the future. It's ascending. It is like that of a candle; it will give you the light to lead the way. You will use your "Z" to light the candles of others, and so on. It is a gift that keeps giving, keeps illuminating. Light travels in a straight line, and so does career and life vision—in parallel. Once you learn to balance them, they will never leave you. They follow you wherever you go.

Every Career Mastermind™ has a nexus, this nexus ties everything together, connecting your careers to your life.

In the mind of a Career Mastermind™, every seemingly unnoticed gesture, no matter how minute or trivial in nature, is a masterful and calculated stroke of the brush. It's a peaceful mindset that brings you peace of mind and clarity.

As the paint falls, although we do not know what the final image will look like, our *masterpiece* is coming into view.

Creative Mastery Coming into View

Let creativity be your life lens, as with it, you will be able to see your unfinished masterpiece. Let truth be your mirror. Have faith in this truth, it will make you a better person.

Each of us have defined success for ourselves. No matter what success means, it is not mastery. Success may be transitory, but mastery means you can repeat your successes. It is an infinite strategy that cultivates success and opens doors to opportunities for more successes.

Mastery is the heart of every Career Mastermind™. It sets you free.

Career mastery is telling the truth and searching for the truth. Without it, there is no purpose.

My father taught me about purpose, how to "master the moment"— to pray and meditate, to be mindful. *Once you master one moment, you will master another, and then, another. This will give you power.*

#CAREERMASTERMIND™

Be a Master of your own life, your own story-maker. Becoming a Career Mastermind™ will give you power to overcome moments of fear, negativity, and limiting beliefs, just as countless others have in the past. It's a mindset, and like ideas, perspectives can change the culture of a society. Focus your electromagnetic power and energy. *This is your moment to brush shoulders with Immortality.*

It's a new year, your year—what are you going to do with your freedom?

"Do not go where the path may lead, go instead where there is no path and leave a trail."

—*Ralph Waldo Emerson*

Change your mindset, change the world.

Chicago, IL: Family Reunion—May 2016

ACKNOWLEDGEMENTS

There are hundreds of people who have inspired me on the road to completing this book.

Allow me to begin by thanking those brilliant individuals who impacted my life and appear between these magical pages, you will be impacting readers of this book for many years to come.

A special thanks to those individuals over the course of my life—at different times in my careers, that encouraged me to find the time (that I didn't have) to write this book. If I can do it, so can you.

To my family—you each have given me love, support, prayers, and understanding at every point in my life. Your compassion, values, and support vibrate in the pages of this book.

Imtiaz Akmal, Dr. Sara Akmal, Shiraz Akmal, Sabah Akmal, Ziya Akmal, King Zaki Sabeel Ayun and Prince Mafaza Aydın Lu'lua

In loving memory of my father, *Muhammad Akmal,* and my grandmother, *Rashida Begum.*

To my extended family—you were always there for me. I could not have written this book without the faith and help of all of you.

Javed Qasim, Kamar Qasim, Faisal Qasim, Ahmar Qasim, Sara Siddiqi, Dr. Abdul Qayyum Ahmed, Dr. Samina Ahmed, Sana Ahmed, Sara Ahmed, Shahnaz Mian, Asif Mian, Arif Mian, Dr. Asma Mian, Imran Qureshi, Zayn Qureshi, Dr. Riaz Ahmad, Teresa Ahmad, Dr. Ayesha Ahmad, Sara Ahmad, Javed Ahmad, Shahnaz Ahmad, Atif Ahmad, Usman Ahmad, Saadia Ahmad-Khan, Mustajab Khan, Fatima Khan, Halima Khan, Ijaz Ahmed, Dr. Rubina Ahmed, Ali Ijaz, Farzaan Ijaz, Kayla Krantman-Mynier, Mohammad Afzal, Babar Afzal, Nargis Babar, Khadijah Babar,

Muqadas Babar, Fatima Babar, Heba Babar, Kashif Ghazi, Dr. Chaudhry Mohammad Anwar, Khuram Ali Anwar, Haider Ali Anwar, and Kudoos Ali Anwar.

In loving memory of my aunt *Tasneem Kausar Anwar,* who was the only person on the face of the earth that could rival my chai recipe.

To those leaders that inspired me:

Richard Saul Wurman: Thank you for helping me hone my craft—by critically assessing my thoughts, being passionate about ignorance, and becoming an expert in the design of my life.

Dr. Ronald Waldman: Thank you for leading by example and teaching me what that means.

Dr. Pedro Manrique: Thank you for mentoring me so many years and for teaching me what leadership means.

Jullien Gordon: Thank you for teaching me how to connect my passion to purpose, and reminding me that the true goal will always be freedom.

Alan St. George: Thank you for living your calling and proving to me that true love still exists—I know she is out there, and I will find her.

www.TitanicClock.com; www.HavencrestCastle.com; www.AlanStGeorge.com

Dr. Kathleen Getz: Thank you for trusting me to build my first state-of-the-art career center under your impeccable leadership and grace.

Nasir Nassiri: Thank you for teaching me that compassion, a sense of humor, and strong work ethic makes an incredible leader.

Dr. Brian Porter: Thank you for teaching me the difference between a manager and a leader.

Dr. Scott Sand: Thank you for pushing me to believe I could (and would) go all the way up the ladder. Thanks for teaching me how to motivate a team.

MaryMargaret Sharp-Pucci, EdD, MPH HSM: Your warmth and leadership are unmatched. Thank you for teaching me how to set the bar high for myself.

Salman Azam: You made and continue to make a difference in my life. Thank you for being there and for being a true brother. You are a role model to every community you enter and to the youth.

To the dear friends that stood by my side:

Oskar Choynowski, Boris Valej, Mustafa Selcik (Muste), Kacem Benyoucef and Sonam Entezari, Awais Chughtai, Omar Haroon, Aurangzeb Husain, Ben Youcef, Cherif A Ndiaye, Anton Khlopotov, Neil Rojas, Farhan Ali, Mohamed Sherif, Nathan Canning, Tia Azhari, Laith Canning, Dr. Devang Thakor, Sanyem Rastogi, Ammar Latif, the A-Team in Chi-Town, Saba Chughtai Azam, Syed Jaffer Hussain, Juned Ali Khan, Akif Ali, Dr. Amjad Akhtar, and the Doormen at 175 E. Delaware Pl—the best doormen in the world.

To my DREAM TEAM—the Career Design Lab, New York City: (Winners of the 2018 Alva Cooper Award: Best Practices in Career Services)

> *Murwa Farah* (my right hand), MBA
> www.linkedin.com/in/murwa-farah/

> *Diane Spizzirro,* MS, LMHC, NCC
> www.linkedin.com/in/dianemspizzirro/

Greg Costanzo, Ed.M
www.linkedin.com/in/costanzogregory/

Onika Richards, MPA, GCDF
www.linkedin.com/in/onikarichardscareerdevelopment/

Barbara McGloin, MA
www.linkedin.com/in/barbaramcgloin/

Nicole Arndt, M.Ed
www.linkedin.com/in/narndt/

Tiya McIver, MS
www.linkedin.com/in/mcivertiya/

Cathy Gibbons, MA
www.linkedin.com/in/cathygibbonslrn/

Brian Brown
www.linkedin.com/in/brianbrowndoubleb/

Jessica Rodgers
www.linkedin.com/in/jessica-rodgers-b5140491/

Evan Smith
www.linkedin.com/in/evan-r-smith/

Also, to:

Titus Willis and our *Student Workers!*

What we accomplished in a very short time span—is absolutely unheard of. We made history at Columbia University. I couldn't have done it without you all!

A special thanks to:

All eleven of our fabulous *Career Design Lab, New York—Student Interns!*

Also to:

JD Schramm, Michael Alvarez, and Jacqulyne Law for joining our ongoing efforts—to build out and sustain the Career Design Lab, San Francisco, following its launch.

To the faculty and staff that helped build my commitment to excellence:

Michael Santa Cruz, Xitlaly Gonzalez, Zohaib Samana, Dr. Martin Boyle, Dr. Michael Oudshoorn, Dr. Adnan Turkey, Dr. Nader Daee, Dr. Jude Lamour, Nirmala Gangadeen, Kristina Gavigan, Ricardo Alonso, Dr. Suk Hun Lee, Dr. Nenad Jukic, Dr. Arup Varma, Dr. Faruk Gudur, Dr. Brian Stanko, Dr. Kevin Lee, Ebony Crump, Justin Sorenson, Mary Ellen Kastenholz, Julie Sells, Brendan Shea, Dr. Mine E. Cenar, Nagaraja Kumar Deevi, Dr. Tiffany Onorato, Thomas Deely, Dr. Paul Bailo, Ben Royce, Joshua Mackey, Karen McFadden, Annette Bhatia, Dr. Manuel Carballo, Dr. Therese Mcginn, and Heather Krasna

Thanks to the academic directors who said to themselves not too long ago: "Let's see what this new guy can do." And then, a year later, thanked me personally for the transformation that occurred.

My sincere thanks go to our Dean's Suite who made it happen—especially our Senior Associate Dean, *Dr. Tatum Thomas,* who sat with me one-on-on to hear my crazy idea of having a career center in the middle of Times Square! Then, after believing in the concept, explored how the letters C, D, and L would come across as an acronym for the Career Design Lab. She charged me with writing the strategic plan and creating a new organizational chart during my first couple weeks, trusting my confidence and expertise—in turn, I trusted her leadership.

To our Senior Vice Dean, *Dr. Steve Cohen*—thank you for your bold and wise direction. Also, for acknowledging my team's hard work in building a new career center where people say: "I have ever seen anything like it, it's an amazing space!"

To other friends that believed in me:

Fernando Vicente-Ferreira, Joan Olivier, the Sultan Family, Dr. Mujahid Mahmood, Dr. Muhammad Ashraf, Atif Ali, Shaheryar Masud Khan, Nadeem Akhtar, Tasha Choi, Yasir Mahar, Ali Khan, UCLA PSA, UCLA MSA, Arijit Nandi, Kishlay Anand, Kamina Singh, Ayesha Khan, Dr. Jason Papin, Dr. Wayne Wong, Dr. Kevin Wright, Jason Paul, Chris Marshall, Daniel Cohen, Neil Amrani, Anya Taormina, Mark J. Carter, the Kendrick family, Martin Ilic, Martin Tajkhan, Jennifer King, Tracy King, Billy Martin, Nazanin Wahid, Affo Sakibou, Dahiana Morel, and Akasa.

Teaching has been hugely influential in shaping this book. You each have taught me a great deal and have provided a *living laboratory* for me to improve my performance and impact towards helping individuals realize their unique potential and purpose. To those students that motivated me and made me proud:

Tania Soris, Tosha Kadakia, Supal Mehta, Caitlin Ebinge, Afshan Hussein, Chao Xu, Mahdi Sahloul, Sameer Sawaqed, Anna Wood, Tania Suárez, Robert Michael, Deanna Cabada, Rachel Oatis, Mehdi Badache, Nischitha Rao, Alicia Sanmoogan, Claudia Tena, Grace Mikus, Ricardo Taveras, and *Hussam Bachour.*

To my marketing team:

You became a part of my family.

Tony Arce and *Miguel Paloma* of Red Ivy Marketing

To my logo designers:

You are among the best talent one can find. Thank you for going the extra mile to tell the story behind the logo.

Anda Hardiansyah (coin operated binoculars) and *Praveen Thomas Cheranellore* (Mastermind Falcon).

To my editors:

Thank you for helping me bring my script to life. You were priceless and the sounding boards I needed to do justice to my vision.

Nathan Hassall
www.linkedin.com/in/nathan-hassall-644064158/

Christopher Lapinski
www.linkedin.com/in/christopher-lapinski-a6981624/

To my proofreaders:

Richard Bowen, Edunjobi Oluwaseun, Dronile Hiraldo, Reed Korr, Murwa Farah, and *Jana Peek*

To my creative design team:

You understood the vision—the Columbia Community embraced it, and our students and alumni loved it.

Desy Suryani, Book Designer; *Ahmed Zaeem,* Graphic Designer; *Kritika Singh,* 2D/3D Generalist; *Md Samsul Huda,* Advanced Wordpress Developer, www.elementorspecialist.com; *Tamta Kondzharia,* Illustrator; *Una Salimovic,* Graphic Designer; *Satya Pamarty, Ramalingam Subramanian, Srinivasan Muneeswaran,* Typesetters, AtriTeX Technologies Pvt Ltd, www.atritex.com; *Ximena Ríos, Graphic Designer, Pixel Gráfico; Alex Melov,* Motion Graphic Designer, Lyric Video Maker, 2D Explainer Video Maker, Video Editor, and Video Animator; (Book Trailer); *Rubaa Jamil,* www.Rubaaj.com; *Daisy Maldonado; Ashley Dupree* (Video Resume); www.theashleydupree.com; *Chris Kopsachilis, So Kim, Chris Rugen, and Savitri Tu*

Special tribute to the passing of Zulfiquar (Z) Bacchus, my Senior Technology Service Technician, who passed away while writing this book. Who would have known that your email to me on 11/21/2018 would be your last. Z, I know you found your "Z" well above this world. You were a Master of your Career. May God elevate your status in the Hereafter. Ameen.

Finally, thank you to the "Friends of the Career Design Lab" that believed in my vision and the *Future of We.*

NOTES

Author's Note

1. Harán Yahya, *The Creation of the Universe*, (Canada: Al-Attique, 2000).

Preface

1. Jena McGregor, "Only 13 percent of people worldwide actually like going to work, The Washington Post, October 10, 2013.

Introduction

1. Jullien Gordon, *The 8 Cylinders of Success* (New York: Department of Motivated Vehicles, 2009).

Chapter 1

1. Mihakly Csikszentmihalyi, *Flow* (New York: Harper Perennial, 2018).

2. Dan Buettner and Ed Diener, *The Blue Zones of Happiness: Lessons From the World's Happiest People (Washington, DC:* National Geographic, October 3, 2017).

3. Héctor García and Francesc Miralles, *Ikigai: The Japanese Secret to a Long and Happy Life (New York: Penguin Books, August 29, 2017).*

Chapter 4

I. Bill Burnett and Dave Evans, *Designing your life: How to Build a Well-Lived, Joyful Life*. (New York: Alfred A. Knopf, 2016).

Chapter 5

I. Alison Alexander, "The Power of Purpose," Academy of Management, December 2015.

2. The Columbia University "YOU Matter" Design Your Career Crown purpose program is based on an original model of hypothesis-driven exploration, reflection, and synthesis as described in this book. A workshop with the same title was previously taught by Andy Chan at the Stanford Graduate School of Business.

3. Liz Mineo, "Harvard Study, almost 80 years old, has proved that embracing community helps us live longer, and be happier", The Harvard Gazette, April 11, 2017.

Chapter 6

I. Dalai Lama and Howard C. Cutler. *The Art of Happiness at Work* (New York, NY: Riverhead Books, September 7, 2004).

2. Emanuel Contomanolis and Trudy Steinfeld (Eds.), *Leadership in Career Services: Voices from the Field* (Seattle, WA: Createspace, Amazon, 2013).

Chapter 8

1. Jeffrey R. Young, "How Many Times Will People Change Jobs? The Myth of the Endlessly-Job-Hopping Millennial", July 20, 2017.

2. "How to Leave a Job You Love," Harvard Business Review, November 15, 2018.

Chapter 9

1. "Career Readiness & Employability: Trends Impacting College Recruiting", NACE 2018.

2. Pulin Sanghvi and Evangeline Kubu, "Reimagining Career Services," NACE Journal, May 1, 2017.

3. Jodi Glickman, *Great on the Job: What to Say, How to Say It. The Secrets of Getting Ahead,* (New York: St. Martin's Griffin, May 10, 2011).

4. Wendy Murphy and Kathy E. Kram, *Strategic Relationships at Work: Creating Your Circle of Mentors, Sponsors, and Peers for Success in Business and Life* (New York: McGraw-Hill Education, July 23, 2014).

5. Daniel Cohen, *The Mentorship Revolution* (Middletown, DE: Graduway, 2018).

6. Farouk Dey and Christine Y. Cruzvergara, "10 Trends in Career Services," LinkedIn Pulse, July 15, 2014.

Chapter 10

1. Gretchen Spreitzer and Christine Porath, "Creating Sustainable Performance," Harvard Business Review, January-February 2012.

Conclusion

1. Ram Doss, Be Here Now, (Lama Foundation, New Mexico, October 12, 1978).

2. May Wong, "Stanford study finds walking improves creativity," Stanford University, April 24, 2014.

GLOSSARY

Affinity Group: A group that pursues a shared interest or common goal, either formally or informally.

Bridge Job: The bridge job is a bridge between full-time work and retirement, or a short-term job following a full-time career. Those most commonly attracted to bridge jobs are workers who are approaching full retirement but are not quite ready to leave the workforce.

C-Sharp: In music, dièse (from French), or diesis (from Greek) means higher in pitch. More specifically, in musical notation, sharp means "higher in pitch by one semitone (half step)." Sharp is the opposite of flat, which is a lowering of pitch.

Design Thinking: A mindset promulgated in Silicon Valley based on the principles of empathetic listening, prototyping, a bias to action, and failing forward.

Drone Perspective / Bird's Eye View: This is a way of viewing or reflecting on every aspect of your life in order to start zooming in/focusing on things that really matter to you and to make adjustments where necessary.

Flash Mentoring (or Situational Mentoring): The quick transmission of vital information about a specific situation from someone, helping you move forward.

Forward Momentum: Strategic foresight and proactive planning combined with positive results and energy; purposeful movement toward a goal, a vision, or a desired destination; a consistent step-by-step process that requires movement in the right direction of states goals; making progress and achieving goals.

Gold Mind: Gold Minds understand themselves before trying to understand the world around them. They think pure, they think sound—collecting nuggets of wisdom from their personal board of directors, but they are independent. They practice making their own purposeful decisions.

Human-Centered Design (HCD): A design and management framework that develops solutions to problems by involving the human perspective in all steps of the problem-solving process.

Image Map (also Concept Map): An image or graphical tool for organizing and representing knowledge. They include concepts and images, usually enclosed in circles, boxes, or another design, and relationships between concepts are indicated by linking concepts.

Innerview: The art of reflecting, exploring, uncovering and discovering the things or people that move you, in order to get closer to knowing your purpose.

Intrapreneurship: The practice of applying entrepreneurial skills, creativity, and approaches within an established company.

Khushboo: An Urdu and Hindi word meaning fragrance.

Master Breeder: A master breeder cultivates new opportunities for people that didn't exist before; these opportunities make a positive impact in the world.

Master Career: The career that aligns most directly with your purpose and serves as a launch pad to other careers.

Mindfulness: The psychological process of bringing one's attention to experiences occurring in the present moment.

Mind Mapping (also Mind Map): A mind map is an easy way to brainstorm thoughts organically without worrying about order and structure. It allows you to visually structure your ideas to help with analysis and recall.

North Star: The direction of your true purpose or your primary goal; the target you are seeking. Your North Star is the point where your purpose meets your faith.

Plus/Delta Assessment Technique: Plus/Delta gives you the opportunity to look at what worked well and to celebrate your success, and also what can be improved upon to make your product or team more effective.

Radical Collaboration: A highly interactive learning lab focused on attitudes, trust, relationship building, and transformation.

Readily-Referable: Typically referring to a resume or cover letter that has been critiqued, edited, polished, and aligned with a targeted employer's needs.

Self-Mastery: Being in control of the internal thought processes that guide your emotions, habits, and behaviors.

See-Sharp: To see with more clarity and at greater distances as you clear your collective life lens and path forward.

Side Hustle: Side hustles are jobs unrelated to your professional background which support your income.

Situational Leadership: This leadership model refers to when leaders or managers of an organization must adjust their styles to fit the development level of the followers they are trying to influence.

Swap Meet: A place where people come to buy, sell and/or trade various goods, including electronics, clothes, and furniture. Similar to a flea market.

The Junto: A club of mutual improvement.

Vision Board: A collage of images, pictures, and affirmations of your dreams, goals, and things that make you happy.

BUSINESS CAREER SERVICES
CONNECTING PASSION TO PURPOSE

Are you ready to connect the dots?

INDEX

A NOTE ON THE TYPE

This font family is a refinement of Roman inscriptional capitals designed by Bruce Rogers as a titling design for signage in the Metropolitan Museum. Rogers later designed for the Monotype Corporation a lowercase based on Jenson's work, turning the titling into a full typeface, Centaur, the most elegant and Aldine of the Jenson derivatives.

Mastermind your peace and share with others.

Hassan Akmal, MBA, MPH

ABOUT THE AUTHOR

Hassan Akmal, MBA, MPH, is the Inaugural Executive Director of Industry Relations and Career Strategies and founder of the Career Design Lab at Columbia University. An alumnus of Columbia University, Akmal blazed a successful path as a visionary, career thought leader, chair of Career Education, and Director of Career Services at several universities in New York, Los Angeles and Chicago. He is a former professional tennis player and International Athlete Ambassador to the United States, and serves on the National Association of Colleges and Employers (NACE) "Future of We"—Think Tank Committee. Additionally, he spearheads Columbia's "Career Week," a five-day premier conference on career disruption, impact, and the future of meaningful work—culminating with a future of career services symposium.

Akmal is the host of the Columbia University "Behind the Scenes" podcast series that consists of in-depth interviews with industry leaders discussing provocative career-related topics that set the stage for students. As a change agent, he is committed to coaching proactive career-seekers who will promote multi-level innovation in our global marketplace. He aims to foster a university-wide career culture that's vibrant and diverse, and breathes success.

In 2015, Akmal pioneered a connector model based on customized connections and communities entitled "BRIDGE: Building Relationships and Interconnectedness Directed towards Graduation and Educational (and Career) Pathways" at Loyola University Chicago. He also re-imagined and re-invented the career services model by directing students to inner-"view" themselves, connecting passion to purpose—thereby crystallizing positive career outcomes in the process. By leveraging the career ecosystem that's readily available, he believes we can help realize dreams and witness their global impact.

Akmal is the CEO, founder, and president of Invitation Relief, Inc., a public-benefit charity for displaced persons and health. He is a former professor of global health, financial advisor for UBS Financial Services Inc., and business development manager. Additionally, he served on the External Advisory Board for Health Systems Management at the Marcella Niehoff School of Nursing, and as a Loyola Chapter faculty advisor for Aahana, a not-for-profit organization dedicated to redressing social inequalities and empowering communities.

With over 10 years' experience leading career and professional development, Akmal teaches individuals the importance of capturing their career and life vision, elevating personal brand in multi-layered social media, leveraging self-awareness, and purpose alignment—he believes these elements are both the keys to maximizing careers and the means of self-fulfillment.

The Falcon Master